Dangerous Weather

# Tornadoes

### Revised Edition

Michael Allaby

ILLUSTRATIONS by Richard Garratt

Facts On File, Inc.

*For Ailsa*
*—M.A.*


*To my late wife, Jen, who gave me inspiration*
*and support for almost 30 years*
*—R.G.*

**Tornadoes, Revised Edition**

Copyright © 2004, 1997 by Michael Allaby

Facts On File, Inc.
132 West 31st Street
New York NY 10001

**Library of Congress Cataloging-in-Publication Data**

Allaby, Michael.
   Tornadoes / Michael Allaby ; illustrations by Richard Garratt.—Rev. ed.
      p. cm.—(Dangerous weather)
Includes index.
   ISBN 0-8160-4796-0 (hardcover : acid-free paper)
   1. Tornadoes. I. Title.
QC955.A45 2004
551.55'3—dc21                                  2003006854

Text design by Erika K. Arroyo
Cover design by Nora Wertz
Illustrations by Richard Garratt

Printed in the United States of America

VB Hermitage 10 9 8 7 6 5 4 3 2 1

This book is printed on acid-free paper.

# Contents

# Preface

## What is a tornado?

Several years have passed since the first edition of this book was published. Much has happened during those years, and the decision to update the book for a second edition gives me a welcome opportunity to report at least some of them. In doing so, I have substantially altered, expanded, and in some places rewritten the original text.

There have been more tornadoes, of course. They happen every year—and not only in the United States. Not long ago there was one in the staid English seaside resort of Bognor Regis, in the course of which a couple driving their car found themselves lifted into the air, shifted sideways, and set down on the opposite side of the road. It is not the sort of thing people expect in Bognor, but it happened.

Climate research has also intensified in recent years. Concern over the possibility that we may be altering the global climate has stimulated funding agencies to increase the resources available for evaluating the likelihood of global warming and its consequences. If we are to understand the extent of this threat—if it is a threat—scientists need to learn much more about the ways the Sun, atmosphere, and oceans interact to produce weather. New discoveries are now being made at an unprecedented rate and, although there is still a long way to go before the global climate is fully understood, we are learning more about it almost every day. This new edition takes account of the most recent relevant findings and discusses whether tornadoes will become more or less frequent in years to come.

Updating the text has also given me an opportunity to expand it in order to provide more detailed explanations. I have added three new chapters. One describes and explains the North Atlantic and Pacific Decadal Oscillations as examples of the periodic changes in climate that occur naturally. Another new chapter deals with tornado outbreaks, and the third discusses climate change and what is known about its influence on the incidence of severe storms.

Sidebars display detailed explanations or interesting items of information without interrupting the main flow of the text. This edition contains many more sidebars than there were in the first edition. These explain concepts from atmospheric science, such as adiabatic cooling and warming, potential temperature, mesocyclones, nonmesocyclone tornadoes, the jet stream, and many more.

Measurements are given in familiar U.S. units, such as pounds, feet, miles, and degrees Fahrenheit, throughout the book, but in each case I have added the metric or scientific equivalent. All scientists now use standard international units of measurement. These may be unfamiliar, so I have added them, with their conversions and the abbreviations used in conjunction with them, as an appendix.

The first edition contained no suggestions for further reading. These have been added in this edition. You will find them listed at the end of the book. The sources include a number of books that you may find useful, but a much larger number of web addresses. If you have access to a computer, these will allow you to learn more about droughts and about climate generally, quickly and free of charge.

We have decided to omit the photographs from the first edition and instead to increase the number of diagrams and maps. These provide more useful information than photographs of tornadoes and the devastation they leave in their wake. My friend and colleague Richard Garratt has drawn all of the illustrations. As always, I am deeply grateful to him for his skill in translating my crude drawings into such accomplished artwork. I am especially pleased and relieved that his home and garden suffered only minor damage when a tornado struck on July 15, 2003.

I am grateful, too, to Frank K. Darmstadt, my editor at Facts On File, for his hard work, cheerful encouragement, and patience.

If this new, improved edition of *Tornadoes* encourages you to pursue your study of the weather further, it will have achieved its aim and fulfilled my highest hopes for it. I hope you enjoy reading the book as much as I have enjoyed writing it for you.

—Michael Allaby
Tighnabruaich
Argyll, Scotland
www.michaelallaby.com

# Introduction

All morning the air over the plain feels heavy, oppressive, and hot. It is almost difficult to breathe. By noon a strong breeze is blowing from the south, but it brings little relief from the sweltering heat. As the afternoon wears on, the sky begins to cloud over from the west, with sheets of thin, white cloud. The cloud is very high. Gradually the sheets merge into a continuous cover.

Far away, scientists studying satellite photographs can see the cloud formation over a very large area and have spotted a developing line of thunderstorms. Meteorologists, responsible for warning people of approaching weather danger, are gathering as much information as they can about these storms. Observations and instrument readings reaching them from weather stations on the ground are augmented by aircraft observations and by radar instruments. Already the meteorologists have issued the first broadcast warnings of approaching storms to people likely to be in their path.

Behind the white cloud, in the far distance, the western horizon darkens. A storm is on its way, and by 3 P.M. people going about their everyday business are pausing now and then to glance nervously at what now appears as a solid wall of dark cloud moving rapidly toward them. It seems to extend, this cloud, from the ground to as high as anyone can see. In fact, its base is a few hundred feet above the ground and its top at about 50,000 feet (15,250 m). Here and there the cloud wall flickers as lightning flickers to and fro inside it, and as it comes closer lightning can be seen streaking to the ground. The breeze is strengthening by the minute. Radio stations continue to broadcast warnings.

Overhead, the cloud thickens and hail begins to fall. Driven by winds that are now fierce, hailstones, some the size of golf balls, send everyone running for shelter. The noise is almost deafening as the hailstones batter buildings and ricochet off cars parked in the street.

## The funnel

Then the hail eases, as though the storm is passing, but it is then that the first sign emerges of the real menace. At the base of the cloud, to the southwest, there are what look like fragments of cloud traveling in opposite directions. Soon it is clear they are the same fragments, moving fast in a tight circle immediately below the main body of the cloud. Probably they are about two miles (3 km) away, but there is no way of estimating their size, so it is difficult to tell.

The twirling cloud grows downward from the cloud base, like a white funnel, swaying erratically this way and that until it reaches the ground. Almost at once its color starts to change. A cloud of darker material surrounds its base, then extends upward, darkening the entire column. With a deep roar, the column moves northeast, straight for the town. Scientists tracking it measure its speed as 45 MPH (72 km/h). By the time it arrives, everyone has taken shelter in the safest places they can find.

This is a tornado, or twister, or whirlwind. It may live no longer than half an hour, often less but occasionally longer, and it is rarely more than half a mile (800 m) wide at the base. Yet this is by far the most ferocious storm known on Earth. During its short life it will expend about as much energy as is used to light all the streets of New York City for one night. Inside it, the wind never blows at less than 90 MPH (145 km/h) and sometimes attains speeds approaching 300 MPH (483 km/h), and it blows in an upward spiral. The funnel carries aloft dust, dirt, and loose material and either hurls it outward with immense force or drops it again. Occasionally it sets objects down very gently, so they survive undamaged, but this is rare.

## The 1974 Super Outbreak

In April 1974 a tornado destroyed 900 houses in 20 minutes. On the same day, and in a shorter time than that, one damaged or demolished nearly 3,000 buildings in the city of Xenia, Ohio. It ripped away the top story of Xenia High School and dropped a bus onto the school stage.

Tornadoes often form in groups, and the storms that give rise to them move, sometimes rapidly, spawning tornadoes as they go. The 1974 Xenia tornado was one of what came to be called the "Super Outbreak." A more recent tornado outbreak caused havoc on Sunday, May 4, 2003, in Missouri, Tennessee, and Kansas. At least 38 people died in those storms and, in the words of Michael Spencer, a local Red Cross official, the small town of Pierce City, Missouri, was "destroyed pretty much."

Tornadoes can form at any time of year and any time of day or night, but they are more likely at certain times. In the United States there are more tornadoes between April and June than in other months and two-thirds of them develop in the afternoon and early evening, one-quarter of all tornadoes striking between 4 P.M. and 6 P.M.

More tornadoes occur in the United States than anywhere else in the world, but they are common in many countries. It seems they are rare in Africa and India, although not unknown. On January 8, 1993, a tornado killed 32 people and injured more than 1,000 in Bangladesh, and on April 9 of the same year one destroyed five villages and killed 100 people in West Bengal. Probably there are about 60 each year in Britain. Most go unreported, because they affect open farmland where no one sees them and British people do not expect them. The many references to whirlwinds in the Old Testament show that people in the Near East have long been familiar with them and think of them as the most destructive forces imaginable.

# WHEN WARM AND COLD AIR COLLIDE

Tornadoes grow out of extremely violent thunderstorms, and thunderstorms develop in air that is highly unstable. *Stable* air lies in layers, like those in a cake. Winds may blow through it horizontally, but there is little or no vertical movement of air. In stable air, as in layer cakes, the layers do not mix. If something forces the air to rise, when it crosses hills, for example, it sinks again as soon as the lifting force is removed. *Unstable* air is quite different. It rises and continues to rise until it reaches a level where its density is equal to the density of the air above it, and it can rise no further. Sometimes the rising air can reach a very great height. That is what happens in a large storm (see the section "Thunderstorms" on pages 37–48).

Stable and unstable air are obviously different. They possess certain characteristics that make them stable or unstable. This suggests that in some way there are different kinds of air. They do not differ chemically, of course. All air contains the same gases in the same proportions, everywhere in the world and all of the time. The difference is in the amount of water vapor contained by stable and unstable air, which can vary widely, and in their temperatures.

## How air masses form

Think of what happens to air that stays in the same place for several weeks. The air need not be stationary, because it might take several weeks for it to cross a large continent or ocean.

Sunlight passes through it, warming the surface of the land or sea, and the air is warmed by contact with the surface. Air is warmed from below, not from above. As the air warms, water evaporates into it, so it will hold water vapor, and the amount of water vapor air can hold depends on the temperature. Warm air can hold more water vapor than cool air, and if moist air is cooled, some of its water vapor condenses into droplets (see the box "Why warm air can hold more moisture than cold air can" on page 2). This is why the windows steam up when you get into a car on a cold day. Your breath is warm and moist, but the windows are cold. When the warm breath reaches the windows it is cooled, so it is able to hold less water vapor and some condenses as droplets onto the windows.

Suppose the air lies over the ocean somewhere in the Tropics. It will be heated strongly, because it is in a warm place, and there is plenty of water

# Why warm air can hold more moisture than cold air can

Water molecules (H₂O) are *polar*. That is to say, there is a small positive charge on the hydrogen side of each molecule (H⁺) and a negative charge on the oxygen side (O⁻). The two charges balance, so the molecule is neutral overall, but the H⁺ atoms of one molecule are attracted to the O⁻ atoms of its neighbors.

In liquid water, this attractive force links molecules together, by *hydrogen bonds*, into small groups. The groups can slide past each other and the bonds are constantly breaking and re-forming.

When its temperature rises, water molecules absorb heat energy. This allows them to move faster and strain against the hydrogen bonds. If they absorb enough energy, they are able to break the bonds completely. Single molecules then leave the liquid. Single water molecules moving freely consti-tute *water vapor*—an invisible gas that is not to be confused with steam, which consists of tiny droplets of liquid water.

If the temperature of the air decreases, the water vapor it contains will also cool. The water molecules then lose energy. If they lose sufficient energy because they are moving slowly enough, when water molecules collide, they sometimes remain close to each other long enough for hydrogen bonds to form between them. They will then exist as liquid water, and some of the water vapor will have condensed.

Consequently, if the air temperature rises, moisture in the air becomes warmer and more of its molecules are able to move freely, as water vapor. If the air temperature falls, water molecules lose energy, hydrogen bonds link them into groups, and the vapor condenses into liquid droplets.

to evaporate into it. It will be warm, moist air. Now imagine it is winter and that the air sits for a time over northern Canada. That air will be cold and dry. Large bodies of air that have remained in one place long enough to become warm or cold, moist or dry, are called *air masses* (see the box "Air masses and the weather they bring" on page 3). As the map in the box shows, air masses of all the principal types form over North America.

# Rising air becomes cooler, subsiding air warmer

Gases consist of molecules, which are atoms joined together. Nitrogen molecules comprise two nitrogen atoms (N–N, written as $N_2$), oxygen molecules comprise two oxygen atoms (O–O, written as $O_2$), and between them nitrogen and oxygen make up about 99 percent of our air (the remaining 1 percent is mostly argon). Gas molecules move freely and at random. They dart here and there, hit one another, and bounce away in new directions. How fast they move depends on how much energy they have. If the gas, or air, is warmed, the heat increases their

# Air masses and the weather they bring

As air moves slowly across the surface it is sometimes warmed and sometimes cooled. In some places water evaporates into it, and in others it loses moisture. Its characteristics change.

When it crosses a very large region, such as a continent or ocean, its principal characteristics are evened out. At any given height, all the air is at about the same temperature and pressure over a vast area, and is equally moist or dry. Such a body of air is called an *air mass*.

Air masses are warm, cool, moist, or dry according to the region over which they formed—known as their *source region*—and they are named accordingly. The names and their abbreviations are straightforward. Continental (c) air masses form over continents, maritime (m) ones over oceans. Depending on the latitude in which they form, air masses may be arctic (A), polar (P), tropical (T), or equatorial (E). Except in the case of equatorial air, these categories are then combined to give continental arctic (cA), maritime arctic (mA), continental

polar (cP), maritime polar (mP), continental tropical (cT), and maritime tropical (mT). Equatorial air is always maritime (mE), because oceans cover most of the equatorial region.

North America is affected by mP, cP, cT, and mT air, the maritime air masses originating over the Pacific, Atlantic, or Gulf of Mexico. These are shown on the map. Air masses change as they move away from their source regions, but they change slowly and at first they bring with them the weather conditions that produced them. As their names suggest, maritime air is moist, continental air is dry, polar air is cool, and tropical air is warm. At the surface there is little difference between polar and arctic air, but there are differences in the upper atmosphere.

It is cP air spilling south when the cT and mT move towards the equator in the fall that brings cold, dry winters to the central United States. It is the meeting of mT air from the Gulf and cT air from inland that produces fierce storms in the southeast area of the country.

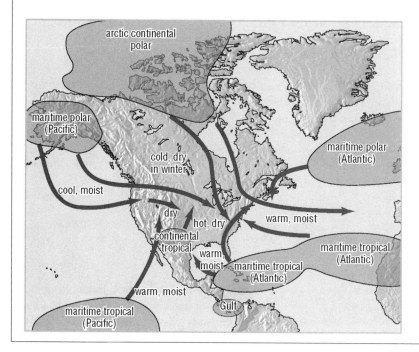

*Air masses that affect North America*

*Less dense air rises through denser air.*

energy and makes them move faster. When they move faster they also move further away from each other and, because they are further apart, they occupy more space. In other words, when air is warmed it expands and when it is cooled it contracts.

Imagine a "parcel" containing one cubic foot of air. If you warm the air, the volume will increase, say to 2 cubic feet. The one cubic foot of cool air weighs the same as the 2 cubic feet of warm air, because the two volumes contain the same quantity of air—no air has been added to the enclosed parcel or removed from it. If you weigh one cubic foot of cold air, warm all the air, then take one cubic foot of warm air and weigh that, the warm air will weigh less than the cool air, because some molecules have moved away, so that the same volume contains less air. Warm air and cold air are different, because equal volumes contain fewer molecules or, to put it another way, they are of different densities.

Place an inflated balloon in a full bathtub and it will float. If you want it to be at the bottom of the tub you will have to push it down and hold it there, because the moment you release it the balloon will bob to the surface. The balloon contains air, air is less dense than water, and in gases and liquids, where they can move freely, dense things sink beneath less dense things and push them upwards. In ordinary air, less dense air will float to the top of denser air. The drawing shows that a bubble (meteorologists call it a *parcel of air*) will rise if it contains fewer molecules than the air surrounding it, and is therefore less dense.

Unstable air is less dense than the air above it, so it rises. As it rises, the air cools. It does so regardless of the temperature of the surrounding air, and without affecting it. This is called *adiabatic* cooling (see the box "Adiabatic cooling and warming" on page 5). Because its temperature falls, the air is less able to hold water vapor. Some of the water vapor condenses, releasing latent heat (see the box "Latent heat and dew point" on page 40). The release of latent heat warms the air again, so it remains less dense than the surrounding air and continues rising. It goes on rising, warmed by the release of latent heat, until it reaches a level where the surrounding air has the same density as itself.

Once the parcel of air has the same density as the air immediately above it, it can rise no further. If the air then settles, with less dense air overlying denser air, it will become stable. After that, there will be very little mixing.

# Fronts

Air masses, each with its own distinct characteristics, form all over the world. Then gradually, but not all at the same speed, they drift away from where they originated. Where two air masses with different densities meet they mix only very slowly. A boundary, or *front*, forms between them

# Adiabatic cooling and warming

Air is compressed by the weight of air above it. Imagine a balloon partly inflated with air and made from some substance that totally insulates the air inside. No matter what the temperature outside the balloon, the temperature of the air inside remains the same.

Imagine the balloon is released into the atmosphere. The air inside is squeezed between the weight of air above it, all the way to the top of the atmosphere, and the denser air below it.

Suppose the air inside the balloon is less dense than the air above it. The balloon will rise. As it rises, the distance to the top of the atmosphere becomes smaller, so there is less air above to weigh down on the air in the balloon. At the same time, as it moves through air that is less dense, it experiences less pressure from below. This causes the air in the balloon to expand.

When air (or any gas) expands, its molecules move farther apart. The amount of air remains the same, but it occupies a bigger volume. As they move apart, the molecules must "push" other molecules out of their way. This uses energy, so as the air expands its molecules lose energy. Because they have less energy they move more slowly.

When a moving molecule strikes something, some of its energy of motion (kinetic energy) is transferred to whatever it strikes, and part of that energy is converted into heat. This raises the temperature of the struck object by an amount related to the number of molecules striking it and their speed.

In expanding air the molecules are moving farther apart, so a smaller number of them strike an object each second. They are also traveling more slowly, so they strike with less force. This means the temperature of the air decreases. As it expands, air cools.

If the air in the balloon is denser than the air below, it will descend. The pressure on it will increase, its volume will decrease, and its molecules will acquire more energy. Its temperature will increase.

This warming and cooling has nothing to do with the temperature of the air surrounding the balloon. It is called *adiabatic* warming and cooling, from the Greek word *adiabatos,* meaning impassable.

(see the box "Weather fronts" on page 6). A front is where warm, less dense air rises over cooler, denser air. This reluctance of masses of air of different densities to mix is what produces a great deal of the weather we experience day by day.

# Storms over the Great Plains

Clouds often form along fronts as warm air rises and its water vapor condenses (see the box "Evaporation, condensation, and the formation of clouds" on page 38 for an explanation of why this happens). Occasionally, though, the effect can be much more dramatic. It sometimes happens that cold air moves beneath very warm, very moist air. The warm air may have been stable, with little or no vertical movement taking place within it. Now, however, it is forced to rise. Its water vapor begins to condense as it cools, releasing latent heat that destabilizes the air. *Conditional instability* is the meteorological term that describes the state of stable air that becomes unstable when it is forced to rise.

Once the conditionally unstable air starts rising it continues to do so, and strong vertical currents develop inside it as air rises, cools, sinks,

# Weather fronts

During World War I, a team of meteorologists led by the Norwegian Vilhelm Bjerknes (1862–1951) discovered that air forms distinct masses. Because each mass differs from adjacent masses in its average temperature, and therefore density, air masses do not mix readily. Using terminology from the daily news at the time, Bjerknes called the boundary between two air masses a *front*.

Air masses move across the surface of land and sea, and so the fronts between them also move. Fronts are named according to the temperature of the air *behind* the front compared with that ahead of it. If the air behind the advancing front is warmer than the air ahead of it, it is a warm front. If the air behind the front is cooler, it is a cold front.

Fronts extend from the surface all the way to the tropopause, which is the boundary between the lower (troposphere) and upper (stratosphere) layers of the atmosphere. Fronts slope upward, like the sides of a bowl, but the slope is very shallow. Warm fronts have a gradient of 1° or less, cold fronts of about 2°. This means that when you first see, high in the sky, the cirrus clouds marking the approach of a warm front, the point where the front touches the surface is about 350–715 miles (570–1,150 km) distant. When you see the first, high-level sign of an approaching cold front, the front is at the surface about 185 miles (300 km) away.

Cold fronts usually move across the surface faster than warm fronts, so cold air tends to undercut warm air, raising it upward along the cold front. If the warm air is already rising, it will be raised even faster along the front separating it from cold air. The front is then called an *ana-front*, and usually thick cloud and heavy rain or snow is associated with it. If the warm air is sinking, an advancing cold front will raise it less. This is a *kata-front*, usually with only low-level cloud and light rain, drizzle, or fine snow. The diagram shows these frontal systems in cross-section, but with the frontal slopes greatly exaggerated.

After a front has formed, waves start to develop along it. These are shown on weather maps and as they become steeper, areas of low pressure form at their crests. These are *frontal depressions*, or *extratropical cyclones*, and they often bring wet weather. Just below the wave crest, there is cold air to either side of a body of warm air. The cold front moves faster than the warm front, lifting the warm air along both fronts until all the warm air is clear of the surface. The fronts are then said to be *occluded* and the pattern they form is called an *occlusion*.

Once the fronts are occluded and the warm air is no longer in contact with the surface, air to both sides of the occlusion is colder than the warm air. Occlusions can still be called cold or warm, however, because what matters is not the actual temperature of the air, but whether air ahead of a front or occlusion is warmer or cooler than the air behind it. In a cold occlusion the air ahead of the front is warmer than the air behind it, and in a warm occlusion the air ahead is cooler, but both of these are cooler than the warm air that has been lifted clear of the surface. The diagram shows this in cross-section. As the warm air is lifted, clouds usually form and often bring precipitation. Eventually both the warm and cold air reach the same temperature, mix, and the frontal system dissipates. Often, however, another similar system is following behind, so frontal depressions commonly occur in families.

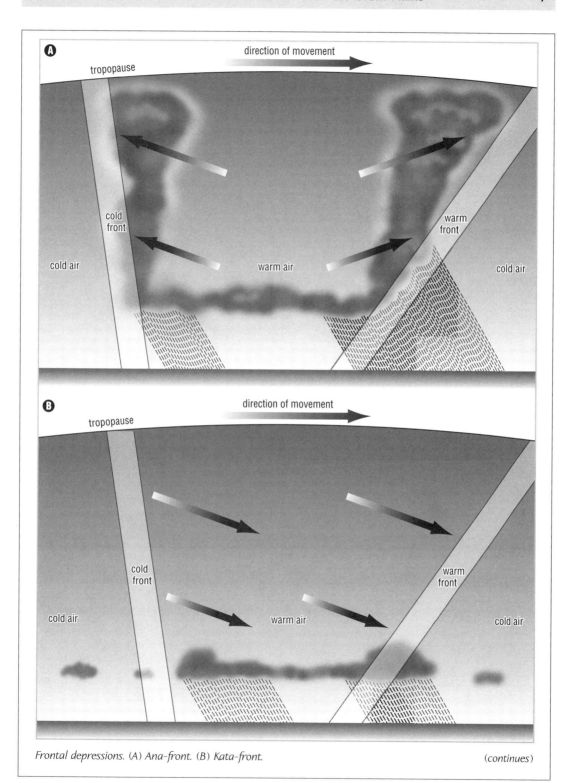

*Frontal depressions. (A) Ana-front. (B) Kata-front.*

(continues)

(continued)

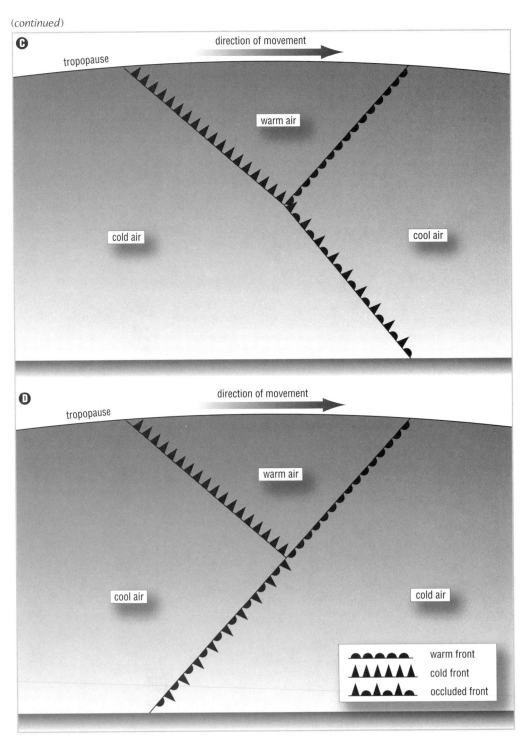

Occluded fronts. (C) cold occlusion. (D) warm occlusion.

warms adiabatically, and then rises again. These are the conditions that can generate towering storm clouds. If they are big enough, violent enough, and there is something to start the air turning, tornadoes may form below them.

These circumstances can and do arise anywhere, but the most violent storms of all arise when more than two air masses collide. This happens fairly often over North America in spring and summer, in the situation illustrated in the map.

In the illustration, one air mass has moved southeastward from the North Pacific, crossed the coast in British Columbia, then crossed the Rockies and entered North Dakota. This is maritime polar (mP) air. It is cold and moist when it crosses the coast, but it loses much of its moisture as it rises over the mountains, so to the east of the Rockies it is dry, but still cold.

A second air mass is moving north from central Mexico. It has spent time over the desert and is warm, dry, continental tropical (cT) air. It meets the cold mP air in the central United States, at a front running from southwest to northeast, approximately along the line of the jet stream (see the section "Jet streams" on pages 27–36). There, the warm air that is moving north rises over the cold air.

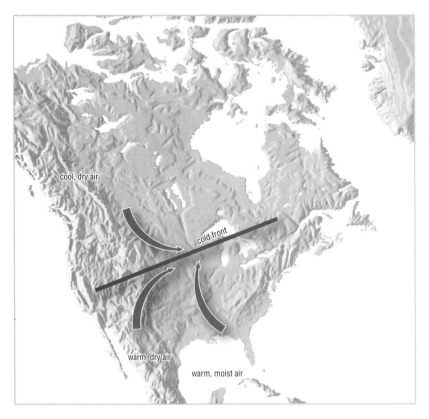

*Meeting of air masses that produces storms*

Air is also moving northwestward from the Gulf of Mexico. This is very warm and very moist maritime tropical (mT) air, and it meets the other two air masses at the front. This is a cold front, moving in a southeasterly direction.

On its journey north, the cT air from Mexico crosses the warm ground of the southern states, which helps it to retain its heat. It meets the advancing cold air, which is denser, and rises over it. Both air masses are dry, so the front produces little or no cloud. The weather is fine below and to either side of it. This boundary is known as the *dry line*.

Then the mT air arrives from the Gulf. It also crosses warm ground, and because in spring and summer the sea is usually cooler than the land, its temperature may rise. It is only slightly unstable until it meets the cold front, but there it is forced to rise and this greatly increases its instability. Heaped clouds develop, it starts to rain, and there may be some thunderstorms.

This would be all that happened, were it not for the cT air from Mexico. It forms a layer of stable air that the rising mT air cannot penetrate, thus trapping the Gulf air between the cold air below and warm air above and preventing the Gulf air from dissipating all its heat.

At the top of the "sandwich," the Mexican cT air is cooling, however, and a point is reached when the Gulf air starts to rise through it. This abruptly releases all the energy of the warm, moist air, producing powerful vertical air currents and clouds that extend almost from ground level to the *tropopause*, the boundary between the lower atmosphere (called the *troposphere*) and the *stratosphere*, at a height of about 50,000 feet (15,250 m). Now the storms become really spectacular, with lightning, thunder, torrential rain, and hail. If the jet stream, just above the cloud tops, sets the air twisting, these huge storm clouds may generate tornadoes.

# HOW WIND CHANGES WITH HEIGHT

Huge thunderstorms are necessary for tornadoes to develop, but a thunderstorm is not enough by itself, no matter how big it is. At the top of the storm, near the cloud tops, the wind must blow from a different direction than the wind lower down. This change in direction is needed to disperse the air that has risen through the cloud and flows out from its top, and to set the air spinning at lower levels.

It is quite usual for the wind at high level to blow from a different direction and at a different speed from the wind we experience on the ground—even in open, exposed places where there are no tall obstructions to deflect it. You can see this sometimes, when a wind vane points in one direction, but high clouds move across the sky in a different direction.

Before they take off on long flights, pilots check the weather they are likely to encounter along their routes. In particular, they are interested in the strength and direction of the winds. To help them, they are supplied with an up-to-date table showing the winds at different heights. They then choose to fly at the altitude where the wind is most favorable, in order to increase the aircraft's speed over the ground and to conserve fuel by shortening the journey time.

## Pressure gradient

Air moves away from areas of high pressure and toward areas of low pressure at a speed that depends on the difference in pressure between the two areas. The pressure difference is called the *pressure gradient* (see the box "Air pressure, highs, and lows" on page 12) and it is what generates the wind. Because the wind speed is proportional to the pressure gradient producing the wind, it is called the *gradient wind*, but the wind does not blow directly toward the center of low pressure and directly away from the center of high pressure. Instead, it blows around these centers (see the box "Christoph Buys Ballot and his law" on page 14).

If you calculate from the pressure gradient what the strength of the gradient wind should be, you will find that the wind at ground level is different. Near the ground, friction with trees, buildings, and the ground surface itself slows the wind and, as it flows and eddies around obstructions, the wind changes direction as well as speed. At weather stations the

# Air pressure, highs, and lows

When air is warmed it expands and becomes less dense. When air is chilled it contracts and becomes more dense.

Air expands by pushing away the air around it. It rises because it is less dense than the air immediately above it. Denser air flows in to replace it, lifting it upward, and the denser air is warmed in turn by contact with the surface, so it also expands and rises. If you imagine a column of air extending all the way from the surface to the top of the atmosphere, warming from below causes air to be pushed out of the column, so the entire column contains less air (fewer molecules of air) than it did when it was cooler. Because there is less air in the column, the pressure its weight exerts at the surface is reduced. The result is an area of low surface pressure—low compared with the pressure elsewhere. The technical term for an area of low surface pressure is *cyclone*, but it is often called simply a *low*.

In chilled air the opposite happens. The air molecules move closer together, so the air contracts, becomes denser, and subsides, drawing more air into the subsiding column. The amount of air in the column increases, therefore its weight increases and the surface atmospheric pressure also increases. This produces an area of high pressure, known as an *anticyclone*, or simply a *high*.

At sea level the atmosphere exerts sufficient pressure to raise a column of mercury about 30 inches (760 mm) in a tube from which the air has been removed. Meteorologists call this pressure one *bar* and they used to measure atmospheric pressure in *millibars* (1,000 millibar (mb) = 1 bar = $10^6$ dynes $cm^{-2}$ = 14.5 lb. $in^{-2}$). Millibars are still the units quoted in newspaper and TV weather forecasts, but the international scientific unit has changed. Scientists now measure atmospheric pressure in pascals (Pa): 1 bar = 0.1 MPa (megapascals or millions of pascals); 1 mb = 100 Pa.

Air pressure decreases with height, because there is less weight of air above to exert pressure. Weather stations that monitor surface air pressure are located in many different places and at different elevations. In order to compare the pressure readings from the network of stations, these are all corrected to give the pressure at sea level, to remove differences that are due only to altitude. Lines are then drawn, linking places where the (sea-level) pressure is the same. These lines, called *isobars*, allow meteorologists to study the distribution of pressure.

Like water flowing downhill, air flows from high to low pressure. Its speed, which we feel as wind strength, depends on the difference in pressure between the two regions. This is called the *pressure*

surface wind is measured by instruments that are sited well clear of obstructions and a standard 33 feet (10 m) above the ground. Wind at higher levels is measured by releasing balloons and tracking them with binoculars or by radar.

Friction is greater over dry land than over the sea, so the wind is always stronger at sea than it is over land. Also, because there are no obstructions at sea, its direction is more constant and closer to that indicated by the pressure gradient.

Wind strength increases with height, because the higher you climb the smaller the influence of friction. The layer of air in which friction significantly affects the wind is known as the *surface* (or *turbulent*) *boundary layer*. Its depth is variable, but it usually extends to between 150 to 3,000 feet (45–1,000 m) above the surface. Above the surface boundary layer the gradient wind is called the *geostrophic wind*.

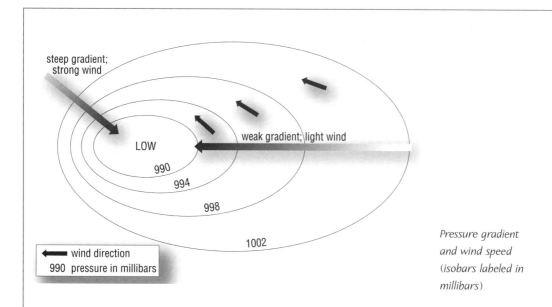

steep gradient; strong wind

LOW

990

994

weak gradient; light wind

998

1002

wind direction
990 pressure in millibars

*Pressure gradient and wind speed (isobars labeled in millibars)*

*gradient.* On a weather map it is calculated from the distance between isobars, just as the distance between contours on an ordinary map allows the steepness of hills to be measured. As the diagram shows, the steeper the gradient, the closer together the isobars are, and the stronger is the wind.

Moving air is subject to the *Coriolis effect* (see the box "The Coriolis effect" on page 78). The Coriolis effect swings the air to the right in the Northern Hemisphere and to the left in the Southern Hemisphere, with the result that clear of the surface, winds flow parallel to the isobars rather than across them. Moving air is also affected by friction with the surface, which slows the wind, reducing the magnitude of the Coriolis effect so that the wind crosses the isobars in the direction of the low pressure. Friction is greater over land than it is over the sea. The result is that surface winds cross the isobars at an angle of about 30° over the oceans and at about 45° over land.

# Balance of forces acting on moving air

The wind does not flow directly from high to low pressure. The rotation of the Earth deflects air moving above it. This phenomenon was first explained by the French physicist Gaspard de Coriolis (1792–1843) and so it came to be called the "Coriolis force," abbreviated as *CorF* (see the box "The Coriolis effect" on page 78). The abbreviation is still used, but CorF is no longer thought of as a force, because nothing pushes the wind to deflect it. What Coriolis discovered was simply the consequence of air (or water, as ocean currents) moving in relation to the Earth, which also moves. The apparent deflection is due to the fact that we observe it from a position that is fixed in relation to the solid Earth. It is an effect, not a force, and today it is called the *Coriolis effect.*

Air moves at all because of a pressure gradient. This is a real force, called the *pressure-gradient force* (PGF). CorF counters the PGF, as though it were a force acting in the opposite direction. The direction of the resulting gradient wind is determined by the relative strengths of these two components. It was a Dutch meteorologist, Christoph Buys Ballot (1817–90), who in 1857 first described what actually happens. His result is summarized as *Buys Ballot's law* (see the box "Christoph Buys Ballot and his law" below). This states that in

# Christoph Buys Ballot and his law

In 1857, the Dutch meteorologist Christoph Buys Ballot (1817–90) published a summary of his observations on the relationship between atmospheric pressure and wind. He had concluded that in the Northern Hemisphere winds flow counterclockwise around areas of low pressure and clockwise around areas of high pressure. These directions are reversed in the Southern Hemisphere.

Unknown to Buys Ballot, a few months earlier the American meteorologist William Ferrel (1817–91) had applied the laws of physics to moving air and calculated that this would be the case. As soon as he learned of this work, Buys Ballot acknowledged Ferrel's prior claim to the discovery, but despite this, the phenomenon is now known as Buys Ballot's law. This states that, in the Northern Hemisphere, if you stand with your back to the wind, the area of low pressure is to your left and the area of high pressure to your right. In the Southern Hemisphere, if you stand with your back to the wind, the area of low pressure is to your right and the area of high pressure is to your left. (The law does not apply very close to the equator.) The diagram illustrates this.

The law is a consequence of the combined effect of the *pressure-gradient force* (PGF) and the *Coriolis effect,* sometimes incorrectly (because no force is involved) called the Coriolis force, and always abbreviated as CorF. Air flows from an area of high

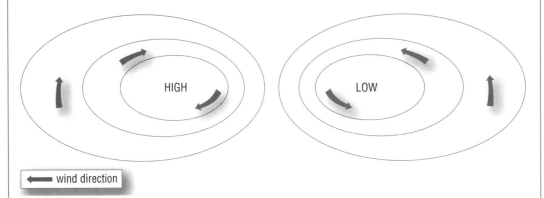

*Buys Ballot's law. In the Northern Hemisphere, winds flow in a clockwise direction around centers of high pressure and counterclockwise around centers of low pressure. Therefore, if you stand with your back to the wind, the center of low pressure is to your left. These directions are reversed in the Southern Hemisphere. This rule of thumb assumes the wind is geostrophic, and not deflected by buildings or other obstructions.*

the Northern Hemisphere winds flow counterclockwise around areas of low pressure and clockwise around areas of high pressure (in the Southern Hemisphere these directions are reversed).

Seen looking down from above the North Pole, the Earth rotates counterclockwise, and this also has an effect. Winds flowing in a clockwise direction are moving in the opposite direction to the Earth's rotation and

pressure to one of low pressure, like water flowing downhill. Just as the speed of flowing water depends on the steepness of the slope (the gradient), so the speed of flowing air depends on the difference in pressure between high and low—the pressure gradient. Gravity is the force that makes water flow downhill. The force making air flow across a pressure gradient is the pressure-gradient force.

As the air flows at right angles to the pressure gradient, the CorF, acting at right angles to the direction of flow, swings it to the right in the Northern Hemisphere and to the left in the Southern Hemisphere. As it starts to swing to the right, the CorF decreases, until the CorF and PGF produce a resultant force that accelerates the moving air. CorF is proportional to the speed of the moving air, so it increases, swinging the air still more to the right. It continues to do so until the air is flowing parallel to the isobars (and at right angles to the pressure gradient). At this point, the PGF and CorF are acting in opposite directions, but with equal magnitude, so they are in balance.

If the PGF were the stronger force, the air would swing to the left and accelerate. This would increase the CorF, swinging it back to the right again. If the CorF were the stronger, the air would swing further to the right, the PGF acting in the opposite direction would slow it, the CorF would decrease, and the air would swing to the left again. The eventual result is to make the air flow parallel to the isobars (pressure gradient) rather than across them. The diagram illustrates this.

Near the ground, friction with the surface and objects on it slows the air. This reduces the magnitude of the CorF (which is proportional to wind speed), altering the balance in favor of the PGF and deflecting the air so it flows at an angle to the isobars, rather than parallel to them. Over land, where the surface is uneven and so friction is greatest, the wind usually blows across the isobars at an angle of about 45°. Over the ocean it crosses at about 30°.

Clear of the surface, the air does flow approximately parallel to the isobars. This is called the *geostrophic wind*.

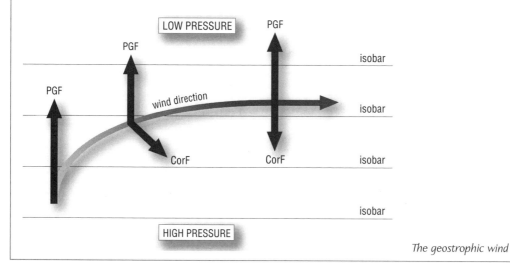

*The geostrophic wind*

this tends to slow them. This means that, in the Northern Hemisphere, winds around areas of high pressure are usually weaker than those around areas of low pressure.

# The Ekman spiral

Friction slows the wind in the surface boundary layer. This affects the balance between the PGF and CorF, causing the wind to flow more in the direction of the pressure gradient. At the surface, over land the wind is deflected by about 25–45° in the direction of the low-pressure region and over sea by 10–30°.

The effect of friction diminishes with increasing height until the wind direction is that of the geostrophic wind, but this happens gradually. Instead of a sudden transition from the gradient wind to the geostrophic wind, wind direction describes a spiral. Wind-driven ocean currents behave in the same way, their direction changing with increasing depth. This spiraling change in direction was first discovered in 1905, by the Swedish oceanographer Vagn Walfrid Ekman (1874–1954). It is known as an *Ekman spiral* whether it occurs in the ocean or the atmosphere. During their climb to cruising altitude, pilots may need to take account of changing wind direction due to the Ekman spiral.

If that were all they had to worry about, air navigation would be a great deal simpler than it is. Modern aircraft climb fast enough for the spiraling change in low-level wind direction to have no significant effect on them. All the pilot would need to know is the wind at cruising height.

Sometimes this is enough, but more often it is not. CorF is greatest at the North and South Pole and it is close to zero near the equator. This causes wind speeds to decrease the farther air moves away from the equator. The PGF that produces a wind of 34 MPH (55 km/h) at 43° latitude, for example, will produce only a 23-MPH (37-km/h) wind at 90°. So, regardless of altitude, the wind speed changes with latitude.

# Wind and air navigation

Remember, too, that the wind flows around centers of high and low pressure. An aircraft flying across a pressure system will, therefore, experience wind blowing first from one direction, then the center itself where winds are light, and finally wind blowing from the opposite direction.

The pilot monitors the aircraft's speed by means of the *airspeed indicator*—an instrument that measures the speed of the aircraft in relation to the air around it. Airspeed is not affected by the wind, but the wind does

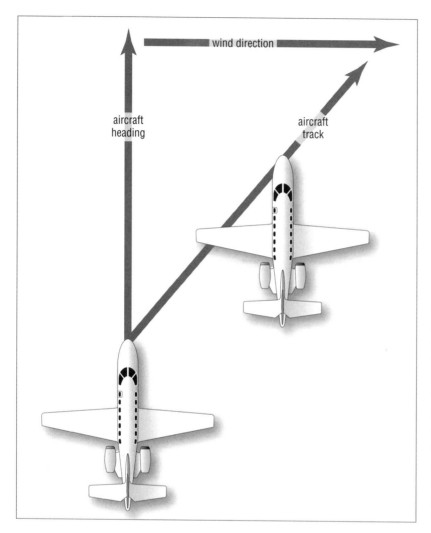

aircraft
heading

aircraft
track

wind direction

*Drift due to wind. The aircraft heading is the direction the aircraft faces and is shown on the cockpit compass. Wind carries the aircraft to one side, by an amount proportional to the wind speed and direction. The resultant of these two forces is the track the aircraft follows over the ground.*

alter the speed of the aircraft in relation to the ground—the *ground speed*—and the track the aircraft follows in relation to the ground below. A tail-wind accelerates the aircraft, a headwind slows it, and a wind from the side causes the aircraft to drift, as shown in the drawing. Drift in one direction as the aircraft approaches the low-pressure center may be corrected by opposite drift as it leaves, but then again it may not.

Drift in one direction will certainly not balance drift from another direction if the aircraft flies through a weather front (see the box "Weather fronts" on page 6). The diagram shows an aircraft that is about to fly through a warm front. The lower part of the drawing shows the aircraft's position as this might appear on a weather map. It is flying into a headwind, caused by the clockwise flow around the high-pressure center. The location of the front on the ground does not agree with its loca-

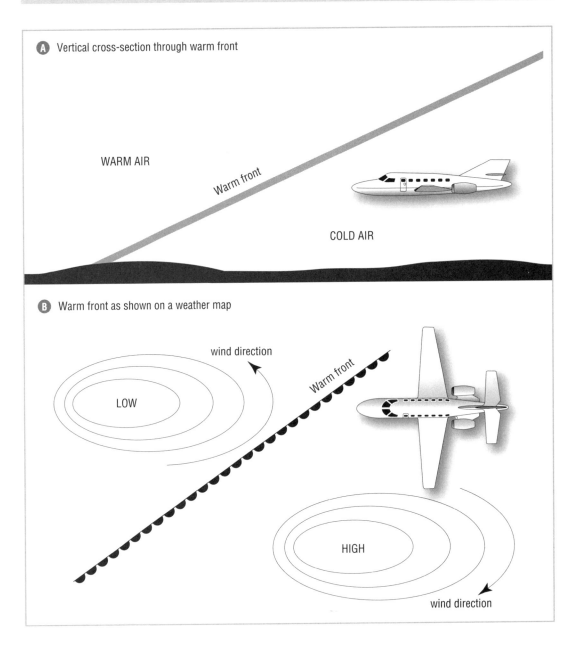

A Vertical cross-section through warm front

WARM AIR

Warm front

COLD AIR

B Warm front as shown on a weather map

wind direction

LOW

Warm front

HIGH

wind direction

*Change in wind direction with height*

tion at the height of the aircraft, however, because the front slopes, as though the cold air is contained beneath an inverted bowl. The aircraft is about to meet the front and, as it crosses, the headwind will become a tailwind.

Now consider the way this will appear to a person standing on the ground watching the plane fly overhead. The surface wind is blowing in one direction. Above the surface, just clear of the surface boundary layer, it is blowing in a different direction and more strongly. Above that again there is yet another wind blowing in the opposite direction and, in all likelihood, at a different speed.

More often than not, the wind varies considerably with increasing height. Moving upward through the surface boundary layer, the speed increases and direction changes through an Ekman spiral as the gradient wind becomes the geostrophic wind. Higher still, the pressure regime may change, with a corresponding change in wind direction and strength. Some hundreds of miles ahead of the surface location of an advancing warm front or retreating cold front, low-level high pressure will lie beneath low pressure, the altitude of the transition depending on distance from the surface position of the front and its angle of slope.

Most weather systems, but especially tornadoes, arise from interactions between atmospheric conditions at low and high levels. For a tornado to develop, the high-level wind must blow strongly from a different direction than the wind at low and medium heights. It is no coincidence, therefore, that tornadoes often occur where air masses meet at fronts, or that many of them form beneath the strongest of all high-level winds, the polar jet stream (see the section "Jet streams" on pages 27–36), associated with the polar front.

# THE NORTH ATLANTIC OSCILLATION AND THE PACIFIC DECADAL OSCILLATION

Every few years the ordinarily dry western coastal regions of Peru and Ecuador are deluged with rain. The parched ground becomes fertile and there is ample grazing for farm livestock. Farmers look forward to a coming *año de abundancia*—a year of plenty. The change in the weather is not good news for everyone, however. At these times the Peruvian fishing fleets may just as well stay tied up in port, because they will not find the huge shoals of anchoveta on which the Peruvian fishing industry depends. The fish have gone elsewhere.

This abrupt and dramatic departure from the usual weather conditions starts in late December, around Christmastime. That is how local people came to call it "the (boy) infant"—in Spanish, *el niño* (see the box "El Niño" below).

El Niño—or *ENSO* (El Niño–Southern Oscillation) to give it its scientific name—happens periodically. The first recorded instance was in

## El Niño

At intervals of between two and seven years, the weather changes across much of the Tropics and especially in southern Asia and western South America. The weather is drier than usual in Indonesia, Papua New Guinea, eastern Australia, northeastern South America, the Horn of Africa, East Africa, Madagascar, and in the northern part of the Indian subcontinent. It is wetter than usual over the central and eastern tropical Pacific, parts of California and the southeastern United States, eastern Argentina, central Africa, southern India, and Sri Lanka. The phenomenon has been occurring for at least 5,000 years.

The change is greatest around Christmastime—midsummer in the Southern Hemisphere, of course. That is how it earned its name of El Niño,

"the Christ child," in Peru, where its effects are most dramatic. Ordinarily, the western coastal regions of South America have one of the driest climates in the world, but El Niño brings heavy rain. Farm crops flourish, but many communities rely on fishing, and the fish disappear.

Most of the time the prevailing low-level winds on either side of the equator are the trade winds, blowing from the northeast in the Northern Hemisphere and from the southeast in the Southern Hemisphere. At high level the winds flow in the opposite direction, from west to east. This is known as the Walker circulation, in memory of Sir Gilbert Walker (1868–1958), who discovered it in 1923. Walker also discovered that air pressure is usually low over the western side of the Pacific, near Indonesia, and

1525. The phenomenon was given the name "El Niño" late in the 19th century. It is a *cyclical* phenomenon that has been occurring for thousands of years and although it is by far the best-known weather cycle, it is not the only one. Changes in the distribution of temperature and atmospheric pressure that occur in one place but affect the weather hundreds or thou-

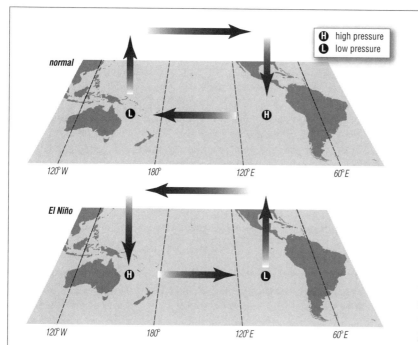

*El Niño. A reversal of pressure distribution allows warm water to flow eastward.*

high on the eastern side, near South America. This pressure distribution helps drive the trade winds, and the trade winds drive the Equatorial Current that flows from east to west, carrying warm surface water toward Indonesia. The warm water accumulates around Indonesia, in a warm pool.

In some years, however, the pressure distribution changes. Pressure rises over the western Pacific and weakens in the east. The trade winds then slacken. They may cease to blow altogether or even reverse direction, so they blow from west to east instead of east to west. This causes the Equatorial Current to weaken or reverse direction. Water then begins to flow out of the warm pool, moving eastward, and the depth of warm water increases off the South American coast. This sup-

presses upwelling cold water in the Peru Current and deprives fish and other marine life of the nutrients in the cold water. Air moving toward South America is warmed and carries a great deal of moisture. This brings heavy rain to the coastal region. This is an El Niño.

In other years the low pressure deepens in the west, and the high pressure in the east rises. This accelerates the trade winds and Equatorial Current, increasing the rainfall over southern Asia and the dry conditions along the South American coast. This is called La Niña. The periodical change in pressure distribution is known as the Southern Oscillation, and the complete cycle is an El Niño–Southern Oscillation (ENSO) event. The diagram illustrates how this happens.

sands of miles away are known as *teleconnections*. They are extremely important in determining the weather we experience from one year to another. Until climatologists understand the way they function, it will remain impossible to make reliable long-term climate predictions.

# North Atlantic Oscillation

The weather in northwestern Europe is strongly affected by another cycle. This one is known as the *North Atlantic Oscillation*.

ENSO episodes affect the weather over a large part of the tropics, but especially in tropical countries bordering the South Pacific Ocean. The North Atlantic Oscillation (NAO) also has widespread effects. Indeed, its effect is felt over such a large area that many climate scientists now call it the *Northern Hemisphere annular mode* (NAM) or, to include both names, NAO/NAM. (*Annular* means "ringlike," referring to the fact that the NAM affects all of the Northern Hemisphere.)

It was Sir Gilbert Walker (1868–1958) who discovered the existence of the NAO in the 1920s. Walker was the British meteorologist who also discovered the Southern Oscillation. The NAO/NAM is a seesaw change in the distribution of surface air pressure between Iceland and the Azores, a group of islands about 800 miles (1,290 km) to the west of Portugal. The map shows the area.

There is a semipermanent area of low pressure centered over Iceland and an area of high pressure centered over the Azores. The Azores high sometimes extends all the way to Bermuda. When this happens it is known in North America as the *Bermuda high*. In practice, the pressures are monitored at Stykkisholmur, Iceland, and Lisbon, Portugal.

Air circulates counterclockwise around areas of low pressure (see the box "Christoph Buys Ballot and his law" on page 14) in the Northern Hemisphere and clockwise around areas of high pressure. Consequently, the prevailing winds are from a westerly direction on the southern side of the Icelandic low and from a westerly direction on the northern side of the Azores (or Bermuda) high. Between them, the Icelandic low and Azores high generate the winds that force weather systems across the ocean from west to east. The greater the difference in pressure between the two systems—the lower the pressure over Iceland and the higher the pressure over the Azores—the stronger the effect will be. Conversely, when the pressure difference decreases weather systems move more sluggishly.

# The NAO Index

Changes in the pressure differences are monitored constantly and are reported as the *NAO Index*, calculated as departures from the average condition. The index is positive when the pressure difference is greater than average and negative when it is smaller than average.

*North Atlantic Oscilla-*
*tion. The NAO refers to*
*the pressure difference*
*between Iceland and*
*the Azores.*

When the index is positive, more winter storms cross the North Atlantic on a more northerly track than the one they follow when the index is negative, and those storms are fiercer. It is fierce storms that trigger tornadoes, so a positive index is likely to mean more tornadoes in northwestern Europe. Winters in Europe are mild and wet during a positive NAO/NAM. The eastern United States also has mild, wet winters, but in Greenland and northern Canada the winters are cold and dry.

Despite bringing wet winters, a positive NAO/NAM can contribute to drought conditions in the eastern United States. This is because during mild winters, less snow falls and thus less remains the following spring. Ordinarily, melting snow releases water slowly into the ground, where it is stored. Rain drains away more quickly than meltwater from snow, so when a spell of dry weather in spring follows a mild winter, the soil can dry out, causing drought.

A negative index means that fewer storms cross the ocean, they are weaker, and they follow a more southerly track. The Mediterranean region as far as the Middle East experiences wet winters, due to the more southerly storm tracks. Greenland and northern Canada also have mild winters, but winters in northern Europe are cold. Cold air masses extend southward over the eastern coast of the United States more frequently, bringing cold, snowy weather.

The NAO/NAM index fluctuates over a period of about 10 years, although the pattern is complicated, with many minor peaks and troughs within the overall cycle. Although each complete oscillation takes the index from a positive peak to a negative trough and back to a second positive peak, the peaks may barely rise above the average or the troughs descend below it. There are records of the index from about 1860 to the present. From 1860 until about 1905, the index was mainly negative—the peaks rose only slightly above the average value. This period was followed by a strongly positive index lasting until about 1930, during which even the troughs were mostly above the average. The index remained close to average until about 1950, when it became strongly negative, but since about 1970 it has been strongly positive.

# The Arctic Oscillation

Scientists are uncertain about what drives the NAO/NAM. It is clearly linked to changes in sea-surface temperatures, but no one understands the nature of that link.

The NAO/NAM may also be linked to a still larger cycle, the *Arctic Oscillation* (AO). The AO is a periodic change in the distribution of surface air pressure between the North Pole and approximately latitude 55°N—the latitude of southern Alaska, Glasgow, Scotland, and Moscow, Russia. When pressure is high over the North Pole it is low at 55°N, and vice versa. The AO is said to be positive when pressure is low over the North Pole.

A positive AO, producing high pressure farther south, directs storms on a northerly track across Scandinavia and Alaska. It also produces dry weather in the Mediterranean region and California, and warm weather across Europe and Asia. When the AO is negative, so that pressure is relatively low in middle latitudes, the Mediterranean region and California have wetter and stormier weather—and more tornadoes. The interior of Europe and Asia is cold.

Some climate scientists suspect that the NAO/NAM may be part of the wider AO. Reflecting this, the overall phenomenon is sometimes called the Arctic Oscillation/North Atlantic Oscillation (AO/NAO).

# Pacific/North American pattern

Periodic climatic changes such as the Arctic Oscillation and North Atlantic Oscillation are not confined to the Atlantic Ocean. They also occur in the North Pacific Ocean. ENSO is one of these, and there are also the Pacific/North American pattern (PNA) and the Pacific Decadal Oscillation (PDO).

Snowfall over the Canadian Rocky Mountains remained constant from about 1700 until 1850. Since then it has increased, and the increase has accelerated since about 1990. Researchers discovered this from ice cores they drilled from a glacier near the peak of Mount Logan, at an elevation of 17,400 feet (5,300 m). They attribute the increasing snowfall to the combined effects of the PNA pattern and the PDO.

The Pacific/North American pattern links variations in the sea-surface temperature in the central and eastern part of the tropical North Pacific Ocean with variations in the high-altitude air pressure over the North Pacific, northwestern North America, and the southeastern United States. When the ocean is warmer than average, high-altitude air pressure will be lower than average over the North Pacific and southeastern U.S., but above average over western Canada and the northern Rocky Mountain area. These changes affect winds, temperatures, and rainfall over a large part of the eastern North Pacific Ocean and North America.

When air pressure is lower than average over the North Pacific and the southeastern United States, and there is high pressure over western Canada and the northern Rockies, the PNA is in its positive phase. It is negative when this pattern is reversed. The PNA affects winds and weather systems over a large part of North America. A positive PNA brings heavy rain to the southwestern United States and northwestern Mexico—within an increased risk of tornadoes.

The PNA is most marked in winter, but it occurs in every month except June and July, and it changes from positive to negative over a period ranging from several weeks to decades. The pattern was negative for several years during the 1960s, positive from 1976 through 1988, negative in 1989 and 1990, and positive through 1992. It remained close to average until 1998, when it was strongly positive, fell to slightly negative in 1999, and it was slightly positive in 2000 and 2001. The 1993 floods in the midwestern states followed the strongly positive PNA of 1992: the positive PNA drove intense storms across the region.

# Pacific Decadal Oscillation (PDO)

The PDO resembles ENSO events, but its cycle is much longer and it affects a different region. It was first identified and given a name in 1996 by Steven Hare, a fisheries scientist studying the effect of climate on salmon production in Alaska. A typical ENSO event lasts for six to 18 months; a PDO lasts for 20–30 years. The effects of an ENSO are felt almost entirely in the Tropics, but with secondary effects elsewhere. The

PDO mainly affects the weather in the North Pacific area and in North America, with secondary effects in the Tropics.

Both ENSO and the PDO involve changes in sea-surface temperatures and sea-level air pressure, but whereas ENSO occurs in the tropical South Pacific, the PDO is measured in the North Pacific. These measurements are used to produce an index of variation from the average values, and because the PDO is related mainly to temperature, its phases are designated "warm" and "cool."

During a warm PDO phase, winter and spring temperatures are higher than normal in northwestern North America, but cooler in the southeastern United States. Winter and spring rainfall is above average in the southern United States and Mexico, but the northwest and Great Lakes regions are relatively dry. There is less snow than usual and less risk of flooding in the northwest. Cool PDO phases produce the reverse of these.

Because the full PDO cycle is so long, there were only two during the past century. Cool phases lasted from 1890 to 1924 and 1947 to 1976. Warm phases lasted from 1925 to 1946 and from 1977 through the middle 1990s. The PDO changed in 1998 from warm to cool, linked to the ending of a very strong El Niño in 1997–98, followed by a La Niña reversal. The cool phase is likely to continue for 20–30 years. We should expect it to bring colder and wetter winters and springs in the Northwest—an area that has experienced marked warming in recent years—but warmer and drier conditions in the southern United States, with a reduction in the frequency of unusually wet years.

No one knows what causes the PDO. This makes its behavior difficult to predict. What we do know is that teleconnections such as the PDO have a large and widespread effect and that they exert their influence by shifting the track of the high-level *jet stream* (see the section "Jet streams" on pages 27–36).

# JET STREAMS

During the 1940s the performance of aircraft improved dramatically. Planes flew faster, farther, and higher than the older ones they replaced. Jet engines were introduced, increasing the speed and operational ceiling of military and later civil aircraft. For the first time, some airplanes flew regularly at altitudes of 30,000 feet (9,000 m) or more. At that height the air is so thin that it offers less resistance than air lower down, so planes use less fuel—provided they are able to reach this height and can fly fast enough to generate the lift needed to support them.

It was while they were flying at these heights during World War II that U.S. bomber crews flying over the Pacific Ocean began to notice something curious. Despite the wind predictions they were given before takeoff, occasionally they found that westward journeys took much longer than they had calculated, and on eastward journeys they arrived ahead of schedule. They concluded that there must sometimes be a very powerful wind at these heights. It was not always in the same place, and sometimes not present at all, but it usually blew from a generally westerly direction. They had discovered a wind blowing like the exhaust from one of the jet airplanes that were starting to come into service. They called it the *jet stream*.

Occasionally, the jet stream reveals itself to people on the ground directly beneath it. If you see long lines of cloud at a very great height, rather like vapor trails but longer and forming parallel streaks, they may have been blown into this shape by the jet stream.

# A ribbon of wind

The jet stream is a narrow band of wind at around 30,000 feet (9,000 m). It is stronger and farther south in winter than in summer. The two maps show its usual location over North America in January and July. The drawing shows it blowing at 95 MPH (153 km/h) at its core, with lower speeds down to 70 MPH (113 km/h) near the edges, but in winter it can be much stronger than this. Then it often exceeds 100 MPH (160 km/h) and sometimes it reaches 300 MPH (483 km/h). It is easy to see how a wind of this force would affect journey times. It is also easy to see how the jet stream can provide the wind, blowing in a different direction from winds at lower altitudes, that is needed to set the air below it spinning to trigger tornadoes.

It also has another important effect. Frontal systems (see the box "Weather fronts" on page 6) tend to develop beneath it. These can cause thunderstorms, so the jet stream is associated with storms that are some-

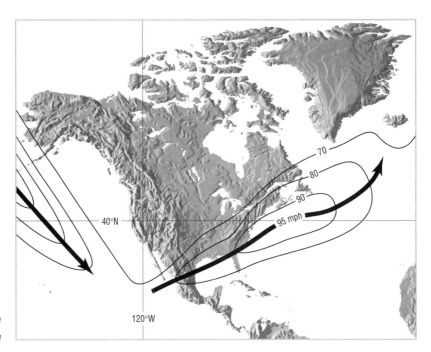

*Jet stream position*
*in January*

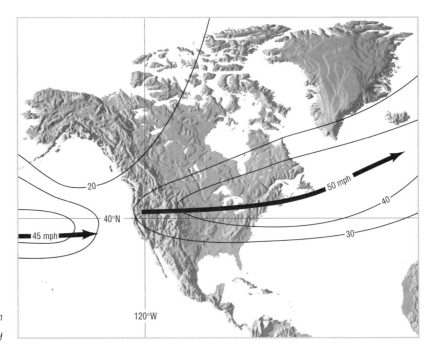

*Jet stream position*
*in July*

times big enough to generate tornadoes. It also provides the mechanism to set rising air spinning.

Although it blows from a generally westerly direction (from west to east), the jet stream is not constant. Indeed, it is a little misleading to think of "the" jet stream, because there can be several in different places at the same time. The principal jet stream over North America and Europe is the Polar Front Jet Stream, but there is also a Subtropical Jet Stream nearer the equator and in summer an Easterly Tropical Jet Stream occurs over Africa and India. The Subtropical Jet Stream is more constant than the Polar Jet Stream, but weaker. As its name suggests, the Easterly Tropical Jet Stream blows from an easterly direction (from east to west).

Air moving horizontally over the Earth's surface tends to follow a curved path, as though it were rotating above a vertical axis through its center. This tendency to rotate is called *vorticity* (see the section "Vortices and angular momentum" on pages 77–83). Vorticity is due to the movement of the air in relation to the Earth's own movement, so it is greatest at the equator, where the Earth is moving fastest. Moving air is also subject to the *Coriolis effect* (see the box "The Coriolis effect" on page 78), which is weakest at the equator and strongest at the North and South Poles.

# Rossby waves

The Polar Jet Stream flows from west to east, but it is readily diverted toward the north or south. If it swings to the north, its own vorticity decreases and the Coriolis effect on it increases. This swings it to the south again, but then the Coriolis effect on it decreases and its own vorticity increases, swinging it back to the north. In this way the jet stream develops very long waves, often measuring more than 1,200 miles (1,900 km) between crests.

It was the Swedish-American meteorologist Carl-Gustav Rossby (1898–1957) who discovered these waves, in 1940, and they are known as Rossby waves. Swings toward the equator are called *troughs* and swings away from the equator are *ridges*. The longer waves tend to remain stationary for most of the time, or sometimes move slowly westward. Shorter waves that form along the long waves travel eastward.

As the jet stream enters a trough it narrows and accelerates, and air converges into it. Convergence at high level produces an area of high pressure in the lower atmosphere. The stream widens and slows around the trough itself, then narrows and accelerates again as it approaches the ridge. This time, however, air diverges from it and the divergence produces an area of low pressure in the lower atmosphere. Undulations in the jet stream are responsible for much of our bad weather, and especially for storms.

# The index cycle

Although the Rossby waves are fairly stable, from time to time they break down in a sequence of steps illustrated in the drawing. This happens when the jet stream and the westerly winds around it are to the north of their usual position. The sequence is called the *index cycle*, because the upper-atmosphere westerly winds are called *zonal* and their strength is known as the *zonal index*. The index is at its maximum when the air flow is clearly from west to east (1 in the diagram).

Over a period of three to eight weeks, the waves grow more and more pronounced (2 in the diagram) until the flow breaks into separate cells, or pockets, of rotating air. When the ridges and troughs are at their most extreme (3 in the diagram) warm air is flowing north and cold air is flowing south. This can bring extreme weather to affected areas. Then, when the index reaches its minimum (4 in the diagram) the jet stream breaks down into a series of cells. Air flows in a clockwise direction (*anti-cyclonically*) around the more northerly cells and counterclockwise (*cyclonically*) around the cells farther south. At this stage the entire system often becomes stationary for several weeks. Until the zonal flow reestablishes itself, in lower latitudes the weather remains dominated by low-pressure regions (*cyclones*) and in high latitudes by high-pressure regions

*The index cycle. (1) Flow is mainly west-to-east (high zonal index). (2) Undulations become more extreme (zonal index weakens). (3) Undulations become still more extreme. so that flow is mainly longitudinal (meridional). (4) Flow has broken into isolated cells (zonal index at its weakest).*

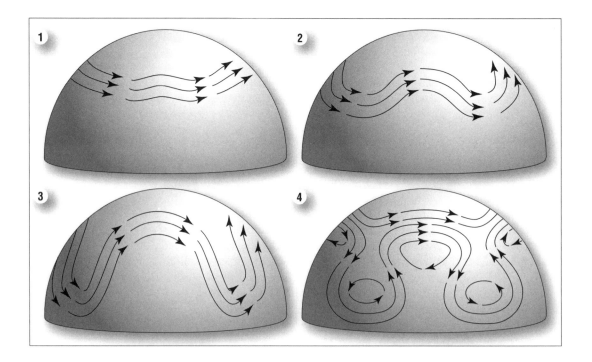

(*anticyclones*). The stationary cyclones and anticyclones divert the weather systems traveling from west to east. This is called *blocking*. Lands on the northern side of the system have anticyclonic weather—usually fine and warm in summer but cold in winter—and those on the southern side have mild, cloudy, and wet cyclonic weather.

# Thermal winds

Winds blow because a pressure gradient exists, and above the surface they blow at right angles to the pressure gradient (see the section "How wind changes with height" on pages 11–19). The jet stream is also produced by a pressure gradient, but it is known as a *thermal wind*.

Weather maps join together places where the atmospheric pressure is the same. The lines they use are called *isobars*. The distance between isobars indicates the steepness of the pressure gradient. If, for example, the surface pressure falls from 1,000 millibars (mb; 14.5 lb. in.$^{-2}$) to 800 mb (11.6 lb. in.$^{-2}$) over a distance of 100 miles (60 km), the pressure gradient is steeper than it would be if pressure fell by the same amount over a distance of 200 miles (124 km). Consequently, the isobars will be closer together, like the contours marking steep and gentle slopes on an ordinary map. This also means the wind will be stronger, because the steeper the gradient, the harder it blows.

Pressure also decreases with height, so it is possible to draw a vertical cross-section of part of the atmosphere, with isobars linking altitudes where the pressure is the same. The diagram captioned "Thermal winds" is a drawing of this kind. It shows three isobars, for 1,000 mb (14.5 lb. in.$^{-2}$), which is the average pressure at sea level, 500 mb (7.2 lb. in.$^{-2}$), and 300 mb (4.3 lb. in.$^{-2}$). As the drawing illustrates, the two isobars are not horizontal. Both of them slope, and the upper one slopes more steeply than the lower one (angle 1 is greater than angle 2). If the diagram showed all the intermediate isobars, it would be clear that the angle of slope increases steadily with height.

The sloping isobars also mark the boundaries of layers in which the air pressure is the same and the layer shown is thicker on the right of the diagram than on the left. The thickness of the layers is proportional to the temperature of the air in them. The air is cold on the left of the diagram and on the right it is warm. Cold air is denser than warm air, because the entire column of air has subsided, packing the molecules closer together near the bottom, but with less air near the top. Consequently, pressure in a column of cold air decreases with height more rapidly than does the pressure in a column of warm air. In cold air the layers are thinner than they are in warm air.

The geostrophic wind (see the section "How wind changes with height" on pages 11–19) blows parallel to isobars drawn across a horizontal surface, with a strength proportional to the pressure gradient. The changing thickness of the layers at different heights is also a gradient, and this also produces a wind. This wind usually blows in a different direction from the geostrophic wind, so the actual wind is a combination of the two. Because the thickness of the layers producing the gradient is proportional to temperature, the wind is called a thermal wind. It blows parallel to the layers. In the diagram this direction is at right angles to the page, so the wind at each level is shown as a circle. The strength of the thermal wind is proportional to the angle of slope (or gradient), so in the diagram the upper wind is stronger than the lower wind (indicated by the larger circle), because the upper slope is steeper than the lower one.

# The Polar Front

Thermal winds blow only where the air temperature changes substantially over a short horizontal distance. Air to one side must be cooler than air to the other side. Where this happens, the thermal wind in the Northern Hemisphere blows with the cool air to its left. A boundary between cool and warm air is a *front* and the front responsible for the strongest of all thermal winds, the Polar Jet Stream, is called the *Polar Front*.

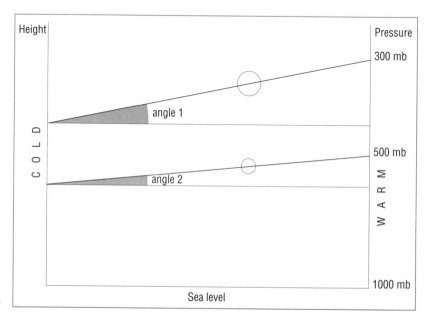

*Thermal winds*

The Polar Front results from the way warm air moves by convection between the equator and poles. This is described by a model of the general circulation of the atmosphere that was developed from the one first suggested in 1735 by the English meteorologist George Hadley (see the box "George Hadley and Hadley cells" below). Hadley wanted to explain why the trade winds blow so reliably from an easterly direction in the Tropics, so his interest was in tropical weather. He suggested that warm air rises over the equator, moves north and south away from the equator at a high level, then descends over the poles and flows back, toward the equator, at low level.

This is not what really happens, but it is close. Very cold, dense air does sink over the poles. It then moves away from the poles at low level until it meets low-level warmer air moving toward the poles. In the

# George Hadley and Hadley cells

When European ships first began venturing far from their home ports into the Tropics and across the equator, sailors learned that the trade winds are very dependable in both strength and direction. They made use of them, and by the end of the 16th century the trade winds' existence was well known. Many years passed, however, before anyone knew why the trade winds blow so reliably. Like many scientific explanations, this one developed in stages.

Edmund Halley (1656–1742), the English astronomer, was the first person to offer an explanation. In 1686 he suggested that air at the equator is heated more strongly than air anywhere else. The warm equatorial air rises, cold air flows in near the surface from either side to replace it, and this inflowing air forms the trade winds. If this were so, however, the trades either side of the equator would flow from due north and south. In fact, they flow from the northeast and southeast.

There the matter rested until 1735. In that year George Hadley (1685–1768), an English meteorologist, proposed a modification of the Halley theory. Hadley agreed that warm equatorial air rises and is

replaced at the surface, but he said that the rotation of the Earth from west to east swings the moving air, making the winds blow from the northeast and southeast.

Hadley was right about what happened, but not about the reason for it. This was discovered in 1856 by the American meteorologist William Ferrel (1817–91), who said the swing is due to the tendency of moving air to rotate about its own axis, like coffee stirred in a cup.

In accounting for the trade winds, Hadley had proposed a general explanation for the way heat is transported away from the equator. He suggested that the warm equatorial air moves at a great height all the way to the poles, where it descends. This vertical movement in a fluid, driven by heating from below, is called a *convection cell*, and the cell Hadley described is known as a *Hadley cell*.

The rotation of the Earth prevents a single, huge Hadley cell from forming. What really happens is more complicated. In various equatorial regions, warm air rises to a height of about 10 miles (16 km), moves away from the equator, cools, and descends between latitudes 25° and

*(continues)*

(continued)

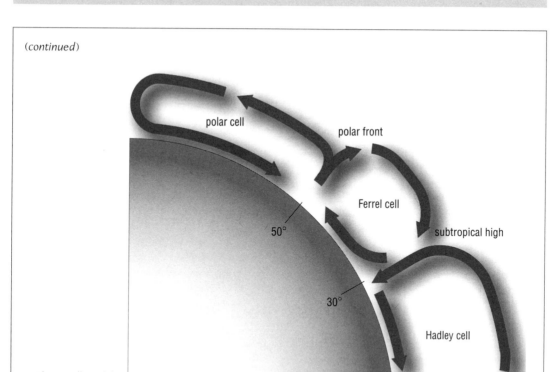

*Three-cell model of atmospheric circulation*

30° N and S. These are the Hadley cells. When it reaches the surface in the Tropics, some of the air flows back toward the equator and some flows away from the equator.

Over the poles, cold air descends and flows away from the poles at low level. At about latitude 50° it meets air flowing away from the equatorial Hadley cells. Where the two types of air meet is called the *polar front.* Air rises again at the polar front. Some flows toward the pole, completing a high-latitude cell, and some flows toward the equa-

tor until it meets the descending air of the Hadley cell, which it joins.

There are three sets of cells in each hemisphere. This is called the *three-cell model* of atmospheric circulation by which warm air moves away from the equator and cool air moves toward the equator. The Hadley cells occur in the Tropics and the polar cells over the Arctic and Antarctic. These are direct cells, driven by convection. Between them the direct cells drive the indirect Ferrel cells, discovered by William Ferrel.

Northern Hemisphere this meeting takes place at about 50° N, although the latitude varies from place to place and with the seasons. In winter, it is a little north of 30° N over the United States, passing across Texas, Louisiana, Alabama, and Georgia. It moves farther north as it crosses the Atlantic and runs along the English Channel, at about 50°

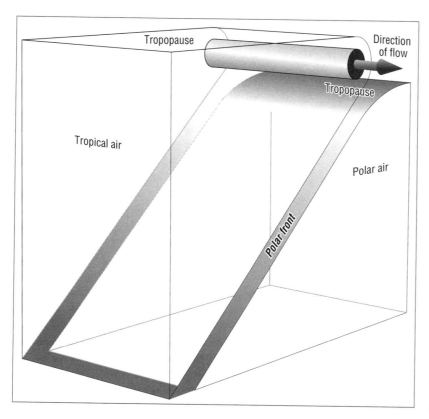

Tropopause

Direction
of flow

Tropopause

Tropical air

Polar air

Polar front

*The Polar Front
Jet Stream*

N. In summer it moves north, to about 37° over the United States and about 51° over Britain. It crosses the Pacific in about the same latitudes, but is farther north over Asia. A similar meeting takes place in the Southern Hemisphere.

It is in these latitudes that polar air moving in one direction meets tropical air moving in the opposite direction. This meeting forms the Polar Front. The diagram is a simple illustration of how this happens and how the Polar Front gives rise to the Polar Front Jet Stream.

Warm air rises and cold air subsides, but air temperature decreases with height. How is it, then, that the cold air near the top of the atmosphere does not simply sink to the surface? Why does it remain aloft? The answer to this conundrum is found in the concept of *potential temperature*—the temperature air would have if it were brought down to the surface (see the box "Potential temperature" on page 36).

Obviously, there is a big difference in temperature between the two types of air on either side of the Polar Front. It is this difference that gives rise to high-level thermal winds. They blow with the cold air to their left in the Northern Hemisphere and to their right in the Southern Hemisphere, so in both cases the winds blow from west to east (they are westerlies).

# Potential temperature

Cold air is denser than warm air, because its molecules are closer together. Consequently, a given volume of cold air has a greater mass than a similar volume of warm air and so it weighs more. Warm air rises because it is less dense than the cold air above it. The cold, dense air sinks beneath the warm, less dense air, and pushes it upwards.

Air temperature decreases with height. If you climb to the top of a mountain, you expect the air to be colder there. High mountaintops are covered in snow, even in summer, and climbers take warm clothes with them. Why is it, then, that the cold, dense air at the top of a mountain, or at the top of the troposphere, does not simply sink to the surface? How does it manage to stay up?

To answer that you must imagine what would happen to the air if it did descend. Suppose, for example, that the air is fairly dry, with no clouds in the sky, and the temperature near to ground level is 80°F (27°C). Near the tropopause, 33,000 feet (10 km) above the surface, suppose the air temperature is –65°F (–54°C). The air near the tropopause is dense, because of its temperature, but this really means it is denser than the air immediately above it. Because air is very compressible, its density also decreases with height.

If the high-level air were to subside all the way to ground level, as it descended it would be compressed and it would heat adiabatically (see the box "Adiabatic cooling and warming" on page 5). Because it is dry, the air would warm by 5.4°F per 1,000 feet (9.8°C per 1,000 m)—this is known as the *dry adiabatic lapse rate* (DALR). As the air descends 33,000 feet (10 km) its temperature will rise by 5.4 × 33 = 178.2°F (98°C). Add this increase to its initial temperature and its temperature when it reaches the ground will be 178.2 – 65 = 113.2°F (44°C). This is much warmer than the actual ground-level temperature of 80°F (27°C). The air could not reach the ground, because it would be less dense, and therefore lighter, than the air below.

The temperature that air at any height above the surface would have if it were subjected to sea-level pressure of 1,000 mb (14.5 lb. in.$^{-2}$) and warmed adiabatically as it was compressed is known as its *potential temperature* (usually symbolized by $\phi$, which is the Greek letter *phi*). Potential temperature depends only on the actual pressure and temperature of the air. Meteorologists calculate the potential temperature of air to determine its stability.

The strength of the upper-air westerlies is proportional to the thickness of the pressure layers in the atmosphere. This increases with height and so the wind speed increases with altitude until, at around 30,000 feet (9,000 m), they reach their greatest strength in the Polar Jet Stream.

# THUNDERSTORMS

All tornadoes are triggered by thunderstorms, but only the very biggest thunderstorms trigger tornadoes. Thunderstorms begin when unstable air rises. To be "unstable," a deep layer of air must be less dense than the air immediately above it. Being less dense, it rises as denser air sinks beneath it and raises it. It goes on rising until it lies beneath air that is less dense than itself, and therefore can rise no higher.

Its rise may begin when the ground in a particular location is warmed strongly by the Sun. The warmed air expands and this makes it less dense than the air above it, so it is pushed upward. That is how summer storms begin. Alternatively, moving air may be forced to rise as it crosses hills or mountains, and warm air may be lifted by denser air at an advancing cold front (see the box "Weather fronts" on page 6).

Just because air is forced to rise, it does not follow that a thunderstorm will develop or, indeed, that any kind of clouds will form. If stable air is made to rise, it will reach a level beyond which it can rise no higher, then sink again. As it rises, the air cools adiabatically and as it sinks it warms adiabatically (see the box "Adiabatic cooling and warming" on page 5).

# Stability and instability

Whether or not air is unstable and continues rising depends on the difference between its rate of adiabatic cooling and that at which the temperature of the surrounding air decreases with height. Air temperature always decreases with height, but not everywhere at the same rate. Suppose, for example, that the temperature at sea level in a particular place is +50°F (+10°C) and that the temperature of the air 10,000 feet (3,000 m) above that place is –10°F (–23°C). This is a drop in temperature of 60°F (33°C) over 10,000 feet (3,000 m), or 6°F for every 1,000 feet (11°C km$^{-1}$). In this example, 6°F per 1,000 feet (11°C km$^{-1}$) is the rate of temperature decrease (or lapse) that is actually measured. It is called the *environmental lapse rate* (ELR).

Rising air cools at the *dry adiabatic lapse rate* (DALR; see the box "Evaporation, condensation, and the formation of clouds" on page 38) of 5.5°F per 1,000 feet (10°C km$^{-1}$). If air in that place is forced to rise, it will cool more slowly than the rate at which the temperature of the surrounding air decreases with height. In other words, the ELR is greater than the DALR. As it rises, therefore, the air will always be just slightly warmer than the air immediately above it. That means it will be less dense and so it will go on rising until it reaches a level where the two lapse rates are the same.

# Evaporation, condensation, and the formation of clouds

When air rises, it cools adiabatically. If it is dry, at first it will cool at the *dry adiabatic lapse rate* of 5.5°F every 1,000 feet (10°C km$^{-1}$). Moving air may be forced to rise if it crosses high ground, such as a mountain or mountain range (1 in the diagram), or it meets a mass of cooler, denser air at a front (3 in the diagram). Locally, air may also rise by convection where the ground is warmed unevenly (2 in the diagram).

There will be a height, called the *condensation level*, at which its temperature falls to its dew point. As the air rises above this level, the water vapor it contains will start to condense. Condensation releases latent heat, warming the air, and once the relative humidity of the air reaches 100 percent and the air continues to rise, it will cool at the *saturated adiabatic lapse rate*, of about 3°F per 1,000 feet (6°C km$^{-1}$).

Water vapor condenses onto minute particles called *cloud condensation nuclei* (CCN). If the air contains CCN consisting of minute particles of a substance that readily dissolves in water, water vapor will condense at a *relative humidity* as low as 78 percent. Salt crystals and sulfate particles are common examples. If the air contains insoluble particles, such as dust, the vapor will condense at about 100 percent relative humidity. If there are no CCN at all, the relative humidity may exceed 100 percent and the air will be *supersaturated*, although the relative humidity in clouds rarely exceeds 101 percent.

Cloud condensation nuclei range in size from 0.001 $\mu$m to more than 10 $\mu$m diameter, but water will condense on to the smallest particles only if the air is strongly supersaturated, and the largest particles are so heavy they do not remain airborne very long. Condensation is most efficient on CCN averaging 0.2 $\mu$m diameter (1 $\mu$m = one-millionth of a meter = 0.00004 inches).

At first, water droplets vary in size according to the size of the nuclei on to which they condensed. After that, the droplets grow, but they also lose water by evaporation, because they are warmed by the latent heat of condensation. Some freeze, grow into snowflakes, then melt as they fall into a lower, warmer region of the cloud. Others grow as large droplets collide and merge with smaller ones.

Air is unstable if the ELR exceeds the DALR. If the situation is reversed and the DALR exceeds the ELR, rising air will cool faster than the rate at which the temperature of the surrounding air decreases with height. This will prevent it from rising, because as soon as it does so it becomes cooler and denser than the air around and above it. This air is stable and if it is forced to rise, it will sink again as soon as the force ceases.

# Condensation and latent heat

Unless it is extremely dry, however, its rate of adiabatic cooling will change long before the air has cooled to −10°F (−23°C), because the water vapor it contains will have started to condense into droplets. Warm air can hold

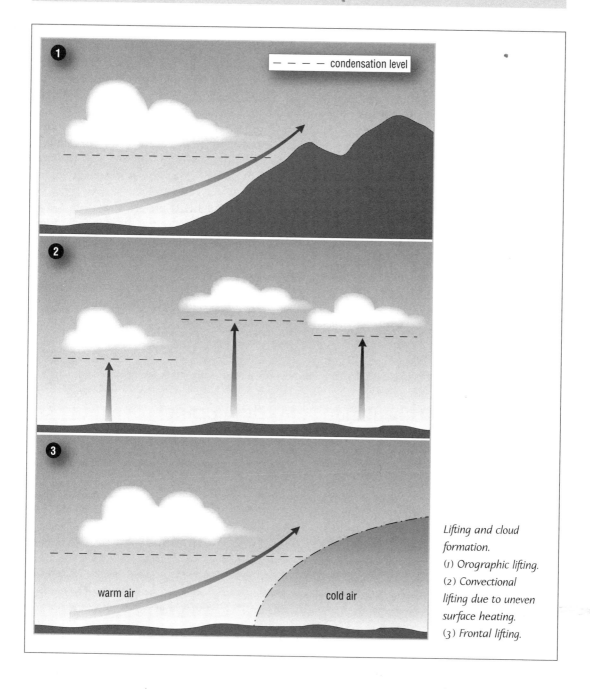

Lifting and cloud formation.
(1) Orographic lifting.
(2) Convectional lifting due to uneven surface heating.
(3) Frontal lifting.

more water vapor than cold air can (see the box "Why warm air can hold more moisture than cold air can" on page 3), so as the air cools it must rid itself of its excess water vapor. The temperature at which condensation begins is called the *dew point temperature*. The dew point temperature varies according to the amount of water vapor present in the air, or, to put it another way, the more water vapor the air contains, the closer it is to being saturated.

The height at which rising air cools to its dew point temperature and water vapor condenses into liquid droplets is called the *lifting condensation level*. It is the height of the cloud base. The height at which air stops rising marks the cloud top.

When water vapor condenses, it releases heat, called the *latent heat of condensation*. This warms the air around it, and if the air is still rising, it slows the rate at which it cools adiabatically from the DALR to the *saturated adiabatic lapse rate* (SALR). The SALR varies, but it averages about 3°F per 1,000 feet (5.5°C km$^{-1}$).

If the air is unstable, meaning the ELR is greater than the DALR, condensation will increase its instability, because the difference between the ELR and the SALR is even greater than that between the ELR and the DALR. So it will continue rising. It is still cooling, so its water vapor will continue to condense, releasing latent heat and maintaining the SALR. When the air temperature falls below freezing, the water vapor will form tiny ice crystals instead of water. This releases even more latent heat (see the box "Latent heat and dew point" below).

# Latent heat and dew point

Water can exist in three different states, or phases, as gas (water vapor), liquid (water), or solid (ice). In the gaseous phase, molecules are free to move in all directions. In the liquid phase, molecules join together in short "strings." In the solid phase, molecules form a closed structure with a space at the center. As water cools, its molecules move closer together and the liquid becomes denser. Pure water at sea-level pressure becomes densest at 30°F (4°C). If the temperature falls lower than this, the molecules start forming ice crystals. Because these have a space at the center, ice is less dense than water and, weight for weight, has a greater volume. That is why water expands when it freezes and why ice floats on the surface of water.

Molecules bond to one another by the attraction of opposite charges, and energy must be supplied to break those bonds. This energy is absorbed by the molecules without changing their temperature, and the same amount of energy is released when the bonds form again. This energy is called *latent heat*.

For pure water, 600 calories of energy are absorbed to change one gram (1 g = 0.035 oz; 600 cal g$^{-1}$ = 2,501 joules per gram; joules are the units scientists use) from liquid to gas (evaporation) at 32°F (0°C). This is the *latent heat of vaporization*. The same amount of latent heat is released when water vapor condenses. When water freezes or ice melts, the *latent heat of fusion* is 80 cal g$^{-1}$ (334 J g$^{-1}$). Sublimation, the direct change from ice to vapor without passing through the liquid phase, absorbs 680 cal g$^{-1}$ (2,835 J g$^{-1}$), equal to the sum of the latent heats of vaporization and fusion. Deposition, the direct change from vapor to ice, releases the same amount of latent heat. The amount of latent heat varies very slightly with temperature, so this should be specified when the value is given. The standard values given here are correct at 32°F (0°C). The diagram illustrates what happens.

Energy to supply the latent heat is taken from the surrounding air or water. When ice melts or

# Upcurrents and downcurrents

Eventually the rising air reaches a ceiling. By then it is very cold. It is also dry, because almost all its water vapor has condensed out of it. Warmer air, rising from below, disturbs it and it starts to sink. As it descends, the air begins to warm adiabatically, but because it is dry it warms at the DALR, so it is warming faster than the rising air is cooling (at the SALR). There

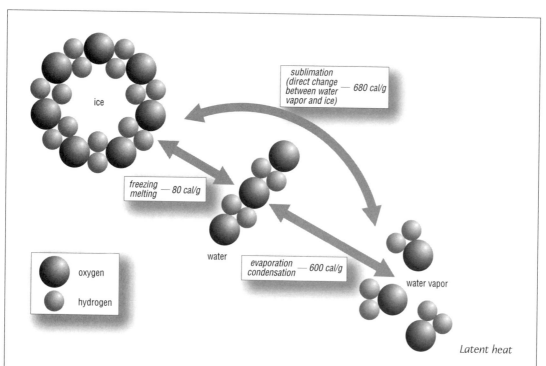

*Latent heat*

water evaporates, the air and water in contact with them are cooled, because energy has been taken from them. That is why it often feels cold during a thaw and why our bodies can cool themselves by sweating and allowing the sweat to evaporate.

When latent heat is released by freezing and condensation, the surroundings are warmed. This is very important in the formation of the storm clouds that can give rise to tornadoes. Warm air rises, its water vapor condenses, and this warms the air still more, making it rise higher.

Warm air is able to hold more water vapor than cool air can, and the amount of water vapor that air can hold depends on its *temperature*. If moist air is cooled, its water vapor will condense into liquid droplets. The temperature at which this occurs is called the *dew point temperature*. It is the temperature at which dew forms on surfaces and evaporates from them.

At the dew point temperature, the air is saturated with water vapor. The amount of moisture in the air is usually expressed as its *relative humidity* (RH). This is the amount of water present in the air, expressed as a percentage of the amount that is needed to saturate the air at that temperature.

are now currents of rising air and currents of sinking air. In a big, towering cloud the upcurrents may be moving at more than 60 MPH (96 km/h), the downcurrents more slowly. As the temperature of the sinking air reaches the dew point temperature, water droplets evaporate into it. Evaporation absorbs latent heat, which cools the air.

Because of these swirling upcurrents and downcurrents, clouds that form in unstable air have heaped shapes, like cotton wool or cauliflowers. Such clouds are called *cumulus*. As they grow wider and taller they become *cumulonimbus*. Cumulonimbus clouds produce rain showers, which are often heavy.

# Inside a cumulonimbus storm cloud

A cumulonimbus cloud, formed in very unstable air, is large and quite complex. There are liquid water droplets in its lower levels. Some of these collide with one another and merge, to form larger droplets. Those that grow too heavy to remain airborne fall as rain.

Near the top of the cloud, there are ice crystals. High-level winds may draw these out into long streamers, shaped rather like a blacksmith's anvil. The anvil ends where the ice crystals are drawn into air that is dry enough for them to change directly into invisible water vapor. They fall as they are drawn out, but once clear of the main cloud they enter dry air and turn

*Inside a storm cloud*

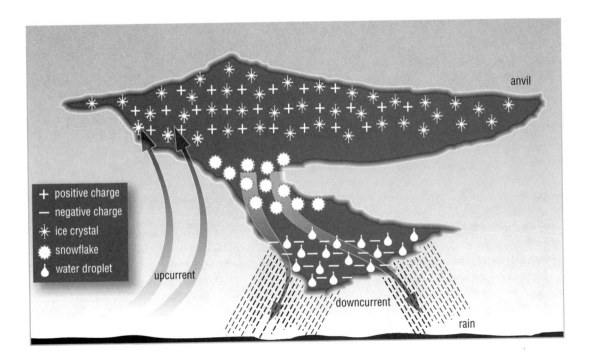

+ positive charge
− negative charge
\* ice crystal
⚹ snowflake
💧 water droplet

anvil

upcurrent

downcurrent

rain

into water vapor. This makes the ice-crystal stream taper, with the thicker end close to the cloud top, and that is what gives this part of the cloud its anvil shape. Thunder was once believed to be the sound of the god Thor beating on this anvil with his hammer.

Some of the ice crystals link together and form snowflakes. The bigger snowflakes are too heavy to remain at the top of the cloud, so they fall, forming a layer of snowflakes in the middle of the cloud. Snowflakes that fall below this level melt and become liquid droplets. The diagram shows what is happening inside a cloud of this type.

Big cumulonimbus clouds often form on really warm summer days. In fact, that is when they are very likely to form. Warmed ground and moist air are all that is needed to trigger their development and these often occur together on a summer afternoon. As you swelter in the humid heat, it may seem strange to think that there is ice in the cloud above you. If you doubt it, a shower of hail ought to convince you, but most ordinary rain begins as ice that melts on its way down.

# Snow and hail

Small ice crystals make ideal condensation nuclei. Near the cloud top, where water vapor turns directly into ice, in addition to the crystals there are many droplets of water that are chilled to below freezing temperature. These *supercooled* droplets freeze onto ice crystals, so the crystals grow at the expense of the water droplets. When they reach a certain size, the crystals start to fall, and they melt as they pass through the warmer air below. If they continue downward and fall from the bottom of the cloud, they will reach the ground as rain. In cold weather, however, they may not pass through air warm enough to melt them and in that case they fall as snow. Snow rarely falls where the air temperature between the cloud base and the ground exceeds 39°F (4°C). If the temperature is very close to this, snow may fall mixed with rain. In Britain this mixture is called "sleet."

Only cumulonimbus clouds produce hail, because these are the only clouds that contain vertical currents that are sufficiently strong to keep the hailstones airborne while they grow. The life of a hailstone begins when a water droplet is carried aloft by an upcurrent, enters much colder air, and freezes. It is now a tiny ball of clear ice. Supercooled water droplets freeze onto it, covering it with rime ice. The hailstone then starts to fall. When it enters slightly warmer air at a lower level, where there are many liquid water droplets, more of these collect around it. The hailstone now comprises a tiny ball of clear ice, surrounded by a layer of white rime ice, and outside that a layer of liquid water. An upcurrent now carries it aloft again, freezing the outer layer of water to form more clear ice, onto which more supercooled droplets freeze as rime ice. The hailstone continues to fall and rise in this way, collecting another layer of clear ice and another layer of rime ice on each trip, until finally it is too heavy to be lifted by the upcurrents. At this point it falls from the cloud, too fast for it to melt significantly. Its size is an indication of the strength of the vertical currents inside the cloud that made it.

Occasionally, hailstones can reach a very large size. There was a hailstorm on September 3, 1970, at Coffeyville, Kansas, in which one hailstone was 5.7 inches (14.4 cm) across and weighed 1.7 lb. (770 g). This may not have been the heaviest. Unconfirmed reports said that a storm at Gopalganj, Bangladesh, on April 14, 1986, produced hailstones weighing 2.25 lb (1 kg). Large hailstones are dangerous. A hailstone about 3.5 in. (8.9 cm) across killed a man in Fort Worth, Texas, in March 2000, and in January 2001, hailstones about 2.9 in. (7.4 cm) across killed one man and injured nearly 30 people in storms that raged along the eastern coast of Australia. A hailstorm with winds up to 40 MPH (64 km/h) killed at least 15 people in northern parts of Henan Province, China, on July 19, 2002. The storms associated with the May 4, 2003 tornado outbreak in Missouri, Tennessee, and Kansas produced hailstones the size of golf balls.

# Birth of a thunderstorm

At this stage, rain or snow, and perhaps hail, are falling heavily enough for people to call it a storm. It is not yet a thunderstorm, but it is rapidly developing into one. Scientists still do not understand exactly how this begins. Several explanations have been proposed, and one seems more likely than the others. The development starts with collisions between hailstones and tiny splinters of ice.

Whether it is a solid (ice), liquid (water), or gas (water vapor), water consists of molecules, each consisting of two hydrogen atoms bonded to one oxygen atom. They are not joined together in a straight line, however, but with both the hydrogens on the same side of the oxygen, separated from each other by an angle of 104.5°. Each oxygen atom carries a negative (–) electric charge and each hydrogen a positive (+) electric charge, so, because of the way the atoms are arranged, a water molecule has a slight negative charge at its oxygen end and a slight positive charge at its hydrogen end. The diagram shows the arrangement. Such molecules are said to be *polar*. Supercooled water droplets freeze inside the cloud, forming hailstones. These burst, producing splinters of ice. The electric charges on the splinters and larger hailstone cores are unequal, and this produces a separation of electric charge inside the cloud (see the box "Charge separation" on page 45).

The effect is tiny, but there are countless millions of hailstones bursting and colliding. Little by little, positively-charged splinters of ice accumulate high in the cloud and negatively-charged droplets accumulate lower down.

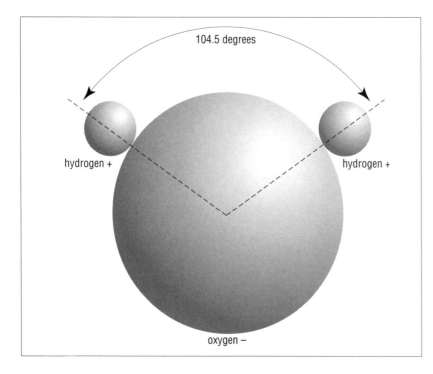

104.5 degrees

hydrogen +                    hydrogen +

oxygen −

*The water molecule*

# Charge separation

A lightning flash is an electric spark and, like any flow of electric current, it travels between two regions of opposite charge. These regions form inside cumulonimbus (and occasionally nimbostratus) clouds, in snowstorms, dust storms, and in the clouds of material ejected by volcanic eruptions.

In a cumulonimbus storm cloud, positive charge usually accumulates near the top of the cloud and negative charge near the bottom. There is also a small area of positive charge, of uncertain origin, at the base of the cloud. The drawing illustrates this distribution of charge.

Scientists are uncertain just how this separation of charge occurs, but probably several processes are involved. Some separation may be due to the fact that the ionosphere, in the upper atmosphere (above about 37 miles; 60 km), is pos-

itively charged and in fine weather the surface of the Earth is negatively charged, with a steady, gentle downward flow of current. This means it is possible that a positive charge is induced on the underside of cloud droplets (by the negative charge below) and a negative charge on their upper surfaces. If the droplets then collide in such a way as to split them, the charges may separate. It is also possible that falling cloud particles may capture negative ions.

The most important mechanism is believed to occur when water freezes to form hail pellets. A hailstone forms when a supercooled water droplet freezes. This happens from the outside inward. Hydrogen ions ($H^+$) then move toward the colder region, so the hailstone contains a preponderance of $H^+$ in its icy outer shell and of hydroxyl ($OH^-$) in

*(continues)*

*(continued)*

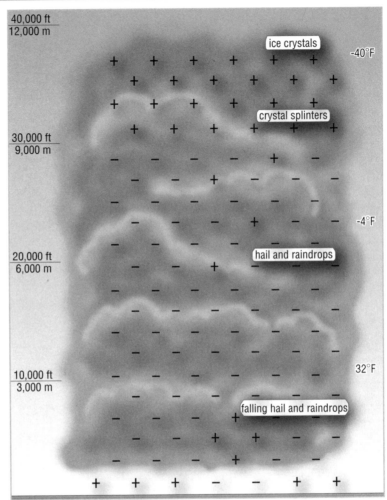

40,000 ft
12,000 m

ice crystals    -40°F

crystal splinters

30,000 ft
9,000 m

20,000 ft
6,000 m

-4°F

hail and raindrops

10,000 ft
3,000 m

32°F

falling hail and raindrops

*Charge separation inside
a thunderstorm*

its liquid interior. As freezing progresses, the interior of the hailstone expands, bursting the outer shell. This releases tiny splinters of ice carrying positive charge (because of the $H^+$). Being so small and light, these splinters are carried to the top of the cloud by updrafts. The heavier hailstone centers, with their negative charge ($OH^-$) sink to a lower level.

Whether or not this is really the way it happens, or all that happens, there is no doubt that the upper part of the cloud comes to carry a positive electric charge and the lower part a negative one. The negative charge near the cloud base may then induce a positive charge on the ground below it. The pattern is not the same everywhere, however. There are local areas of positive charge in the base of the cloud and negative charge on the ground immediately beneath them.

# Lightning

Air is a good electric insulator, so these separated charges cannot equalize themselves by a flow of current through the air from the positive to the negative regions. The charges continue to accumulate until there are places where the strength of the electric field inside the cloud, and between the cloud base and the ground, is enough to trigger a huge spark, flashing from positive to negative and neutralizing the charge.

What we see as lightning is this electric spark. It may flash from one part of the cloud to another, in which case we see it as "sheet" lightning— a bright flash with no visible center. It may flash from one cloud to another. Or it may flash between a cloud and the ground, as a "fork" of lightning.

Lightning comprises three or four separate strokes following one another at intervals of about 50 milliseconds (thousandths of a second). The interval between them is so short that we usually see them as a single flash, lasting up to one-fifth of a second. Some people are able to see the separate strokes and for them the lightning flash appears to flicker.

The first flash is called the *stepped leader*. It carries excess electrons— negative charge—from the base of the cloud to the positive charge on the ground. The stepped leader follows a line of least resistance among the air molecules. This makes it jump from side to side and gives the "fork" its jagged shape. As it moves, the spark releases so much energy that it knocks electrons away from the air molecules it touches, leaving an invisible line through the air in which the air is *ionized*—electrically charged. The ionized path is about 8 inches (20 cm) wide and it is a good electrical conductor.

As the stepped leader nears the ground, the charge on the ground ionizes the final section of the path. Electrons then flow to the ground from the lower part of the lightning stroke. This draws more electrons down from the cloud and so the electron path extends upward. This is called the *return stroke*. It illuminates the ionized path and carries the charge downward from the cloud, neutralizing the charge at the base of the cloud.

The base of the cloud and the induced charge on the ground are both neutralized, but there is still an excess of negative charge higher in the cloud. This produces a fresh stroke, called a *dart leader*. It follows the same ionized path and is met by another return stroke. The process continues until the charge in the cloud has been completely neutralized.

Energy released by the lightning flash heats the air along its path. Heating causes the air to expand, but the heat is so intense and so sudden, there is no time for the surrounding air to move aside for it. It takes less than one second for the air temperature along the lightning path to rise by 14,000–60,000°F (7,800–33,000°C). Quite literally, the air explodes, sending out the shock waves we hear as thunder.

If you are close to the storm, the thunder sounds like a huge crash, but if you are farther away, it rumbles. This is because of the time it takes for the sound to travel from the source to your ears. Thunder is produced all the way along the lightning path, which is jagged and up to 1 mile (1.6 km) long. Some parts of the path are closer to you than others, so sound from them reaches you a fraction of a second before the sound from the more distant parts. Consequently, the sound of the thunder continues for a short time.

Sound waves are damped by their passage through the air. The high-pitched frequencies are lost first, and so the farther you are from the storm, the deeper the sound of the thunder will be. If you are more than about 6 miles (10 km) from the storm, you are unlikely to hear the thunder at all, because all of the sound waves will have been absorbed by the air before they reach you.

Light from the lightning flash travels at the speed of light. Sound from the thunderclap travels at the speed of sound, about 1 million times more slowly. This means that light from the flash will reach you before sound from the thunder and you can use the difference in journey times to estimate the distance between you and the storm. Count the seconds from the moment you see the flash until the moment you hear the thunder. Five seconds represents a distance of one mile (3 seconds represents one kilometer).

# SQUALL LINES

*Shenandoah* was the pride of the U.S. Navy. In 1919, the ship was built in Philadelphia, and *Shenandoah* was assembled at Lakehurst, New Jersey, in 1923. That is when it made its maiden flight. *Shenandoah* was an airship, and in those days most people believed airships were the flying machines of the future (see the box "Airships" on page 50). The ship's design was based on that of the German zeppelins, but it avoided some of the dangers inherent in the zeppelin design. In particular, *Shenandoah* used helium as a lifting gas, rather than hydrogen. It was its 7 million cubic feet (198,000 m³) of hydrogen that was to cause the *Hindenburg* airship to burst into flames spectacularly at Lakehurst in 1937. Helium is rare and costs much more than hydrogen, but it does not burn. *Shenandoah* was hailed as a very safe ship.

Following its first flight, *Shenandoah* made a trip all the way across the United States and back, a total of 9,000 miles (14,480 km), that took her 235 hours. It made many other journeys, mainly so that the navy could show it off to the public. It was an impressive sight. The airship was nearly 700 feet (213 m) long, nearly 80 feet (24 m) wide, and powered by six 300-horsepower (224-kW) engines.

## The final journey

A little before 3 P.M. on September 2, 1925, *Shenandoah* cast off from the mooring masts at Lakehurst, bound for Detroit on its 57th flight. The ship sailed westward into the evening and through the night, but early the following morning, before dawn, the captain noticed lightning to the north and east. *Shenandoah* turned south, away from the storm, only to be confronted by a bank of fast-moving cloud. There was no time to take evasive action, and the airship was caught in a violent upcurrent. The crew released some of the helium to slow the ascent, but then a downcurrent sent them plunging toward the ground and they released some of the water that was used as ballast. It was all to no avail. Another upcurrent broke the airship into two pieces. Both pieces quickly disintegrated and *Shenandoah* crashed in eastern Ohio. It was not a single, isolated thunderstorm that had destroyed the airship, but something much bigger and a good deal more violent.

*Shenandoah* had flown directly into a squall line. A *squall* is a short-lived but violent storm in which the wind speed increases by at least 30 MPH (48 km/h). As its name suggests, a *squall line*, or *line squall*, is a line of squalls. These are usually thunderstorms, several miles thick, produced by clouds that are more than 30,000 feet (9,150 m) tall, and sometimes hundreds of miles long, but with gaps between clusters of storms. A squall line moves, as a line of storms, at speeds of 30 MPH (48 km/h) or more. One crossed southern England in 1959 traveling at about 44 MPH (71 km/h).

# Airships

An airship consists of a rigid frame covered with a skin to provide a large, enclosed space that is filled with a lifting gas. This is a gas that is lighter than air. The earliest airships used hydrogen as a lifting gas. All modern airships use helium because, although it provides less lift and is much more expensive, it is nonflammable. The vessel is powered by engines and is equipped to carry passengers, freight, or both, either suspended beneath the vessel in a gondola, or accommodated inside the frame. It is the rigid frame and the fact that it can be steered that distinguish an airship from a gas-filled or hot-air balloon and the powered balloon known as a blimp.

The first airship was designed and built by the French engineer Henri Giffard (1825–82). It was 144 feet (44 m) long, 52 feet (12 m) in diameter, and held 88,300 cubic feet (2,500 m³) of hydrogen. It was powered by a 3 horsepower (2 kW) steam engine with a three-bladed propeller 11 feet (3.4 m) in diameter turning at 110 r.p.m. On September 24, 1852, Giffard took it on its maiden flight from the Hippodrome in Paris, flying at about 6 MPH (10 km/h) in a light wind.

Airships possess positive buoyancy. That is to say, the total mass of the airship, including its lifting gas, is less than the mass of the air that its volume displaces. Therefore, the airship experiences a buoyancy force acting upward.

At 32°F (0°C) and an atmospheric pressure of 29.92 inches of mercury (1,000 mb), 1,000 cubic feet of air weigh 80.72 pounds (1,000 m³ weigh 1.29 tonnes), and 1,000 cubic feet of helium weigh 11.14 pounds (1,000 m³ weigh 178.6 kg). Hydrogen is about half as heavy as helium. Consequently, 1,000 cubic feet of helium will lift 62 to 65 pounds (1,000 m³ will lift 994 to 1,042 kg).

Its buoyancy means that the engines of an airship are not required to raise it from the surface or to propel it at a sufficient speed for it to experience lift from aerofoil surfaces. The engines need only propel the vessel at a speed that is convenient, so they can be quieter than those of a conventional aircraft and consume much less fuel.

Rigid airships do not depend on the internal gas pressure to maintain their shape. There are openings in the hull to allow air to enter and leave freely in order to equalize the pressure inside and out. Ballonets are containers filled with air and separated from the lifting gas by flexible diaphragms. Varying the pressure in the ballonets accommodates the changes in the volume of the lifting gas due to changing temperature. There are usually two ballonets, located fore and aft, and they are also used to trim (control the attitude of) the vessel.

In middle latitudes, over North America and Europe, most squall lines move from west to east or northwest to southeast. In the Tropics they tend to travel in an easterly direction. This is because they move with the prevailing winds, which are westerly in middle latitudes and easterly in the Tropics.

# The storm cloud

High-level cloud often provides the first advance warning of an approaching squall line. This is the *anvil*, blown ahead of the main mass of the storm cloud by the high-level wind. Cloud covers much of the sky, thinly at first but quickly thickening and becoming lower.

It may not be possible to distinguish it from below, but there is a second layer of cloud below the high-level anvil. This is the *shelf cloud*. Rain falls from the high-level cloud into the shelf cloud, but this rain is carried aloft again by rising air currents inside the cloud and so it does not reach the ground. Ragged fragments of cloud drift below the main mass of cloud, but if it is possible to see beyond them, in the distance there will be what looks like a solid wall of cloud reaching almost to the ground. Its base may be parallel to the ground, or shaped like an arch. The arched section of the cloud is called the *arcus*.

As the edge of the shelf cloud passes overhead, the wind will change direction, strengthen, and become gusty. This is the *gust front*, where air is being drawn into the base of the storm and spilling out from it. Wind speeds in a severe squall can reach 100 MPH (160 km/h), with even stronger gusts along the gust front. The temperature will drop rapidly, often by 10°F (5.5°C) a minute or more, and the air pressure will suddenly rise.

After that the rain will start. Precipitation falls in the region behind the main cloud mass, where air is descending. The heaviest fall will come first and may be accompanied or preceded by hail. There will probably be thunder and lightning. The diagram shows a cross-section of how a squall-line storm might appear to someone watching it pass from a safe distance.

*Squall line storm*

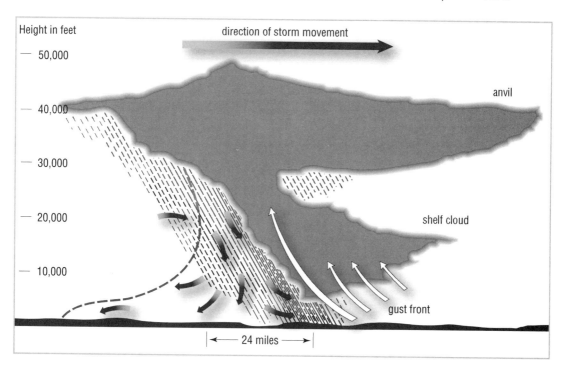

Squall lines also generate tornadoes. On May 2 and 3, 1956, a squall line crossing the United States triggered about 30 tornadoes, and the 148 tornadoes of the "Super Outbreak" on April 3 and 4, 1974, were produced by three separate squall lines that all developed at the same time. Between them, these squall lines extended from the southern shores of Lake Michigan to central Alabama.

Sometimes the storms generate swirling upcurrents below the cloud, along the leading edge of the gust front. These resemble tornadoes, but are much weaker. They are called *gustnadoes* to distinguish them (see the box "Gustnadoes" below).

# Conditions for a squall line

Two air masses with different characteristics must collide in order for a squall line to develop. Most commonly it is cold air that collides with warm air, but sometimes it is a collision between dry air and moist air. In either case, there must also be wind shear at high level. *Wind shear* occurs where one wind blows in a different direction or at a different speed from an adjacent wind. Wind shear is needed to carry rising air away from the top of the cloud.

Most squall lines begin when a mass of cold, dry, dense air moves forward very fast against a mass of warm, moist, less dense air. This pro-

## Gustnadoes

Supercell cumulonimbus clouds and storm clouds that develop along squall lines are fed by convection. Warm air rises through them, generating strong upcurrents. Raindrops and hailstones falling from the cloud drag cold air down with them. This generates strong downdrafts. In nonsupercell clouds, the downdrafts cool the rising air. After a time this suppresses the upcurrents and the cloud dissipates.

Supercell and squall-line clouds survive longer and the downdrafts emerge from them beneath an arched or bowed section of the cloud called the *arcus*. The downdrafts leave the cloud as strong winds that gust to 22–44 MPH (36–72 km/h). They are much colder than the warm air that is being drawn into the base of the cloud. As it passes, the downdraft can cause a temperature drop of 18°F (10°C) in a few seconds. The boundary between the cold and warm air is so sharply defined, it is known as the *gust front*.

Gust fronts can sometimes produce whirling air along the edge of the front. These often pick up dust to form *dust whirls*. The pockets of whirling air resemble tornadoes, but there is no funnel connecting them to the cloud overhead and they are seldom strong enough to cause any serious damage. They are known as *gustnadoes* to distinguish them from tornadoes.

duces a cold front (see the box "Weather fronts" on page 6) that is very vigorous, due to its speed. The dense air pushes beneath the less dense air, forcing it to rise. As it rises, the pressure acting on the air from above decreases, because it is the weight of the overlying air that exerts the pressure, and the greater the altitude, the smaller the amount of air above. With the pressure reduced, the air expands, and when air expands it cools adiabatically (see the box "Adiabatic cooling and warming" on page 5).

Warm air can hold more water vapor than cold air can (see the box "Why warm air can hold more moisture than cold air can" on page 2). Consequently, when air cools to below the dew point temperature, the water vapor it contains starts to condense into liquid droplets. Condensation produces clouds (see the box "Evaporation, condensation, and the formation of clouds" on page 38) and also releases latent heat (see the box "Latent heat and dew point" on page 40). The latent heat warms the surrounding air, making it rise further and cool again, causing still more water vapor to condense. The clouds grow bigger and bigger. Above the *freezing level*—the height at which the temperature is at freezing—the cloud contains a mixture of ice crystals and very cold water droplets, and near the top of the cloud all of the water is in the form of ice.

In a squall line, the wind above the clouds blows from a different direction to the wind lower down, carrying away the rising air. This is called *divergence* and, because air is being removed, it produces a region of low atmospheric pressure in the lower part of the clouds. Air at ground level is drawn into the low-pressure area and immediately rises, feeding the cloud with air and moisture.

At the same time, hailstones, snowflakes, and very cold raindrops are falling from the cloud. They drag cold air down with them. There are then two sets of air currents inside and beneath the cloud, one entering the cloud and rising, the other sinking from the cloud and leaving. While all this is happening, the dense air is still advancing, churning up the air ahead of it and pushing it into the upcurrents. The diagram shows how the entire system moves.

# The squall line appears

This is when the squall line earns its name. By now the clouds have become storm clouds, called *cumulonimbus*, and they tower to a great height. Then, for reasons scientists do not really understand, they form groups along a line and the strong, gusting wind at their leading edges, where air is being drawn into the low-pressure region, becomes continuous over long distances. This is the squall line itself—the narrow belt of strong, blustery winds.

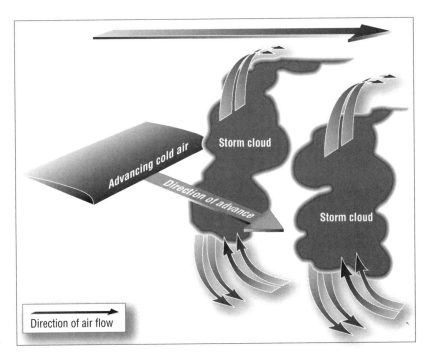

*Squall line*

Squall lines are not entirely straight. Often they are curved, and straight squall lines sometimes have curved sections within them. The curved sections are called *bowing line segments* or *bow echoes*—a name that refers to the characteristic radar echoes they produce.

During the early stages of its development, the cold downcurrents in the cloud meet the updrafts and start to slow them. Cold, descending air starts to spread horizontally, but the rising air flows over its edge and forms a new upcurrent to one side. After a time this upcurrent also meets its own spreading downcurrent, flows around its edge, and becomes another new upcurrent.

Eventually, the upcurrents and downcurrents separate completely. Upcurrents draw in air from ahead of the squall line. Downcurrents emerge to the rear of the line, but the sinking air then diverges, some of it flowing forward beneath the upcurrents and out of the front of the line. The downcurrents consist of air that is being dragged downwards by precipitation. That is why the rain and hail fall at the rear of the cloud mass.

The stream of cold, sinking air that flows beneath the less dense air ahead of the storm line forces more air to rise and new clouds to form. As they form, downcurrents from the new clouds produce still more clouds ahead of them. This movement, which triggers the formation of new cloud, is also what produces the strong gustiness of the wind.

# The squall line perpetuates itself

Not even huge storm clouds last for more than a few hours, but those in a squall line constantly regenerate themselves. They do so at first by producing new upcurrents to the side of their own downcurrents, and later by triggering new cloud formation in front of themselves. As the line advances, it looks like a solid mass of clouds all moving together—in effect a single, immense cloud. In fact, old clouds are constantly disappearing at the rear of the line and new ones are forming at the front. This is how the line moves.

The storm system is now perpetuating itself. It was an advancing mass of dense air that started the process, but now it can continue independently. The line of storms starts to move faster than the air mass behind it. If it lasts long enough, the squall line can move hundreds of miles ahead of the cold front.

It can happen that the collision triggering the formation of a squall line occurs between dry and moist air, both at much the same temperature. When this happens, the dry air may flow over the top of the moist air, trapping it beneath. This will cause clouds to form as moist air rises through the overlying dry air. The effect is usually fairly mild, but if the moist air is already cloudy, cumulus and then cumulonimbus clouds will develop. These are "heaped" clouds, produced by vigorous convection. Alternatively, if the dry air flows beneath the moist air, the moist air will be forced upward and the effect will be the same as that produced by a cold front.

# Nonfrontal squall lines

Squall lines advance because individual storm clouds are feeding one another. This mechanism also makes it possible for squall lines to develop even when there is no front to trigger them.

The process often begins with a single huge storm. Within the cloud, upcurrents of warm air conflict with the downcurrents of cold air being swept down with the rain and hail. If the cloud is big enough, the currents tend to separate (see the section "Supercells" on pages 69–76), so that warm air is being drawn into one region of the cloud and cold air is sinking and moving outward from another area. The sinking air may then flow beneath the warmer surrounding air, just as it does ahead of a squall line and with similar results. One cloud supplies cold air at ground level to lift warmer air and start it cooling. In effect, the outflow of air creates a kind of artificial cold front, with each storm cloud triggering the formation of others along it. Once formed, this type of squall line behaves in exactly the same way as one triggered by a real cold front.

Storms can also merge into one another if several form independently but fairly close together. Again, no cold front is needed to start them growing, because they can begin as ordinary thunderstorms (see the section "Thunderstorms" on pages 37–48). When they merge, however, they may align themselves and grow into a squall line.

Cold fronts are by far the commonest trigger, however, and the most vigorous cold fronts occur where tropical and polar air masses meet. This most often happens close to the Polar Front and it is at the Polar Front that the jet stream provides a strong wind shear to start squall lines forming. These most often occur in spring, which is when the Polar Front and its jet stream are moving northward across North America (see the section "Jet streams" on pages 27–36).

Tornadoes that are linked to squall-line storms are usually fairly short-lived and weak, but squall lines are only one source of tornadoes. Isolated supercell thunderstorms can produce stronger and longer-lasting tornadoes, and these are much less predictable.

# TORNADO OUTBREAKS

Squall lines comprise many thunderstorms, all of them active at the same time and many of them vigorous enough to trigger tornadoes—a storm of this kind is called *tornadic*. When a single weather system, such as a squall line, triggers more than about a dozen tornadoes, the event is known as a *tornado outbreak*. The outbreak of 1974 (see the section "What is a tornado?" on pages xv–xvi) was the biggest outbreak ever recorded anywhere in the world. In the space of 24 hours on April 3–4, it generated 148 tornadoes. That one was called the "Super Outbreak." It was unique because of the number of tornadoes it produced, but tornado outbreaks are not uncommon and some of them generate many individual tornadoes and cause devastation over a wide area.

At about 7 A.M. on September 20, 1967, for example, Hurricane Beulah crossed the coast near the mouth of the Rio Grande, in Texas. Near the center of the storm, the winds were blowing at about 136 MPH (219 km/h), although they quickly weakened. Beulah briefly attained category 4 on the Saffir-Simpson hurricane scale, but for most of its time over land Beulah was rated as no more than category 1—the weakest—and at times the winds dropped to less than 75 MPH (121 km/h). This is the lower limit for a hurricane, and when the wind speed decreased to below it, Beulah had to be reclassified as a tropical storm.

Beulah was not an especially ferocious hurricane, but it forced some communities to evacuate and caused a great deal of damage to property. Floods due to tidal surges and the heavy rain were responsible for most of this—the cost of the flood damage exceeded $100 million. Several places recorded more than 14 inches (356 mm) of rain.

Despite the relatively low wind speeds, Beulah was remarkable for the number of tornadoes it produced. Some reports said there were 95, but others placed the figure as high as 115 or 141—not far short of the Super Outbreak—and one even claimed 150, although this estimate is probably too high. If there were about 100 tornadoes, this would be the highest number that any tropical cyclone has ever been known to cause.

Individually, these tornadoes were quite small. Many of them were no more than 20–40 feet (6–12 m) in diameter at the base and they remained in contact with the ground for less than one minute—some for only a few seconds. They traveled fast, however. At times some of them were moving over the ground at 60 MPH (96 km/h). All tornadoes are dangerous, and those accompanying Beulah caused five fatalities. Four of these occurred in Palacios, Texas, soon after the hurricane made landfall. The other person died near Louise, in Wharton County, Texas.

Tropical cyclones—the storms that are also known as *hurricanes, typhoons, cyclones,* and by various other names, depending on where they occur—can and do trigger tornadoes, but there seems to be no way of predicting whether a particular storm will do so. Beulah, a fairly weak storm, produced a record number. Andrew, one of the most violent storms ever known, produced far fewer.

Hurricane Andrew was the most destructive storm ever to strike the United States. It roared its way through southern Florida on August 24, 1992, with winds that produced one gust measured at 177 MPH (285 km/h). Andrew was rated category 5—the highest—on the Saffir-Simpson scale and it caused damage costing $26.5 billion. Yet, despite its ferocity, Andrew triggered only 62 tornadoes.

# The 1999 outbreak

An outbreak on May 3–4, 1999 generated 78 tornadoes in the course of 21 hours over Oklahoma and Kansas. One of those tornadoes, rated F-5 on the Fujita scale (see the section "Measuring the severity of tornadoes" on pages 141–147) caused damage costing about $1 billion, making it the costliest tornado in U.S. history. The "Oklahoma City Tornado," as it came to be known, traveled 38 miles (61 km) from Chickasha, through the southern side of Oklahoma City and Bridge Creek, then through Moore, Midwest City, and Del City. It demolished or damaged about 8,000 buildings. Damage from the May 1999 outbreak as a whole amounted to about $1.5 billion.

The May outbreak was the worst of the year, but 1999 was a bad year for outbreaks. An outbreak of 70 tornadoes began on the evening of April 8 and lasted through the following day. Those storms crossed Nebraska, Iowa, Missouri, Illinois, Indiana, and Ohio. There were small outbreaks on September 4 and September 16, in Virginia and North Carolina, caused by Tropical Storms Dennis and Floyd, and six tornadoes—not strictly an outbreak—caused two deaths in Chico, Texas, on December 2. Although there were so many tornado outbreaks in 1999, there is no evident pattern to their occurrence—no more than there is to the incidence of tornadoes themselves.

Perhaps the frequency of outbreaks is not surprising in light of the number of tornadoes the United States experiences. The 78 tornadoes of the May 1999 Oklahoma and Kansas outbreak contributed to the 325 tornadoes that month in various parts of the country. There were 1,225 tornadoes in the whole of 1999—and that total was down from the 1,424 that struck in 1998. The 1999 total included six major tornado outbreaks and several smaller ones.

According to unofficial reports, there were only 451 tornadoes in the United States by the end of July 2002. The traditional tornado season runs from March until July and the small number made 2002 an unusually quiet year. There were fewer than half the 10-year annual average of 914 tornadoes and the 451 total was the lowest midyear number since 1988. This was because the season started late, due to an outbreak of cold air in February and March that suppressed the development of tornadic storms in the Southeast. There were up to 100 tornadoes later in the year and outside the season, however, including the November outbreak described below. These increased the 2002 annual total, but it remained well below the 10-year average.

The first major outbreak of 2002 was on January 1 and 2, when 26 tornadoes occurred in Texas and Louisiana. This was unusually early. Warm, moist air from the Gulf had moved northward near the surface. This produced strong convection currents and storm clouds. At the time, the winds in the upper atmosphere were blowing strongly from west to east. Strong convection and wind shear provided ideal conditions for setting the air turning, but although it is fairly common in late spring, this weather pattern rarely develops so early in the year.

A second January outbreak soon followed the first. It occurred on January 17, in Arkansas, Tennessee, and Missouri. There were 25 tornadoes in the second outbreak and they killed eight people. Six people lost their lives on January 21 and 22, when a third outbreak, this time of 104 tornadoes, struck Arkansas, Louisiana, and Tennessee. Those tornadoes produced hailstones the size of softballs—almost 4 inches (10 cm) across—and, as with many tornadoes, there were stories of lucky escapes. A girls' basketball game in the gym at Beebe High School was abandoned when word arrived of an approaching tornado. Between 200 and 300 people left. Thirty minutes later a tornado with winds of more than 160 MPH (257 km/h) totally demolished the gym—but injured no one.

# Enigma and Tri-State

Severe though it was, the Super Outbreak was not the most lethal of all tornado outbreaks. That dubious distinction probably belongs to an outbreak of 60 tornadoes that crossed the southeastern United States on February 19, 1884. The tornadoes lasted for 12 hours, from 11 A.M. until 11 P.M., caused damage costing an estimated $3 million—a vast sum in 1884 money—and killed possibly 420 people. The "possibly" is the reason the outbreak is called Enigma. Estimates of the number of deaths range from 182 to 1,200. That is the enigma.

There is no doubt about the number of people who lost their lives during the Tri-State Outbreak on March 18, 1925. The total was 747, but 695 of those were killed by a single tornado—the Tri-State itself. In all there were nine tornadoes on that day, however, and the remaining eight killed an additional 52 people.

The Tri-State tornado was remarkable for the distance it traveled. It covered 219 miles (352 km) at about 60 MPH (96 km/h) along a track that took it across parts of three states—Missouri, Illinois, and Indiana (see the section "How a tornado travels" on pages 91–95).

# Palm Sunday and Easter Sunday

Tornadic storms often occur around Easter and there have been two outbreaks on Palm Sunday. The 1965 Palm Sunday Outbreak was the second deadliest of the 20th century, killing 258 people and injuring 3,148. On April 11–12 a total of 51 tornadoes moved through parts of Wisconsin, Illinois, Michigan, Indiana, and Ohio. In lower Michigan, two tornadoes crossed Steuben and Monroe Counties, one after the other. A large tornado destroyed or damaged 90 percent of the buildings in Russiaville, Indiana, and Goshen, Indiana, was struck by two tornadoes at the same time.

In 1994, Palm Sunday fell on March 27. On that day 12 tornadoes occurred in Alabama and Georgia between 10:45 A.M. and 8:15 P.M. These were triggered by violent storms that affected Alabama, Georgia, North Carolina, South Carolina, and Tennessee. Piedmont, Alabama, was the town that suffered the greatest loss, when a tornado killed at least 19 worshipers at the Goshen Methodist Church.

There have also been two outbreaks on Easter Sunday. The first happened on March 23, 1913, in eastern Nebraska and western Iowa. In the space of 1.5 hours, between 4:30 and 6:00 P.M., eight tornadoes caused damage costing $4 million and killed 181 people.

There was a much bigger outbreak on April 23, 2000. In the second Easter Sunday Outbreak, a total of 28 tornadoes struck in southeastern Oklahoma, southwestern Arkansas, northeastern Texas, and northwestern Louisiana. Six supercell (see the section "Supercells" on pages 69–76) thunderstorms triggered most of these tornadoes, and isolated thunderstorms accounted for all but one of the remainder. The exception was a twister that began as a waterspout (see the section "Waterspouts and water devils" on pages 106–110) over Cross Lake, Louisiana, and became a tornado when it crossed onto land. It then passed through Shreveport and Bossier City. The tornadic thunderstorms formed a line ahead of a cold front advancing from Oklahoma. A second line of storms formed later behind the first line; it was a storm on the second line that produced the waterspout.

Fortunately, most of the tornadoes were of only moderate strength, rated F-1 and F-2 on the Fujita scale (see the section "Measuring the severity of tornadoes" on pages 141–147), although a few were F3. No lives were lost, but there was considerable damage to property. Some of the tornadoes caused damage up to 2 miles (3 km) on either side of their track, and although most were in contact with the ground only briefly, some covered a considerable distance. One tornado traveled 37 miles (59.5 km) from Bossier Parish to Minden, Louisiana, and another covered 32.5 miles (52 km) from close to Greenwood to the southern side of Shreveport and then to Elm Grove, Louisiana.

# Mother's Day

In 1999, a total of 199 tornadoes touched down in the United States between May 1 and May 10, but that record was broken in 2003, when 395 tornadoes struck during this period. One of the outbreaks occurred on Sunday, May 11—Mother's Day.

The first outbreak of the month struck Missouri, Tennessee, and Kansas on Sunday, May 5th. The area worst affected was Pierce City, a small Missouri town with a population of a little more than 1,000. Almost every building was damaged or destroyed.

Tornadoes struck again on Mother's Day weekend. The second outbreak of the month crossed Illinois, Indiana, Iowa, Kentucky, Missouri, North Carolina, Oklahoma, Tennessee, and Wisconsin. One twister lifted a farmhouse in Iowa and set it down again more than 30 feet (9 m) away—complete with three teenage occupants, two of whom were unharmed; the third boy suffered scratches from broken glass. Dan McCarthy, a meteorologist at the federal Storm Prediction Center said it was the longest tornado outbreak he could recall. By the time it ended, at least 38 people had been killed and hundreds were injured.

# Winter tornadoes

The tornado season ends in July, but this does not mean tornadoes never occur in winter. A tornado outbreak began in the middle of the day on November 21, 1992, and by the time it ended, early on the morning of November 23, it had produced a total of 94 tornadoes. Crossing parts of 13 states, between them these twisters killed 26 people, injured 641, and caused $291 million of damage. The deadliest of the tornadoes, rated F-4—meaning its winds were 207–260 MPH (333–418 km/h)—traveled 128 miles (206 km) through Mississippi and killed 12 people. Another F-4 tracked 20 miles (32 km) through the suburbs of Houston, Texas, demolishing 200 homes and damaging a further 1,000.

Another November outbreak occurred in 2001. On Saturday, November 24, approximately 24 tornadoes struck in Alabama and others caused damage in Mississippi and Arkansas. A total of 11 people died in that outbreak.

One of the worst November outbreaks on record happened on November 10–11, 2002. A cold front stretching from Texas to New York and advancing eastward at 110 MPH (177 km/h) met warm, moist air moving northward from the Gulf of Mexico and producing temperatures that were 20°F (11°C) higher than normal. The collision between the two air masses produced a squall line with storms that triggered at least

66 tornadoes, some registering F-4 and F-5—winds of 207–318 MPH (333–512 km/h). At least 36 people lost their lives, 17 in Tennessee, 12 in Alabama, five in Ohio, and one each in Mississippi and Pennsylvania. One tornado left a track 50 miles (80 km) long in Walker County, Alabama. Mossy Grove, Tennessee, was one of the towns that suffered most. A tornado wrecked everything along a track 5–6 miles (8–10 km) long through the town.

As with so many tornadoes, this crop generated stories of lucky survivals. A family of four living near Knoxville, Tennessee, sheltered in a neighbor's house. Minutes after they took cover, two cars crashed into the house, collapsing a wall onto their 17-year-old daughter. The wind blew away the rubble of the wall and then lifted the girl's 9-year-old brother into the air, pulling his shoes from his feet. Both parents and the daughter grabbed the boy's ankles and held him. The daughter was stripped of her clothes. It was a terrifying ordeal, but the family survived.

Two people died but many more were saved in a cinema complex in Van Wert, Ohio, when an F-4 tornado, 3,000 feet (915 m) across struck the building. The manager had just enough time to move the audiences into relatively secure corridors and bathrooms before the twister demolished one theater, dropping three cars into it, and tore the roofs from two more.

On January 24, 1967, an outbreak of 30 tornadoes moved through Iowa, Missouri, Illinois, and Wisconsin. The outbreak lasted for nine hours. Seven people died and 268 were injured.

Tornadoes are associated with violent storms. The fact that a single weather system can generate an outbreak of dozens of tornadoes, some of them reaching F-4 strength, illustrates dramatically the power that convection can release in unstable air and the vast area the resulting storms can affect.

# HOW A TORNADO BEGINS

Any thunderstorm that is capable of generating tornadoes is said to be *tornadic*. The appearance of tornadic storms is a little different from that of squall-line storms (see the section "Squall lines" on pages 49–56), but both types produce similar effects.

When you are beneath a big cloud it is almost impossible to estimate the height of its base or, in the case of a cumulonimbus, its bases, for a cumulonimbus cloud extends to the side with sections that look like shelves. One of those shelves, joining the really huge tower of a tornadic storm at a quite low level, may be the inner edge of the *anvil*—the scientific name is *incus*, which is the Latin word for "anvil." The rest of the anvil, its base sloping upward, stretches away from the tower for several miles. If you are standing directly in the path of the approaching cloud and facing it, in the Northern Hemisphere the anvil will stretch toward you and to your right, as shown in the drawing. In the Southern Hemisphere the anvil will stretch to your left.

## Mammatus

On the lowest part of the anvil base there may be a quite unmistakable feature. Many smooth, udder-shaped clouds may look as though they are suspended from the base of the main cloud. This is a supplementary cloud feature called *mammatus*, from the Old English version of the Latin word for breast.

Mammatus forms when ice crystals at the top of the anvil sublime—change directly from ice to water vapor without passing through a liquid phase—and the water vapor moves into the dry air above the anvil. Sublimation absorbs a large amount of latent heat (see the box "Latent heat and dew point" on page 40) from the surrounding air, rapidly producing small pools of air at the top of the anvil that are colder than the surrounding air. Being colder, the small pools are also denser than the surrounding air, and they contain ice crystals, just like the rest of the anvil. They sink through the anvil until they protrude from its base just far enough to produce the mammatus effect.

Mammatus can form only where the anvil is very large. Very large anvils indicate the presence of very violent upcurrents and a layer of stable air above the cloud. Rising air, carried in the upcurrents, cannot penetrate the stable layer and so it spills sideways. That is what forms the anvil. The size of the anvil is a measure of the amount of water vapor the upcurrents are feeding into it. The bigger it is, the more water it contains, and so the more vigorous the upcurrents must be.

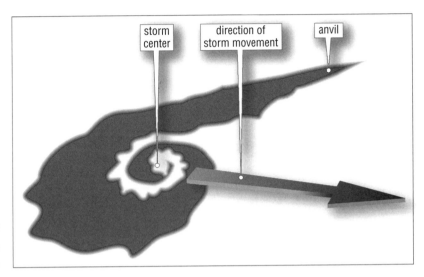

*Location of the anvil and direction of movement in a tornadic storm*

Violent upcurrents are necessary for the formation of tornadoes, so the appearance of mammatus beneath an approaching cloud is a clear warning. It does not mean tornadoes are present, but it does mean they are possible or even likely.

Squall-line storm clouds rarely produce mammatus. With them, the early warning sign is the appearance of fragments of cloud that are moving in a circle beneath the main cloud.

# Vertical currents

Ordinary cumulonimbus, of the kind that produces heavy showers and sometimes thunderstorms, is not tornadic. Within this type of cumulonimbus, the upcurrents and downcurrents are in the same place, so they compete.

The downcurrents are made by cold air that is dragged downward by falling rain and hailstones. The upcurrents rise vertically through the cloud and the precipitation and downcurrents fall directly into them. This cools the rising air, making it less buoyant, and within an hour or so it suppresses the upcurrents completely. Once that happens, the storm begins to die and before long the storm cloud dissipates. As the storm dies, the main part of the cloud falls as rain or snow, with smaller drops or flakes than fell earlier, and after a few minutes nothing may remain of the cloud except for its anvil, drifting off by itself. While the storm lasts you feel the downcurrents as gusts of cold wind, and the combination of air entering and leaving the base of the cloud makes the wind strong and variable in direction.

Where the upcurrents are strong enough to feed a really big anvil, however, the sweep of air into the anvil produces a *wind shear* that bends over the upper part of the upcurrents, carrying them clear of the downcurrents, as shown in the diagram. This allows the upcurrents and downcurrents to separate, with the upcurrents overhanging the downcurrents. The cloud then contains a *supercell* (see the section "Supercells" on pages 69–76). This process can convert an isolated thunderstorm into a tornadic storm. Upcurrents and downcurrents also separate in squall-line storms, but the mechanism is different (see the section "Squall lines" on pages 49–56 for an explanation).

# Wind shear and the mesocyclone

Even at this stage the emergence of tornadoes is not inevitable. A third factor is needed to set the entire system spinning on its axis. That factor is a change in wind speed and direction with height, called wind shear.

There is usually some wind shear. Because of friction, surface winds over land are always weaker than the winds a few hundred feet above the ground and their direction is less constant (see the section "How wind changes with height" on pages 11–19). In itself, this is not enough to provide the necessary amount of wind shear, but if the storm cloud lies beneath the jet stream or across a weather front, the high-level wind

*Upcurrents and downcurrents in a tornadic storm*

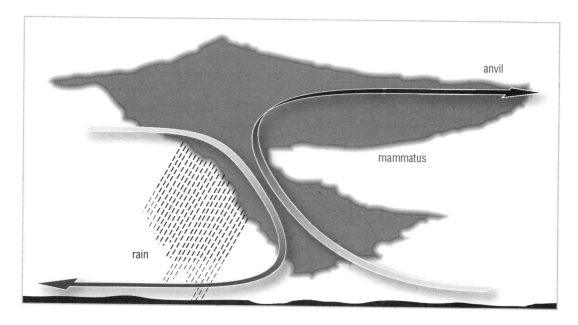

direction and speed will be quite different from those of the wind at lower levels. The jet stream (see the section "Jet streams" on pages 27–36) is certainly strong enough to provide considerable wind shear and frontal winds may be strong enough.

Upcurrents, rising through the cloud, flow in the direction of the wind. As they rise, they encounter wind from a different direction, which deflects them. Moving air tends to rotate about an axis (see the section "Vortices and angular momentum" on pages 77–83) and this deflection either starts the upcurrents rotating or intensifies their rotation if they are already spiraling upward.

Air near the center of the cloud, containing cloud particles and raindrops or ice crystals, then starts to rotate. The rotating air turns counterclockwise in the Northern Hemisphere. Counterclockwise rotation is called *cyclonic* and at its center there is a *cyclone* or region of low air pressure. At this stage a *mesocyclone* has developed in the interior of the cloud (see the box "Mesocyclones" below).

# Mesocyclones

A large cumulonimbus storm cloud derives its energy from convection. Warm air is drawn into the base of the cloud, and the condensation of water vapor inside the cloud releases latent heat energy that sustains the convection. Convection generates updrafts of air.

Precipitation falling from the upper parts of the cloud drags cold air downwards. This generates downdrafts of air. In most clouds, the downdrafts fall into the updrafts, cooling and suppressing them. If there is wind shear in the upper part of the cloud, the updrafts and downdrafts are tilted so that the downdraft no longer falls into the updraft. This forms a *supercell*, in which the air rotates about a horizontal axis, rising on one side and descending on the other side.

Along the edge of the updraft, the rotating air then starts to tilt. It continues to tilt until the horizontal rotation has been translated into vertical rotation—rotation about a vertical axis—with two vortices spinning side by side, one turning clockwise and the other counterclockwise. The storm is then likely to divide into two. In the Northern Hemisphere, the one with internal counterclockwise (*cyclonic*) rotation is the stronger.

Cyclonic rotation produces a region of low air pressure at its center. Air is drawn into the low-pressure region. This is called *convergence*. Converging air spins in a counterclockwise direction, intensifying the existing rotation, as shown in the diagram. There is then a mass of spinning cloud and precipitation particles inside the cloud at about the middle level. This is the midlevel *mesocyclone*. It is usually 2–5 miles (3–8 km) across.

Below the cloud, the downdraft is still rotating about a horizontal axis. If part of this rotation is transferred to air approaching the updraft, the horizontal rotation of the rising air is tilted until it becomes vertical. This produces a second, low-level mesocyclone near the base of the cloud. The low-level mesocyclone may become stronger than the midlevel mesocyclone.

# Tornadoes without tornadic storms

Not every tornado grows from a tornadic storm. This seems like a contradiction—after all, calling a storm "tornadic" implies that it is capable of triggering a tornado. Tornadic storms are identified by radar, however. Radar can detect the mesocyclone inside the cloud, heralding the formation of a tornado. Mesocyclones develop in supercell clouds. Consequently, a storm emanating from a supercell cloud becomes tornadic when the cloud acquires a mesocyclone.

This process explains the formation of most tornadoes, but there are exceptions. Some tornadoes occur in the absence of a mesocyclone. These *nonmesocyclone* tornadoes occur when there is little rain or hail falling. Sometimes they develop when the air is quite dry. They are smaller than ordinary tornadoes and less violent, but nevertheless they can be strong enough to damage property (see the box "Nonmesocyclone tornadoes" on page 68).

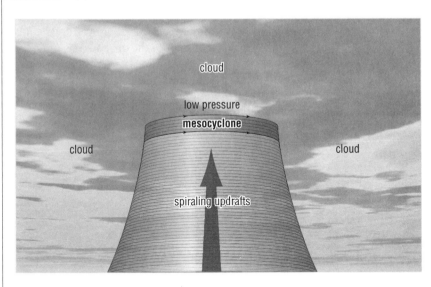

*Mesocyclone*

If the mesocyclones extend downward, the funnel of spiraling air may emerge beneath the cloud base. If it extends all the way to the ground it becomes a tornado.

Mesocyclones are invisible, because they are located inside the cloud, but they produce a distinctive radar echo and so meteorologists are able to detect them. Warnings of the likelihood of tornadoes are based on these radar echoes.

# Nonmesocyclone tornadoes

Most tornadoes develop from mesocyclones inside supercell storm clouds, but there are exceptions. Tornadoes that develop in the absence of mesocyclones are known as *landspouts, nonsupercell tornadoes,* or *nonmesocyclone tornadoes.*

Nonmesocyclone tornadoes grow from the ground upward, into the storm cloud rather than out of it. Scientists believe they begin as swirls of air close to the ground, similar to dust devils and probably generated by the convergence of air into the updraft entering a cloud that is still growing and has not yet reached its mature stage as a storm cloud. The swirls of air extend upward until they join the cloud above them.

The storm has not yet broken, and so nonmesocyclone tornadoes develop in fairly dry air. If precipitation is falling, it is usually light and the tornado funnel is much narrower than the funnel of a mesocyclone tornado. The air may be so dry that very little water vapor condenses in the funnel. In that case the funnel may be visible only because of the dust it has gathered.

Most nonmesocyclone tornadoes are fairly weak, but occasionally they can be strong enough to cause damage. For reasons scientists do not yet understand, these tornadoes are much more common in Colorado than they are in Oklahoma.

However they develop, from a mesocyclone or from the ground, at this stage small wind eddies may lift dust from the ground, raising it a foot or two, twisting as it goes. If you see these miniature twisters beneath an approaching storm cloud you can be sure all the necessary ingredients for a tornado are assembled. They tell you that rising air in the cloud is spinning strongly. At any moment one or more tornadoes may appear.

# SUPERCELLS

Inside a storm cloud, warm air is rising in upcurrents and cool air is sinking in downcurrents. This is what happens in a *convection cell*. It is a very common phenomenon. When you heat a pan of water on the stove, convection cells usually form in it. Warmed water rises, cools at the surface, and sinks to the bottom, where it is warmed and rises again. Many homes have central heating systems that work in this way.

Convection is due to gravity. When a fluid (gas or liquid) absorbs heat, its molecules move farther apart and therefore it becomes less dense. This means that a unit volume—one cubic inch, for example—of a warm fluid contains fewer molecules and therefore weighs less than it would if the fluid were colder and contained more molecules. Because it is less dense, the warm fluid is displaced by denser and therefore heavier fluid that sinks by gravity, flows beneath it, and lifts it upward. We think of warm air rising, but this is misleading. It is true that warm air rises, but this is not because it is defying gravity and simply floating away. It is because colder air, being denser and heavier, is sinking beneath it and pushing it upward.

Inside an ordinary cumulonimbus storm cloud, the convection cells are unstable and last no more than an hour or two. The upcurrents and downcurrents interfere with one another until the downcurrents smother the upcurrents and the cold rain and snow, together with the cold air they drag down with them, cool the rising air. When that happens, the storm dies down and the cloud quickly starts to dissipate. If the conditions that led to the formation of the cloud remain, however, even as it is dying another storm cloud will be forming to take its place. Consequently, a storm can last much longer and travel farther than the individual clouds that compose it.

# Separating the vertical currents

If the upcurrents and downcurrents separate, however, so that they flow in different parts of the cloud, the resulting convection cell is much more stable. A cloud in which this happens can live for many hours.

The two currents will separate if wind shear in the upper part of the cloud tilts the upcurrent so it no longer rises vertically. Hail, rain, and ice that form near the top of the upcurrent continue to fall approximately vertically through the cloud, but because the upcurrent is tilted, they fall to one side of it. When this happens, the downcurrents no longer interfere with the upcurrents (see the box "Mesocyclones" on page 66).

Often there is not just a single convection cell in a large cumulonimbus, but several. Sometimes these form when adjacent cumulonimbus clouds merge. This can happen when unstable air extends to a considerable height and there is high-level wind shear.

More often, multiple convection cells develop along squall lines (see the section "Squall lines" on pages 49–56). The strong downcurrent of cold air leaving a convection cell produces a very small area close to ground level in which the atmospheric pressure is just a little higher than that of the surrounding air. The denser air moves beneath the less dense air, causing it to rise. The lifted air is *conditionally unstable*. Once it starts rising it becomes unstable (see the box "Lapse rates and stability" on page 71). The downcurrents beside it continue to push more and more air into it, making the air rise with increasing intensity until there is enough of it to form the upcurrent of a new convective cell, with its own downcurrent to repeat the process.

Just by looking at it you cannot tell where one cloud ends and the next begins. It looks like, and is, a single, vast mass of cloud, but it is cloud that contains whole clusters of convection cells. When fully developed, each individual convection cell is usually about 0.5 mile (0.8 km) in diameter.

# Giant cells and firestorms

Some convection cells grow much larger than this. They can be up to 6 miles (10 km) across. A cloud containing such large convection cells reaches much greater heights than an ordinary storm cloud and it lasts far longer. These very large, stable, convective cells are called *supercells*. The upcurrents in supercells often rise at 100 MPH (160 km/h) or more.

If they are big enough and hot enough, surface fires can cause intense convection cells. After the atomic bomb was dropped on Hiroshima in 1945, and also after fires that followed an earthquake in Tokyo in 1923, the strong convection produced *firestorms*. The heat at the center of the fire was so intense that it drew in air from a wide surrounding area and sent it spiraling upward. The inflowing air carried debris, adding fuel to the fire. These storms triggered several tornadoes.

Tornadoes also occurred around firestorms in other cities, in Germany as well as Japan, but those caused by the Hiroshima atomic explosion led a young Japanese scientist, Tetsuya Theodore Fujita (he took his middle name in 1968), to embark on what became a lifelong study of tornadoes. Based at the University of Chicago, Professor Fujita (1920–98) was recognized as probably the world's leading authority on the subject. It was Professor Fujita who proposed, in 1957, that tornadoes might occur in clouds of a particular type—he called them "supercell clouds"—all of which have a similar structure, or "architecture."

# Lapse rates and stability

Air temperature decreases (or lapses) with increasing height. The rate at which it does so is called the lapse rate. When dry air cools adiabatically, it does so at about 5.5°F for every 1,000 feet (10°C per km). This is known as the dry adiabatic lapse rate (DALR).

When the temperature of the rising air has fallen sufficiently, its water vapor will start to condense into droplets. This temperature is known as the dew point temperature, and the height at which it is reached is called the lifting condensation level. Condensation releases latent heat, which warms the air. Consequently, the air cools at a slower rate, known as the saturated adiabatic lapse rate (SALR). The SALR varies, but averages 3°F per 1,000 ft. (6°C per km).

The actual rate at which the temperature decreases with height is called the environmental lapse rate (ELR). It is calculated by comparing the surface temperature, the temperature at the tropopause (about −67°F; −55°C in middle latitudes),

and the height of the tropopause (about 7 miles; 11 km in middle latitudes).

If the ELR is less than both the DALR and SALR, rising air will cool faster than the surrounding air, so it will always be cooler and will tend to subside to a lower height. Such air is said to be absolutely stable.

If the ELR is greater than the SALR, air that is rising and cooling at the DALR and later at the SALR will always be warmer than the surrounding air. Consequently, it will continue to rise. The air is then absolutely unstable.

If the ELR is greater than the DALR but less than the SALR, rising air will cool faster than the surrounding air while it remains dry, but more slowly once it rises above the lifting condensation level. At first it is stable, but above the lifting condensation level it becomes unstable. This air is said to be conditionally unstable. It is stable unless a condition (rising above its lifting condensation level) is met, whereupon it becomes unstable.

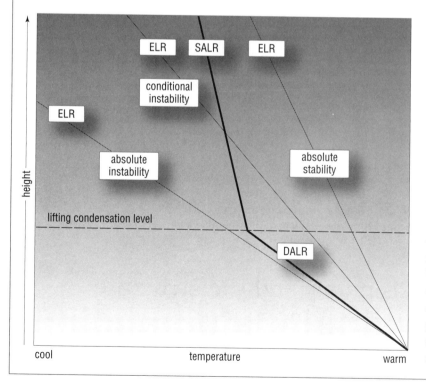

*Lapse rates and stability. If the environmental lapse rate (ELR) is less than both the dry (DALR) and wet (SALR) adiabatic lapse rates, the air is absolutely stable. If the ELR is greater than the SALR, the air is absolutely unstable. If the ELR is less than the SALR but greater than the DALR, the air is conditionally unstable.*

# Danger to aircraft

Inside a big cumulonimbus, never mind a fully grown supercell cloud, conditions are extremely violent and it is for good reason that aircraft will detour many miles to avoid them. In his book *Wellington, Mainstay of Bomber Command*, Peter G. Cooksley described what can happen to a plane that accidentally flies through one.

One morning in 1944, a Wellington bomber of the Royal Air Force took off from its field to the northwest of London on what should have been a routine training mission. At 12,000 feet (3,660 m) the plane entered what the pilot took to be cumulus cloud. As the crew soon discovered, however, the cumulus exterior hid a core of vigorous cumulonimbus storm cloud and they flew directly into it.

Bucking and swinging about wildly, the plane was bombarded with hail and sheets of rain. The pilot and copilot were strapped into their seats, but the other members of the crew found themselves floating weightless one moment as the machine dropped from beneath them, then pressed hard into their seats as it leapt upward. Equipment that was not tied down did the same. Heavy ammunition boxes floated, then crashed to the floor, and the navigator's maps and pencils rose into the air and scattered everywhere. The needle on the airspeed indicator spun crazily and then the instrument broke. All the windows suddenly went white as they were covered with rime ice, and ice started accumulating on the wings. The pilot tried to turn back to fly out of the cloud, but his attempt to do this sent the bomber into an uncontrolled, spiraling dive. At this point he ordered the crew to prepare to bail out.

It was the dive that saved them. The pilot was able to regain control by throwing the plane out of the bottom of the cloud, where the ice melted from the wings and blew away. They had plunged 7,000 feet (2,135 m), most of the time with the plane completely out of control. Miraculously, none of the crew was injured, and their plane, said to be one of the strongest types of aircraft ever built, sustained only minor damage.

At least one pilot has ejected inside a thunderstorm, when the engine of his jet fighter failed and the fire warning light made him fear it was burning. He ejected at 47,000 feet (14,335 m), fell, then was swept upward at tremendous speed, fell again, and repeated this several times before falling from the bottom of the cloud. He spent more than half an hour inside the cloud, alternately suspended from his parachute and dragged upwards by it, before finally he reached the ground.

# Rising air and the structure of the atmosphere

Both of these were "merely" isolated thunderstorms. A supercell storm is much fiercer. Large storms are often severe, but supercell storms are always severe, terrifying, and usually very dangerous. They can tear the wings from any plane that is not specially strengthened to survive them and, beneath them, they can generate tornadoes, and often do.

As air races up the main core of an upcurrent, more air is drawn in at the base. This is *convergence* and it has two effects. The first is that converging air tends to start turning about a vertical axis. This is due to *vorticity* (see the section "Vortices and angular momentum" on pages 77–83). The second effect is to produce a region of intensely low pressure beneath the cloud, where the air is converging. The speed of the moving air generates gale force, gusting winds. Air entering the cloud is already moist, and as it rises and cools its water vapor condenses. It rises so fast, however, that water vapor is carried to a great height.

There is a limit to the height rising air can reach, no matter how warm it is. Air is warmed from below by contact with the land and sea surface. It is this warming that makes air rise by convection, and as it rises it cools adiabatically (see the box "Adiabatic cooling and warming" on page 5).

Atmospheric processes are often described in terms of their effects on a "parcel" of air—a body of air that is completely isolated from the air around it. Rising air is not really confined to "parcels," because there is a great deal of mixing due to air turbulence, but the concept is useful in describing what happens. Rising air does cool adiabatically, and latent heat, released and absorbed by the condensation and evaporation of water in air that is moving vertically and at the same time mixing with the surrounding air, affects the temperature inside the cloud.

The greater the altitude, however, the farther away the air is from the source of warming and the less affected it is by warmth carried aloft by convection. Its temperature decreases with height. The influence of latent heat also decreases with height, because as the temperature continues to fall, more and more water vapor is "squeezed" out of the air. The graph illustrates this fall in temperature with height (the lapse rate) in a very simplified way. In fact, the lapse rate varies from place to place and from one day to the next in the same place, so the diagram shows the principle of what happens, rather than being a literal description of it.

Eventually, a height is reached where the temperature either remains constant with further increase in altitude or gradually increases, as shown in the diagram. Ordinarily, rising air cannot surpass this height, because the air above it is at the same temperature and density as itself. A boundary called the *tropopause* divides the atmosphere into two distinct layers. In the lower layer, the *troposphere*, temperature decreases with height. In the layer above the tropopause, the *stratosphere*, temperature is at first constant with increasing height, then increases, due mainly to the absorption of incoming solar ultraviolet radiation by oxygen and ozone. It is this absorption that forms the ozone layer. The stratosphere, too, ends with a boundary called the *stratopause*, above which, in the *mesosphere*, temperature once more decreases with height.

The name *troposphere* is from the Greek word *tropos*, which means "turning." The troposphere is the region of the atmosphere in which air

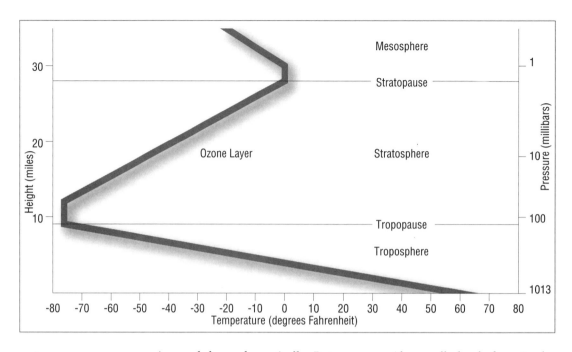

*Pressure, temperature, and height through the atmosphere*

rises and descends vertically: It turns over. Almost all clouds form in the troposphere (a few special kinds of cloud occasionally form in the stratosphere) and it is where weather happens. Because air is easily compressed, the weight of the overlying atmosphere presses down so much that 84 percent of the air making up the entire atmosphere lies below a height of 8 miles (13 km), and 94 percent of it lies below 18 miles (29 km). Atmospheric water vapor is confined almost wholly to the troposphere. Air in the stratosphere is very dry. The "strato" in *stratosphere* is from a Latin word meaning "strewn about," or "laid down." In the stratosphere there is very little vertical movement of air, but that is not how the stratosphere acquired its name. Léon-Philippe Teisserenc de Bort (1855–1913), the French meteorologist who discovered the stratosphere, believed that the air was so still at this height that its constituent gases would separate, with the heaviest at the bottom and the lighter ones above. This does not happen. Gases in the stratosphere are as thoroughly mixed as those in the troposphere.

The height of the tropopause varies, but on average it is at about 10 miles (16 km) over the equator and 5 miles (8 km) over the poles. The difference is due to the much greater surface heating over the equator and the resulting convection.

In a supercell cloud, the upcurrents rise so fast, with so much energy, that they overshoot the tropopause, sometimes by as much as two miles (3 km), with ice-crystal cloud still forming in air with an average temperature of about –76°F (–60°C). Not even a supercell cloud can extend farther than this. Its upward motion checked, the rising air steadies, then sinks to just below the tropopause as the cloud spreads downwind to form the upper part of the anvil. Seen from an aircraft flying in the stratosphere, the top of the storm cloud has a clearly marked hump.

# Downcurrents and precipitation

The supercell downcurrent is also very strong. It originates at about mid-height, as shown in the drawing of a storm cloud, and it loses none of its speed as it leaves the base of the cloud. Downcurrents can emerge as 75-MPH (121-km/h) winds. Technically, this is a hurricane-force wind and it can do considerable damage, especially to farm crops. Combined with the torrential rain that accompanies it, the downdraft can flatten crops on the ground (farmers call this *lodging*), leaving them soaked and almost impossible to harvest.

Hail, too, can cause severe crop damage. Hailstones begin to form in the upcurrent and grow by repeated freezing and partial melting (see the section "Thunderstorms" on pages 37–48 for an explanation of how hail-

*Structure of a supercell*

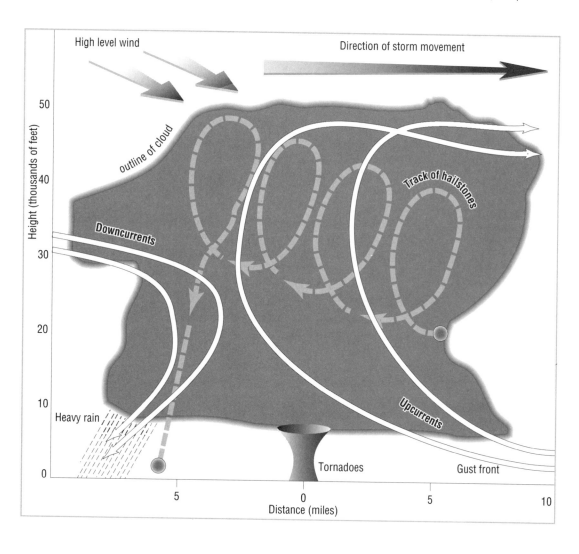

stones form). As they rise and fall, the hailstones move progressively toward the rear of the cloud, eventually falling in the downcurrent. Hail falls when the weight of a hailstone is greater than the updraft can lift, so the size it can attain is directly related to the strength of the updraft and that, in turn, depends on the size and vigor of the convective cell. An ordinary cumulonimbus cloud usually releases hailstones about the size of peppercorns. In a supercell cloud, where many times more energy is being used, hailstones can sometimes grow much bigger. There have been many reports of hailstones the size of golf balls and of rare specimens that are even bigger. Fortunately, these seldom cause much damage, because there are few of them. Most hailstones are caught in the downcurrent before they can grow to this size. What does cause damage is the intensity of a supercell hailstorm. Individual hailstones are quite small, but they fall in huge numbers and are accelerated toward the ground by the downdraft carrying them. They can strip the ears from corn and destroy other cereal crops. A scientist once traced the path of a particular storm from fields identified by the farmers who had filed insurance claims for damage to the crops in them.

# Rotation

The diagram gives the misleading impression that the upcurrents and downcurrents blow like winds. You might imagine the air blowing directly along invisible tunnels, with the flow in a direction parallel to the tunnels themselves. In fact, the air spirals its way upward through the storm, usually moving counterclockwise.

This rotation starts where wind shear deflects the upcurrent, usually at about the midheight of the cloud. Moving air (and liquid) has a natural tendency to turn around an axis at right angles to its direction of movement. This behavior is called *vorticity* (see the section "Vortices and angular momentum" on pages 77–83). The rotation spreads downward from the middle of the cloud, where the upcurrent is bending away from the vertical, until it sets the whole of the *mesocyclone* beneath it rotating all the way to the bottom of the cloud (see the box "Mesocyclones" on page 66).

Rotation at the base of the mesocyclone is what makes fragments of cloud turn and, as it speeds up, part of the cloud descends below the base of the main cloud. This descended cloud, projecting from the rear of the storm, turning slowly, and from which no rain falls, is what appears as a wall cloud. To people far enough away to see the whole width of the storm passing across their line of sight it is clearly marked, as a solid-looking cloud attached to the bottom of the main cloud. It is not a tornado, but it is beneath the wall cloud that tornadoes may appear.

# VORTICES AND ANGULAR MOMENTUM

Have you ever wondered how a soldier manages to steer a tank? A car is steered by moving its front wheels, but tanks run on caterpillar tracks and have neither front wheels nor steering wheels. All the same, tanks can turn corners. This is possible because tank tracks can be controlled independently to run at different speeds. The tank turns when the driver slows down the track on one side and speeds up the track on the other side. This makes the tank follow a path that curves in the direction of the slower track. A rowboat is steered in the same way. Row on one side of the boat only and the boat will turn away from the side you are rowing. Taxiing airliners also steer by means of their engines. In each of these cases, increasing or decreasing power to one side makes the two sides of the tank, boat, or plane try to move at different speeds and the result is a turn in the direction of the slower side.

There is a general rule here that is rather similar to one that applies to fluids—liquids and gases. If there are two streams, side by side and flowing in the same direction but at different speeds, the faster stream will curve in the direction of the slower. When air (or water) moves it does so in relation to the air (or water) to either side. This means there is always a stream flowing faster than the stream next to it (which may not be moving at all) and, therefore, all moving streams will tend to follow curved paths. Assuming there is nothing confining them, such as the banks of a river or the sides of a valley, eventually streams will flow more or less in circles. This tendency of a moving stream to curve is called *vorticity*. Vorticity may cause the moving gas or liquid to rotate about any axis, but since winds, rivers, and ocean currents flow horizontally, the most important axes are vertical. The flow that affects weather systems, including tornadoes, tends to make air rotate about a vertical axis.

## Coriolis effect and the "bath plug vortex"

The Earth spins on its own axis. Its motion deflects liquids and gases that are moving over its surface into curved paths. This process is called the *Coriolis effect* (see the box). Coriolis deflection induces vorticity and, because its vorticity is due to the movement of the planet, it is called *planetary vorticity*.

Planetary vorticity is significant only where the movement is large. It affects air masses moving across continents and oceans, but very small streams, flowing only a short distance, also curve. They have a vorticity of their own.

# The Coriolis effect

Any object that is moving toward or away from the equator and that is not firmly attached to the surface does not travel in a straight line. As the diagram illustrates, it is deflected to the right in the Northern Hemisphere and to the left in the Southern Hemisphere. Moving air and water tend to follow a clockwise path in the Northern Hemisphere and a counterclockwise path in the Southern Hemisphere.

The French physicist Gaspard-Gustave de Coriolis (1792–1843) discovered the reason for this in 1835 and so it is called the *Coriolis effect*. It happens because the Earth is a rotating sphere and as an object moves above the surface, the Earth below is also moving. The effect used to be called the Coriolis "force" and it is still abbreviated as "CorF," but it is not a force. It results simply from the fact that we observe motion in relation to fixed points on the surface.

The Earth makes one complete turn on its axis every 24 hours. This means that every point on the surface is constantly moving and returns to its original position (relative to the Sun) every 24 hours, but because the Earth is a sphere, different points on the surface travel different distances to do so. Consequently, they travel at different speeds. If you find it difficult to imagine that New York and Bogotá—or any other two places in different latitudes—are moving through space at different speeds, consider what would happen if this were not so: The world would tear itself apart.

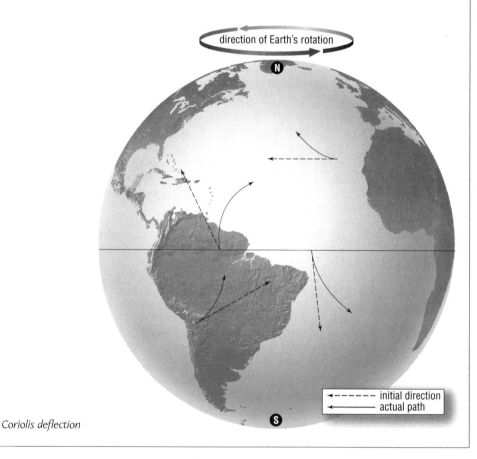

*Coriolis deflection*

direction of Earth's rotation

N

S

- - - - - - - initial direction
——— actual path

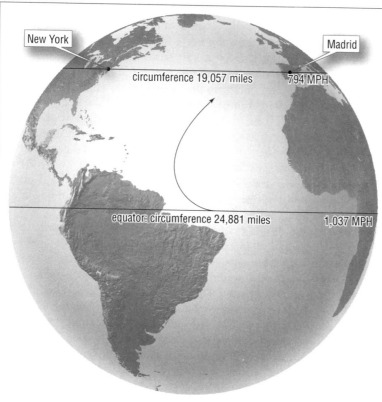

New York

Madrid

circumference 19,057 miles

794 MPH

equator: circumference 24,881 miles

1,037 MPH

*Coriolis effect*

Take two points on the surface, one at the equator and the other at 40°N, which is the approximate latitude of New York and Madrid. The equator, latitude 0°, is about 24,881 miles (40,033 km) long. That is how far a point on the equator must travel in 24 hours, which means it moves at about 1,037 MPH (1,668 km/h). At 40°N, the circumference parallel to the equator is about 19,057 miles (30,663 km). The point there has less distance to travel and so it moves at about 794 MPH (1,277 km/h).

Suppose you planned to fly an aircraft to New York from the point on the equator due south of New York (and could ignore the winds). If you headed due north you would not reach New York. At the equator you are already traveling eastward at 1,037 MPH (1,668 km/h). As you fly north, the surface beneath you is also traveling east, but at a slower speed the farther you travel. If the journey from 0° to 40°N took you six hours, in that time you would also move about 6,000 miles (9,654 km) to the east,

relative to the position of the surface beneath you, but the surface itself would also move, at New York by about 4,700 miles (7,562 km). Consequently, you would end not at New York, but (6,000 – 4,700 =) 1,300 miles (2,092 km) to the east of New York, way out over the Atlantic. The diagram illustrates this.

The size of the Coriolis effect is directly proportional to the speed at which the body moves and the sine of its latitude. The effect on a body moving at 100 MPH (160 km/h) is 10 times greater than that on one moving at 10 MPH (16 km/h). Sin 0° = 0 (the equator) and sin 90° = 1 (the poles), so the Coriolis effect is greatest at the poles and zero at the Equator. This is because as a body on the surface or at a constant height above it moves away from the equator, its distance from the Earth's rotational axis decreases. As its radius of rotation decreases, its rate of rotation accelerates, although most of the increased velocity is lost due to friction with the surface.

There is an example of this that is familiar to everyone. When water flows out of a bathtub it usually forms a spiral as it goes down the drain, and the closer it is to the drain the faster it turns. The bath water spirals because of its own vorticity, and it is easy to understand why.

The weight of the water in the bath exerts a pressure on the bottom of the tub. This pressure is distributed evenly everywhere except at the drain, where water flowing out of the tub creates a region where the pressure is much lower. All the bath water is drawn toward the low pressure at the drain, and you can picture it as forming many small streams flowing side by side. To reach the drain, the streams nearest to the center of the tub have a shorter distance to travel than the streams near the sides. All the streams must reach the drain at the same time, however, so those that have farther to travel must travel faster. Consequently, the streams near the sides of the tub travel faster than the streams closer to the center. They tend to curve in the direction of the slower ones until they form a circle or, in this case, a spiral called a *vortex*. This is very like the way a tornado spins and the tornado mechanism is sometimes called a "bath plug vortex."

Many people believe that water invariably spirals counterclockwise down the drain in the Northern Hemisphere and clockwise in the Southern Hemisphere. Some go even farther, and would have you believe you can tell which hemisphere you are in by watching the water leave the bathtub, because the direction changes the instant you cross the equator. It is a lovely idea, but unfortunately it is nonsense. Both sides of the tub are the same distance from the drain, so the water approaches equally from either side and there are two fast streams tending to curve around slow streams. The stream from one side tends to curve to the left and the stream from the other side tends to turn to the right. Which tendency wins is a matter of chance. The water usually forms a vortex, but it may turn in either direction and occasionally it does not spiral at all. You can test it for yourself. Each time you take a bath, make a note of the way the water spirals. Over a large number of trials you will find you have recorded about as many clockwise spirals as counterclockwise ones.

Water spirals down the drain because of its own vorticity, not because of planetary vorticity. If the tub were the size of an ocean, then the Coriolis effect would determine the direction the water turned, but a real bathtub is far too small to be influenced in this way. Even if it were, there is no Coriolis effect at the equator, so tropical bathtubs would be no help in telling you where you were, although water spirals out of them there as it does everywhere.

# Planetary vorticity, relative vorticity, and absolute vorticity

Vorticity therefore has two components. There is planetary vorticity and the vorticity of the moving stream itself. This is known as *relative vorticity*. Add the two together and the result is called the *absolute vorticity*.

Absolute vorticity tells you how a moving stream will really behave. Planetary vorticity deflects streams to the right in the Northern Hemisphere and to the left in the Southern Hemisphere. This is called *cyclonic* motion and, by convention, it is known as *positive vorticity*. Cyclonic flow moves counterclockwise in the Northern Hemisphere and clockwise in the Southern Hemisphere. Rotation in the opposite directions is called *anticyclonic* and results from *negative vorticity*.

On a scale large enough for planetary vorticity to be significant, if relative vorticity is positive it adds to planetary vorticity, so the absolute vorticity will be the sum of the two. If relative vorticity is negative, on the other hand, it may disappear altogether; overwhelmed by the much stronger planetary vorticity acting in the opposite direction and from which it must be subtracted.

Air converges into an area of low pressure, for which the technical term is a *cyclone*, and its convergence produces a cyclonic flow and therefore a strongly positive absolute vorticity. Diverging air, flowing away from an area of high pressure, or *anticyclone*, has negative relative vorticity and, provided the divergence continues at a constant rate, its absolute vorticity decreases, eventually to zero.

Inside a supercell (see "Supercells," pages 69–76), or each of the convective cells in a multicell cloud, air is moving rapidly upward in the upcurrents. This draws in air at the base. Air flowing inward is converging over a distance that is large enough for planetary vorticity to be significant, so as the air is drawn into the cloud, it acquires positive absolute vorticity. In other words, it starts to spin in a counterclockwise direction (in the Northern Hemisphere) about its own axis and it continues spinning as it rises, moving in an upward spiral. Wind shear aloft sets the rising column rotating in the middle of the cloud, but the positive vorticity of the converging air increases the rate of spin. Almost all tornadoes in the Northern Hemisphere spin counterclockwise, although occasionally they have been known to spin clockwise. Scientists believe that clockwise tornadoes are set spinning by the downcurrent from the divergence of air leaving the supercell.

At the top of the cloud, rising air forms a region of high pressure. Air flows away from it. This is divergence, with negative relative vorticity, and so its absolute vorticity is very small. The outflowing air moves in more or less straight lines, rapidly carrying air away from the top of the upcurrents and drawing more air upward to take its place.

# Conservation of angular momentum

Now another effect becomes influential. This has the forbidding name of the *conservation of angular momentum*. The principle is much less alarming than it sounds.

When any body spins about its own axis, three factors describe its motion. These are the mass of the body (on Earth this is equivalent to its weight), its spinning radius, and the rate at which it is turning. This is measured as the number of degrees through which it turns in a given time and is known as its *angular velocity*. The Earth, for example, makes one complete turn, through 360°, every 24 hours, so it has an angular velocity of 360 ÷ 24 = 15° per hour. If you multiply these three factors together—mass × radius × angular velocity—the product is the *angular momentum* of the body. This is a number that remains constant should any of the factors change. If one of the factors increases, for example, one or both of the others must decrease so the product remains the same when they are multiplied together. Suppose an orbiting satellite, which is spinning about the center of the Earth, broke in two. Each piece would have less mass than the whole satellite. To conserve angular momentum the pieces might accelerate to increase their angular velocity, or move into higher orbits to increase their orbital radius.

There is a more familiar example that you may have seen. Figure skaters sometimes perform accelerating pirouettes. The skater starts the spin with her arms fully outstretched. Once the spin has begun, she gradually draws in her arms toward her body. As she does so she spins faster. Her spin accelerates because, by withdrawing her arms, she reduces her radius of spin. To conserve her angular momentum, either her mass or her angular velocity must increase. Clearly, she cannot suddenly gain weight, so she spins faster. The spin accelerates without any extra effort from her. It is an entirely automatic consequence of reducing her spin radius.

# The tornado vortex

Think now of the shape of a tornado. It extends from the base of the cloud to the ground and it is much narrower at the bottom than it is at the top. This is only the visible part of the tornado. It also extends upward, to about the middle of the cloud, and it is spinning all the way. It is a vortex, like a drain vortex, but one that is upside down, because it draws air upward. Low pressure stretches the vortex downward (see "Structure of a tornado," pages 84–87 for an explanation of why this happens). Stretching makes the funnel taper, but it does not alter the mass of air at each level within it. Tapering reduces the radius of the vortex.

The vortex is a mass of air that starts rotating in the middle of the cloud. It forms in an upcurrent, through which air is rising, but the rotating mass remains constant. The upcurrent merely feeds it by adding air at the bottom as it is removed at the top. What matters is the rotation, not the fact that individual air molecules are moving through the vortex.

When the air in the middle of the cloud starts to rotate, it has a certain mass, a certain angular velocity (rate of spin), and a certain radius. If

*Conservation of angular momentum in a tornado. As the rotating air at the center of the cloud extends downward, it becomes narrower. This reduces its radius of rotation. Consequently, its angular velocity increases: it spins faster.*

any one of these is altered, the others must change as well in order to conserve angular momentum. The tornado forms when the vortex is drawn towards the ground and tapers as a result of stretching. The illustration shows how its angular momentum is conserved. The mass of the air remains unchanged, but tapering reduces its radius and, therefore, its angular velocity increases at the narrow bottom of the funnel. In the center of the cloud, at the top of the vortex, the air is turning relatively slowly, but at ground level it is turning at a ferocious speed and the air being drawn into it is accelerated by its own convergence to the same rotational speed.

The tremendous winds of a tornado result from vorticity and the conservation of angular momentum. The effect is the same as that which makes a figure skater spin faster when she draws in her arms.

# THE STRUCTURE OF A TORNADO

When you think about it, it seems odd that a liquid can be made to move uphill. Yet this is what happens when you suck a drink through a straw. The drink moves up the straw. Inside the glass or can, the weight of the atmosphere exerts the same amount of pressure on every part of the surface of the drink. Sucking removes some of the air from inside the straw, thus reducing the air pressure and, therefore, the pressure acting on the drink at the bottom of the straw. The drink is being pushed down less strongly there than everywhere else, so it rises. To put this another way, the liquid moves from a region of relatively high pressure at the bottom of the straw to one of relatively low pressure—in this case, in your mouth.

A supercell is rather like a drinking straw, with the divergence of air at the top sucking the air upward. It spins as it rises because there is so much of it. If you could suck on a straw about six miles (10 km) across, your drink would spin through the straw, too. Air rushes into the bottom of the supercell. If the individual molecules of your drink were big enough to be visible, you would see them rushing towards the bottom of the straw in just the same way, sweeping tiny dust particles along with them, and rushing up into the straw, like a tornado picking up debris.

The harder you suck on a straw the faster the drink flows into your mouth, because the harder you suck the lower you make the air pressure in the straw. How fast the drink flows depends on the difference between the air pressure at the bottom of the straw and the air pressure surrounding it.

Tornadoes are also driven by differences in air pressure, but with a difference. When you drink from a straw the vertical distance between your head and the bottom of the straw is very small, but the top of a tornado vortex is a considerable distance above ground level. This is important because of the decrease of atmospheric pressure with height.

## Why the funnel extends downward, and how it becomes visible

Pressure is lowest at the center of the vortex. As the bottom of the vortex reaches the base of the wall cloud, the pressure at its center may be about 100 millibars lower than the ground-level atmospheric pressure well clear of the vortex. This amounts to a difference of only 1.5 pounds per square inch ($105 \text{ g cm}^{-2}$). It sounds very small, but it makes the core pressure equal to the ordinary atmospheric pressure at a height of about 3,000 feet (900 m). That is enough to pull the surrounding part of the wall cloud all the way to the ground. The tornado is an extension of the wall cloud.

As it descends, the tornado funnel consists only of air, but it is moist air and the pressure within it is relatively low. The low pressure causes some of the water vapor in the air to condense into liquid droplets. These are exactly similar to cloud droplets, but they form in the tornado funnel and they are not part of the cloud itself. How much water vapor condenses depends on the amount the air contains, and this varies. It is the water droplets that make the descending funnel visible and, therefore, most funnels are white—the color of cloud droplets—when they first appear. Storm clouds look black only because they contain enough droplets to block out a considerable proportion of the sunlight, making the sky dark. The droplets themselves are not black.

# Dust and debris

Not all tornadoes appear as clearly defined white funnels, however. If the air descending in the funnel is relatively dry, there will be less condensation in it than there would be in moister air. The density of water droplets in the funnel will be low, and the funnel will appear faint. It may even be invisible. Sometimes tornadoes form behind heavy rain, which hides them.

Even then, faint or invisible tornadoes often reveal themselves. Before the funnel reaches the ground, the air at ground level is already rotating vigorously as it is drawn into the upcurrent. Its rotation raises a cloud of dust and small debris a few hundred yards wide to a height of a few tens of feet. This cloud is often visible from a considerable distance, provided, of course, the visibility is not reduced by rain. If you see a cloud of this kind in the distance, apparently sitting on the ground with a dark storm cloud low above it, expect a tornado at any moment, because the funnel has already started its descent. Many tornadoes fail to develop, so the funnel may not complete its descent all the way to the ground before disappearing, but even if that tornado fails another may be about to appear nearby.

Whether you can see it or not, you are very likely to hear it. When so much air moves with so much energy it makes a great deal of noise. At a distance, the rumbling, roaring sound is like that of a freight train.

Soon after it touches the ground, the color of the funnel changes. Air flowing into the base of the upcurrent with the force of a gale carries dust, dirt, and any loose material in its path, sending it all spiraling upward. This gives the funnel a brown or gray color, and it is light or dark depending on the composition of the material being swept into it. Eventually the dust and fragments of debris envelop the funnel in a cloud, making it clearly visible. Fully developed, the tornado may retain its funnel shape, but the dust cloud surrounding it may alter its appearance greatly. A tornado can look like a ballooning cloud.

While it is forming, its funnel descends more or less vertically, but in most cases its alignment quickly changes. The funnel curves over, often until its upper part is almost horizontal, and as it moves the funnel twists and snakes.

At its center, the vortex is open and the air clear, like the eye of a hurricane. Around the eye, wind speeds can exceed 200 MPH (320 km/h) and sometimes they reach more than 300 MPH (480 km/h), though it is understandably difficult to make precise measurements. At its base, the tornado funnel is up to about 400 yards (366 m) in diameter, but it can be much smaller. Most of the damage a tornado causes is due to the force of its winds, but it is the difference in pressure that generates the fierce upcurrent, and it is the upcurrent that lifts large objects, sometimes to a considerable height. The tornado itself is moving forward (see "How a tornado travels," on pages 91–95) and so the objects it lifts are carried with it. That is how they can be transported from one place to another.

# Suction vortices

Tornadoes are renowned for their freakish effects. Some of these are due not to the main tornado, but to smaller ones that surround it and are triggered by it. These are called *suction vortices* and they are often hidden in the dust cloud surrounding the base of the main tornado.

Air rushing in to join the upcurrent crosses uneven ground and encounters buildings, trees, and other obstacles. The wind destroys some of these, but it expends some of its energy in doing so and is deflected from its course. The airflow is by no means as even as you might expect it to be. The wind gusts, changes direction this way and that, and makes all the moving air around the tornado extremely turbulent. Turbulence produces eddies, like the eddies you can make by drawing your hand through water, but these eddies form in air that is already rotating strongly and accelerating as it approaches the vortex.

Eddies can rotate in either direction, but some of them turn cyclonically, in the same counterclockwise direction as the wall cloud and the tornado reaching down from it. These eddies have their own rotational speeds, or angular velocities, but they also have the angular velocity of the main tornado and the mesocyclone above it, as well as the forward movement of the tornado. All of these add to their speed, which means they turn much faster than the tornado itself. If the tornado generates winds of 200 MPH (320 km/h), its suction vortices can blow at 300 MPH (480 km/h).

Suction vortices are very small, some no more than 10 feet (3 m) across and few ever reach a diameter of more than 100 feet (30 m). They are also short-lived. Few last longer than about three minutes. They travel around their parent tornado in the same direction as it is spinning, usually counterclockwise, but a suction vortex rarely completes even one full orbit. Finally, because they form so close to their parent tornado, the suction vortices are often hidden inside its dust cloud. No one sees them as they come and go. No one hears them, either, in the general roaring tumult of the storm.

In most cases it is only after they pass that evidence can be found for their brief existence, although they have been seen and even photographed. On April 10, 1979, a tornado at Wichita Falls, Texas, produced six suction vortices that can clearly be seen in a photograph. That tornado, or set of tornadoes, destroyed nearly 8,000 homes and killed 44 people.

Sometimes a suction vortex strikes a house, but it is so small that only part of the house is damaged by it. Suction vortices have been known to demolish half a house, leaving the remainder untouched, and then to vanish before reaching the neighboring house, so that the damaged house is left standing by itself amid undamaged houses. When they move over crops, suction vortices make spiral or circular patterns. They may be responsible for some of the "crop circles" that from time to time make the news (although most are deliberate hoaxes) and they have also left long, spiraling tracks of flattened corn. Where they occur on open ground, suction vortices can make *suction scars*—shallow holes, just a few feet across—by drawing up dirt from the surface. At one time, people believed these were the footprints of giants.

# WHAT HAPPENS INSIDE A TORNADO

Few people have gazed into the heart of a tornado and lived to tell what they saw. Yet there are a very few exceptions. In 1991 a man was sitting in his car in Colorado when a tornado passed directly over him. True, he did not look upward into it, but he did experience the passing of the funnel. It began, he reported, in absolute calm. Then the car was hit by what he described as a "slam of wind" hurling hailstones the size of marbles and he ducked instinctively, fearing the windows of the car would be smashed. The wind, which he guessed was moving faster than 70 MPH (113 km/h), ceased almost at once. He looked out and there was the funnel, moving away.

One person who did stare directly into a tornado funnel was able to do so safely because, as it approached, the funnel lifted from the ground. Tornadoes are dangerous only while they are touching the ground. Once the bottom of the funnel lifts well clear of the ground it loses contact with the buildings and other structures and objects it can destroy. The tornado still twists and roars, but it is harmless.

This does not mean you can afford to take risks. If you see an approaching tornado lift, so that its base is above the ground, on no account should you wait for a chance to gaze into it. Tornadoes often raise themselves in this way, only to descend to ground level again in a matter of moments. The apparently safe tornado that is coming toward you could have turned back into a killer by the time it reaches you. Even if the tornado you are watching is harmless, there may be another one that you failed to notice. It may be a monster and it may be approaching fast. You might not see or hear it in the general roar and confusion of the storm. If there are tornadoes around, even "safe" ones, head for shelter at once.

## Will Keller's story

Will Keller was familiar with tornadoes and thought he knew what he was doing. In fact, he was lucky—but he did gaze right into the heart of a tornado. He described his experience in an article published in the magazine *Monthly Weather*.

Mr. Keller was a Kansas farmer, out in his fields on the afternoon of June 22, 1928. A hailstorm had just totally destroyed his wheat crop and Mr. Keller and his family were looking at its remains. His attention was fixed on the ruined crop, so he took little notice of the umbrella-shaped cloud in the distance. It looked as though it might conceal a tornado, and the air felt oppressively humid in a way he had learned to associate with an approaching tornado. Then he took another look. Dangling from the greenish-black base of the cloud there was not one tornado, but three—and one of them was heading directly for them and was already very close.

He immediately called his family together and led them to the prepared cyclone cellar. They entered ahead of him and Mr. Keller was about to follow them and shut the door when he glanced back at the storm. Two of the tornadoes were clearly visible in the distance across the flat fields. He said they looked "like great ropes dangling from the clouds." The third and closest tornado was funnel-shaped, with ragged clouds around it. It hung from the center of the storm cloud and appeared to be the biggest and most vigorous of the three. It was now quite close, but as he watched, its base began to lift clear of the ground. He knew this meant the tornado would not harm him, but he also knew that he could jump into the cellar in an instant if the base started to descend again.

The tornado continued to lift as it slowly approached. Mr. Keller had seen many tornadoes. He was not frightened and was confident he was safe. Eventually the funnel was directly overhead and Mr. Keller found himself gazing straight up into it.

He said the air was very, very still, but the end of the funnel made a loud screaming, hissing noise. There was a strong, "gassy" smell and he found it difficult to breathe.

It was the lightning, constantly zigzagging back and forth across the inside of the funnel, that allowed Mr. Keller to see what was happening. Above him there was a circular opening, 50–100 feet (15–30 m) across, and he was able to see up it to what he estimated was a height of at least 2,600 feet (790 m). Its walls were clouds rotating about the center. The hissing noise was made by small tornadoes that were forming like tails around the lower rim of the funnel, then breaking away and disappearing. The funnel itself, he said, was rotating counterclockwise, but some of the "tails" rotated counterclockwise, others clockwise.

Mr. Keller was very lucky. Although the tornado he watched was safe, one of the others might suddenly have descended on him, leaving him no time to leap into the cellar and shut the door. The oppressive air he associated with tornadoes is not always evident and his suspicion that the "umbrella-shaped" cloud might conceal a tornado was not well founded. You cannot tell whether a storm will trigger a tornado just by its appearance. Most tornadoes do not make a "screaming, hissing noise" and they do not emit a distinctive smell. It is impossible to say what the smell may have been. Perhaps it was ozone—the acrid smell produced by electric sparks—formed by the lightning inside the funnel.

# Illuminated tornadoes

Like the eye of a hurricane, the center of a tornado funnel is fairly calm, with air descending slowly through it, and the atmospheric pressure is very low. This core is surrounded by air spiraling upward, and it is here that the winds occur. Clouds form as moist air is drawn into the spiral, the pressure falls abruptly, and its water vapor condenses. Wind speeds fall with increasing distance from the core.

Electrical activity is intense. The base of the parent supercell carries a negative charge and sparking between this and the positive charge at a higher level probably accounts for much of the lightning seen inside the tornado funnel. It is also possible that the rapid rotation of the funnel acts like a dynamo, generating its own electricity.

Sometimes the entire funnel is illuminated. People watching from several miles away said that a tornado in Oklahoma in May 1955 had what looked like a pinwheel of fire spinning at its top. Others said the funnel was lit from inside, blue near the top and orange lower down, with orange fire spitting from its base.

So far, scientists do not have a complete explanation for these lights, but there have been reports of them since Old Testament times. The prophet Ezekiel certainly knew about them: "And I looked, and, behold, a whirlwind came out of the north, a great cloud, and a fire infolding itself, and a brightness was about it, and out of the midst thereof as the color of amber, out of the midst of the fire." (Ezekiel 1:4.)

# HOW A TORNADO TRAVELS

Watch the ordinary cumulus clouds that often dot the sky like tangles of clean cotton wool on a fine afternoon as they drift across the sky, carried by the wind. Check their direction with a nearby wind vane and usually you will find that the clouds are traveling in a different direction from the way the wind vane points. It is the wind at the height of the clouds that carries them, not the wind at ground level or at the top of a tower or church steeple.

There is a layer of air, the *planetary boundary layer*, that extends from the ground to an average height of about 1,700 feet (519 m)—the precise height varying according to the nature of the surface. Within this layer, all moving air is affected by friction with the ground and objects on the ground, such as hills, trees, and buildings. Friction slows the movement of air and it also changes the direction of the wind. Air above the planetary boundary layer is not affected by friction with the surface and, consequently the wind at that height is from a different direction.

Cumulonimbus storm clouds are very much bigger than fair-weather cumulus. It is more difficult to see them move because they occupy such a large proportion of the sky. All the same, they do move and, like the smaller cumulus, it is the wind that carries them. In their case, it is the wind at about the height of the middle of the cloud. With a massive storm cloud, this will be the wind at about 20,000 feet (6 km).

# Multicell storms

Clouds that produce tornadoes move differently. Like an ordinary thunderstorm, a multicell storm cloud is driven by the wind at about 20,000 feet (6 km). The cloud as a whole moves with the midaltitude wind, and air flows into it from its right, at an angle of about 45°. Multicell clouds are deceptive, however. The upcurrents inside them are repeatedly stifled by their own downcurrents. Sinking air spills out of the cloud to the right of the direction in which the cloud itself is moving. This spillage triggers a new upcurrent by moving beneath warmer, ground-level air and lifting it. The warm air is *conditionally unstable*. Lifting triggers its instability and produces a new convection cell to the right of the previous one. The old cell then dies. As the part of the diagram labeled "A" shows, the result is a series of steps in which, relative to the direction of its forward motion, the active convection cell shifts diagonally to the right.

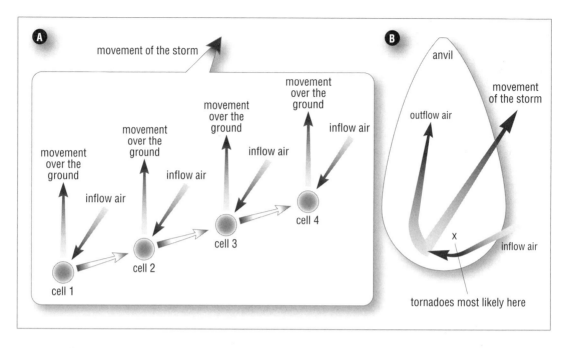

*Direction of movement of (A) multicell and (B) supercell storm*

Although cells are dying all the time and being replaced by new ones forming next to them, the individual cells are not obviously visible, and that is what makes these clouds deceptive. What you see appears as just one huge storm cloud. Overall, therefore, the apparent effect is that the storm travels to the right of the midaltitude wind.

In other words, a multicell cumulonimbus seems to move almost directly into the inflowing wind. Provided meteorologists can track the movement of the whole storm cloud and measure the direction of the inflowing air, this allows them to distinguish an ordinary, single-cell thunderstorm from a multicell cumulonimbus and to calculate from the inflow the direction the storm cloud is moving.

Multicell storms often develop along squall lines (see "Squall lines," on pages 49–56). This adds a further complication, because the cold front that produces the squall line is also moving. Most weather fronts travel in a generally easterly direction in the middle latitudes of both hemispheres. They are propelled by the high-level winds, which in these latitudes are westerlies (blowing from west to east). Over the United States, the prevailing high-level winds are from the southwest. Since this is the direction the cold front travels, it is also the direction of travel of its associated squall line and the storms along it.

In 1925, for example, a very severe outbreak of about seven tornadoes started in Missouri, then moved northeastward across Illinois and Indiana for a total distance of nearly 440 miles (708 km). The squall line that produced the 1974 Super Outbreak traveled eastward and was very long. At one point it extended from the Gulf of Mexico into Canada and 148 tornadoes occurred at various points along it.

Individual storms move with the front that causes them, but at the same time they move with the midaltitude wind and apparently crab to the right of the wind direction because of the continual formation of new cells. The result is that the squall line as a whole moves in a generally easterly direction, but the storms it produces tend to move along the front. This means tornadoes can occur anywhere along a cold front that has a squall line.

Although in North America the high-level westerly winds usually blow from southwest to northeast, in late spring and early summer they occasionally blow from the northwest, and the storms move the other way. On May 27, 1896, for example, an outbreak of 18 tornadoes around St. Louis, Missouri, traveled from northwest to southeast.

# Supercell storms

A supercell cumulonimbus is very like an ordinary cumulonimbus in many respects and so you might expect it to travel the same way, in the direction of the midaltitude wind. Some supercells do just that, but most do not. For reasons scientists are so far unable to explain, most supercell storms travel in a direction to the right of the midaltitude wind, and a few travel to the left of it. If you can see the direction in which the cloud anvil points, this indicates the direction in which air at the top of the cloud is being swept away from the upcurrents. This is approximately at right angles to the direction of inflowing air. A supercell cloud usually travels at about 45° to the right (shown in the part of the diagram labeled "B"), or more rarely to the left, of the axis of the anvil.

Not all supercell storms need fronts to trigger their development. Isolated ones can form wherever the ground is heated strongly by the Sun and the air is moist. There is no front to direct the movement of these storms, but nevertheless the midaltitude wind that drives them forward is often westerly, so, like multicell storms, they tend to move from west to east.

# Tracking storms

Supercell storms usually last for several hours. This is much longer than the lifespan of an ordinary storm cloud but, nevertheless, it is not very long. The storms move fast, however, and during their brief lives they can travel tens of miles, wreaking havoc as they go with their hail, rain, and tornadoes.

Squall lines live for much longer than supercell storms and a single squall line can carry 50 or more multicell cumulonimbus clouds spread along it. During the period in which it was generating tornadoes, the 1974 Super Outbreak squall line traveled more than 550 miles (885 km) in 16 hours and 10 minutes, at an average speed of about 35 MPH (56 km/h).

The movement of isolated supercell clouds and squall-line cold fronts can be tracked (see "Tracking and forecasting tornadoes," on pages 155–163) and people can be given ample warning of their approach, but predicting the track of an individual tornado is much more difficult. They form beneath storm clouds, but their movement over the ground is very erratic. Most of those associated with a cold front move along the front or parallel to it, traveling from southwest to northeast, which is the usual orientation of cold fronts, but this is no more than a generalization and there are many exceptions. Some tornadoes stay over one spot, hardly moving at all. Others move in circles, or describe figures-of-eight, and they can change the pattern without warning. If you see a tornado, even in what seems to be the far distance and even if you think it is stationary, the only sensible rule is to assume it will come for you and take appropriate action. With tornadoes, safety lies in expecting the worst while hoping for the best.

Their tracks are erratic, and their speeds and the distances they cover are no less so. Obviously, those that are stationary have no forward speed. While they are moving, most tornadoes travel at between about 25 and 40 MPH (40–64 km/h). In 1977 a tornado crossed Illinois and Indiana at an average speed of 46 MPH (74 km/h), covering 340 miles in seven hours and 20 minutes. It is not unknown, however, for a tornado to travel at 65 MPH (105 km/h).

# Tornadoes rarely travel very far

Tornadoes seldom last very long, so even if they travel fast they rarely have time to travel very far. Few cover more than 25 miles (40 km). The average track of the tornadoes in the 1974 Super Outbreak was 18.7 miles (30 km), which was thought to be rather long. In 1973 the average track length for all tornadoes in the United States was 4.7 miles (7.6 km), and in 1972 it was 3.3 miles (5.3 km). Three small tornadoes crossed central Arkansas on the evening of December 7, 2001. Their tracks were 5, 7, and 6 miles (8, 11, and 10 km) long. The present average track length is 1–4 miles (1.6–6.4 km).

Even so, there are exceptions. The 340-mile (547-km) track of the 1977 tornado may be the longest ever recorded, but the Tri-State Outbreak (so called because it crossed Missouri, Illinois, and Indiana) in March 1925 included one tornado that traveled 219 miles (352 km) at a speed of 60 MPH (96 km/h). In April 1908 an outbreak in Louisiana and Georgia included one tornado that covered 158 miles (254 km), from Weiss, Louisiana, to Winchester, Mississippi, at about 45 MPH (72 km/h).

The distance a tornado travels depends, at least partly, on the terrain it covers. Tornadoes move best over level, open ground and they tend to dissipate when they meet hills and steep-sided valleys. There are exceptions, as you might expect, for tornadoes that possess more energy than most. One of the Super Outbreak tornadoes was seen to descend to the bottom of a canyon, 1,000 feet (300 m) deep, cross it, and climb 3,300 feet (1,006 m) to the top of the ridge on the other side. It was estimated that the wind speeds around the core of that tornado may have reached about 260 MPH (418 km/h). It was so energetic that even a deep canyon could not stop it.

At its base, a tornado funnel is narrow. It is the diameter of the funnel base that determines the width of the track a tornado makes. Damage occurs only within this track and tornadoes are almost surgically precise. Properties even a foot or two outside the track are likely to be unharmed by the wind, although they may be severely damaged by debris dropped from a considerable height or hurled with great force. Few tracks are more than about half a mile (800 m) wide, and the width of many is no more than 100 to 400 yards (90–370 m). The three Arkansas tornadoes of December 7, 2001, left tracks 25 yards (23 m) wide. There is always a tornado that breaks the rules, of course. For part of its journey, the track of the 1908 Louisiana-Georgia tornado that covered 158 miles (254 km) was 2.5 miles (4 km) wide.

Although most tracks are narrow, groups of tornadoes often appear together and their tracks overlap, so the actual trail of damage is much wider than the track of a single tornado. Suction vortices (see "What happens inside a tornado," on pages 88–90) just outside the main funnel can cause appalling damage, but full-scale tornadoes can divide into several separate funnels and adjacent funnels can merge. This produces confused tracks that vary in width greatly from place to place. A tornado that struck Viroqua, Wisconsin, in 1865 comprised several main vortices that later merged into a single funnel, and in April 1974, Tanner, Alabama, was hit by two tornadoes that arrived half an hour apart.

# HOW A TORNADO DIES

Tornadoes rarely live for very long. The one in 1977 that lasted more than seven hours and traveled some 340 miles (547 km) across Illinois and Indiana was highly unusual. Few last longer than 20 minutes and many disappear within one minute or less. They spend an average of five minutes in contact with the ground. One consequence of this is that many tornadoes go unreported. They occur in remote, sparsely populated areas and disappear quickly. No one notices them until later, when the damage they caused to plants is discovered and the culprit identified. Today, when atmospheric conditions over many countries are monitored much more closely than was possible in the past, many tornadoes are observed that formerly would have been missed. This does not mean that more tornadoes are happening.

How long a tornado lasts depends on the amount of energy that is available to it. The more energy it has the more intense it will be. This suggests that severe tornadoes are likely to continue for longer than mild ones. This is true in principle, but many intense tornadoes divide into several vortices, sharing the total amount of energy among them. Once this happens, the individually weaker tornadoes may dissipate quickly, but then two or more of them may rejoin, combining their energy once more. As always with tornadoes, it is impossible to predict their behavior accurately.

# A huge concentration of energy

Tornadoes represent a huge concentration of energy. It is not that they release so much. An ordinary summer shower releases 10 times more energy than an average tornado and most thunderstorms release 1,000 times more without being thought especially severe.

The ferocity of a tornado is due entirely to its ability to concentrate energy into a small area. The volume of an average thunderstorm cumulonimbus is about 280 cubic miles (1,166 km$^3$) and that of an average tornado is about 1 cubic mile (4 km$^3$). A thunderstorm possesses much more energy than a tornado, but its energy is distributed throughout a much greater volume of air.

What is remarkable is not that the life of a tornado is so brief, but that enough energy can be concentrated for it to form in the first place. Huge concentrations of energy are difficult to achieve and are almost always unstable. Think of what happens when you boil water to make a hot drink, for example. Heating the water increases its energy. The boiling water has more energy than the surrounding air, because the air is much cooler than the water, so the hot water represents a concentration of energy, or, to put it another way, it has a higher energy density. The increase was achieved by burning fuel to "pump" energy into it. Once your drink is ready, however, it starts to cool at once. Unless you drink it while it is hot, it will continue to cool until it reaches the same temperature as the air in the room (which will have been warmed by it, but so slightly you will not notice the effect). The concentration of energy was difficult to achieve and unstable. It did not last for very long.

This instability occurs because energy always flows from regions of higher concentration to regions of lower concentration. Heating cold water until it boils does not contradict this principle, because the stove burner on which the water is heated also has a high energy density and energy flows from it to the lower energy density of the water. The burner, in its turn, is heated by burning fuel, which has an even higher energy density. That energy flows in only one direction is one of the most basic of scientific principles, known as the second law of thermodynamics (see the box).

Energy to drive the cumulonimbus cloud and, therefore, the tornadoes that form beneath it, is supplied by the Sun (and its energy, too, will eventually be dissipated, some billions of years from now). The energy is concentrated either by uneven heating of the ground, which produces isolated cumulonimbus clouds, or by the interaction of air masses at a front (see the sidebar "Weather fronts" on page 6). The concentration cannot be sustained, however. Ordinary thunderstorms exhaust themselves and disappear in an hour or two; supercell and multicell storms die within a few hours. Cold air at a front eventually lifts the warm air completely above the ground to a height at which it can rise no farther and all the air stabilizes.

A tornado requires a large additional concentration of energy, which occurs when the drop in pressure between outside air and air in the center of the vortex of rising air (the horizontal pressure gradient) is more than 8 millibars per 100 feet (0.26 mb m$^{-1}$). It is very rare for such a sharp drop to develop to so low a core pressure, but in some tornadoes the core pressure is 200–250 mb lower than the air pressure outside the vortex. Some scientists believe electrical discharges inside the funnel may provide some of the energy driving the movement of air that produces the low pressure, but they do not know how this might work.

# The energy dissipates

It cannot last. Air spills into the low-pressure core, raising its pressure. This process starts at the bottom of the funnel, where it is narrowest and the pressure gradient is steepest. Many tornadoes start to weaken when they move across uneven ground, perhaps because friction with the rough surface slows the inflowing air and causes eddies that spill air directly into

# The laws of thermodynamics

Thermodynamics is the scientific study of energy, the ways it can be transformed from one form into another, the ways it moves, and its ability to do work. All of these are governed by four laws of thermodynamics. Their numbering is unusual. Laws 1 and 2 were discovered in 1850 by the German physicist Rudolf Clausius (1822–88). He developed the first law from earlier work by the French physicist Nicolas-Léonard-Sadi Carnot (1796–1832) and the English physicist James Prescott Joule (1818–89). This led Clausius and William Thomson (Lord Kelvin, 1824–1907) to the second law. The third law was discovered in 1906 by the German physical chemist Walter Hermann Nernst (1864–1941), for which he was awarded the 1920 Nobel Prize in chemistry. Another principle, which follows from the second law and had been accepted for centuries, was recognized later as a law of thermodynamics. It was more fundamental than the others, however, so it could not properly be called the fourth law. At the same time, calling it the first law and renumbering the three established laws would cause confusion. The English physicist Sir Ralph Howard Fowler (1889–1944) proposed that it should be called the zeroth law.

0 **(the zeroth law)** This states that if two bodies are in thermal equilibrium (for instance, at the same temperature) as each other and both are in thermal equilibrium with a third body, then all three are in thermal equilibrium and no energy will pass among them. This is the most fundamental of the laws.

1 **(the first law)** This states that energy can be neither created nor lost, but it can change its form (for example, chemical energy in a fuel can be changed to heat and in an engine, heat can be changed into motion). The first law is often called the law of the conservation of energy, because this follows from it. The law also proves the impossibility of a perpetual motion machine, because energy cannot be created to power such a device.

2 **(the second law)** This states that heat cannot move from one body to another body at a higher temperature without producing some other effect. For example, if two bodies at different temperatures are placed side by side, the temperature of the cooler will rise and that of the warmer will fall until both are at the same temperature (if you leave a cup of coffee standing on the table, it will cool until it is at room temperature; it never grows hotter and the air in the room cooler). Heat pumps, refrigerators, and freezers remove heat from a cool body and pass it to a warmer body, but this does not contradict the second law, because work is done to effect the transfer of heat. The second law also means that where energy is concentrated it will flow to regions of lower concentration until it becomes evenly distributed. This dispersion of energy is called *entropy*.

3 **(the third law)** This states that in a perfectly crystalline solid there is a temperature at which no further change in entropy occurs. This temperature is called absolute zero, 0 on the kelvin (K) scale ($1K = 1°C = 1.8°F$; $0K = -273.15°C = -459.67°F$). Absolute zero cannot be attained, although modern physicists have cooled substances to within a few millionths of a degree of it.

the base of the vortex. Towns usually destroy tornadoes in this way, although not before suffering damage.

There are exceptions, of course. On June 13, 1968, a tornado appeared 8 miles (13 km) southwest of Tracy, Minnesota, and traveled northeast at 35 MPH (56 km/h) for a distance of 13 miles (21 km). It passed right through the town, without lifting from the ground, killing nine people, injuring 125, and leaving a trail of damage 300 to 500 feet (90–150 m) wide that cost $3 million.

As it fills with air, the bottom of the funnel disappears. To an observer some distance away, it looks as though the funnel raises itself above the ground, but in fact the lower part of the funnel has filled with air and vanished as the pressure gradient disappeared. Air is still swirling into the funnel, but it is air that is being drawn from above ground level and it has no effect on objects on the ground. As Will Keller knew when he gazed up into a funnel in 1928 (see "What happens inside a tornado," on pages 88–90), once its funnel no longer reaches all the way to the ground, a tornado is harmless and below it the air is relatively calm.

Unless the funnel descends again, which some do, the tornado is now doomed. Its energy dissipates as air pressure in the core equalizes with the pressure outside. When the core pressure is no longer low enough to make water vapor condense as air expands and cools adiabatically (see the sidebar "Adiabatic cooling and warming" on page 5) in the inflowing air, the funnel fades until it is invisible. Soon after that, the concentration of energy driving the tornado is lost, the energy of the storm becomes more evenly distributed, and the tornado disappears.

# DUST DEVILS AND WHIRLWINDS

In the scorching heat of the desert it appears like a wraith, a pale, writhing, shrieking column reaching to the sky. At first it is alone, but then another rises from the ground, and another. They are individuals, no two quite alike. There are fat ones and thin ones, tall ones and short ones, and all of them move unpredictably, wandering hither and thither as though searching for something lost. They rise, screaming yet insubstantial, then each vanishes as suddenly as it appeared until, eventually and for no apparent reason, all of them are gone. While they remain they seem to hunt and anything they capture they try to destroy. They are angry and very strong. Tents and flimsy buildings may not withstand them. They will tear doors from their hinges. They can kill people and livestock.

This, rather than the tornado, is the true whirlwind, familiar throughout history to all those who live in deserts or on the dry plains, and it has always been mysterious. God spoke to the prophet Job out of the whirlwind (Job 38:1). Job said that whirlwinds come from the south. From where he lived, that is the direction of the desert, although he did not mention it. In the many Old Testament references to whirlwinds, they are described as fierce, terrible destroyers. Armies descend on their foes like a whirlwind and the whirlwind sweeps away everything in its path. It was the prophet Hosea who famously warned idolaters and the impious that "they have sown the wind, and they shall reap the whirlwind" (Hosea 8:7).

Its awesome reputation is not surprising. A tornado gives warning of its approach. No one can miss the vast, dark cloud that heralds most tornadoes (although some storm clouds are pale and indistinct). Dust devils, on the other hand, are whirlwinds that spring from nowhere. There is no cloud to generate them. They appear suddenly beneath a clear blue sky, with no warning, as towers of furiously swirling dirt and air, sometimes reaching to a great height. Nor do they appear alone. Where there is one, usually there will be more, and sometimes a small army of them may advance, as though living up to the biblical descriptions.

## A whirlwind is not a tornado

A whirlwind looks much like a tornado, but in fact it is not a tornado at all in the strict sense. A dust devil grows from the bottom up, rather than from the top down as a tornado does, and it is dust particles, not water droplets, that make it visible. There are other differences. Not every tornado grows from a mesocyclone. Waterspouts and landspouts, for example, often form in clouds that contain no mesocyclone or supercell (see "Waterspouts and water devils," on pages 106–110), but dust devils do not need even a parent cloud. A tornado seems to hang beneath a cloud, but dust devils form in cloudless conditions. This makes a dust devil look like a freestanding variety of tornado. It is as though the earth itself becomes alive and rises, howling.

It is obvious, when you think about it, that tornadoes and dust devils must form in different ways. A tornado is part of the huge cumulonimbus cloud from which it descends. The cloud grows because its upcurrents are driven by convection, fed partly by the latent heat released by the condensation of water vapor. The vaporization and condensation of water power storm clouds. A full-size cumulonimbus holds up to half a million tons (454,000 tonnes) of water. That is its "fuel," and unless it receives a constant supply of moisture, the storm quickly dies. Dust devils occur only in deserts and other very dry places. All air contains some water vapor, even over the driest desert where rain never falls, but tornadoes need moist ground to supply water that evaporates from the surface. This is something no desert can provide in anything like the amount required. Water plays no part in the life of the whirlwind.

Whirlwinds and tornadoes are different but, nevertheless, they share one important similarity. Both are caused by convection.

# Convection and specific heat capacity

If you have ever tried to walk barefoot across sand or bare rock in the middle of the afternoon on a really blazing summer day, you will know that the ground can be very hot. It can be so hot that walking is impossible and the only way to avoid being burned is to run as fast as you can. You do not pause anywhere until you reach a cool, shaded spot, or, if you are on a beach, the edge of the sea or lake. The fact that all of the bare ground exposed directly to the heat of the Sun is hot enough to hurt your feet may lead you to assume that the ground is at the same temperature everywhere. This is not necessarily so. Some materials conduct more heat downward than others, to lower levels, removing it from the surface, and some surfaces reflect more heat than others. Sand and different types of rock vary widely in these respects—and both are very different from water.

When the Sun shines strongly on rock, sand, water, or any other material, the material absorbs the heat and its temperature rises. The amount of heat any substance must absorb before its temperature rises by a specified amount is known as the *specific heat capacity* for that substance, and it varies widely from one substance to another (see the sidebar).

# Specific heat capacity

When a substance is heated, it absorbs heat energy and its temperature rises. The amount of heat it must absorb in order to raise its temperature by one degree varies from one substance to another, however. The ratio of the heat applied to a substance to the extent of the rise in its temperature is called the *specific heat capacity* for that substance. It is measured in calories per gram per degree Celsius (cal $g^{-1}$ $°C^{-1}$) or in the scientific units of joules per kilogram per kelvin (J $kg^{-1}$ $K^{-1}$; $1K = 1°C = 1.8°F$). Specific heat capacity varies slightly according to the temperature, so when quoting the specific heat capacity of a substance it is customary to specify the temperature or temperature range to which this value refers.

Pure water has a specific heat capacity of 1 cal $g^{-1}$ $°C^{-1}$ (4,180 J $kg^{-1}$ $K^{-1}$) at 59°F (15°C). This means that at 59°F (15°C) one gram of water must absorb 1 calorie of heat in order for its temperature to rise by 1 degree Celsius (or 0.56 cal to raise its temperature by 1°F). Seawater at 17°C (62.6°F) has a specific heat capacity of 0.94 cal $g^{-1}$ $°C^{-1}$ (3,930 J $kg^{-1}$ $K^{-1}$).

The desert surface consists of granite and basalt rock, sandstone, and sand. At temperatures between 68°F and 212°F (20–100°C), the specific heat capacity of granite is 0.19–0.20 cal $g^{-1}$ $°C^{-1}$ (800–840 J $kg^{-1}$ $K^{-1}$). That of basalt over the same temperature range is 0.20–0.24 cal $g^{-1}$ $°C^{-1}$ (840–1,000 J $kg^{-1}$ $K^{-1}$), and the specific heat capacity of sand is 0.20 cal $g^{-1}$ $°C^{-1}$ (800 J $kg^{-1}$ $K^{-1}$). These values are typical for most types of rock.

Water has a specific heat capacity about five times that of rock. This means water must absorb five times more heat than rock to produce a similar rise in temperature. It is why water warms up so much more slowly than sand and rock. Visit the beach on a really hot day in summer and by lunchtime the sand will be so hot you have to run across it to avoid hurting your bare feet, but when you splash into the water, it is refreshingly cool. The reason for this is the difference in the specific heat capacities of water and sand.

In the desert, the rock and sand, with a low specific heat capacity, heat up rapidly. By the middle of the day the dry surface is extremely hot. Specific heat capacity works both ways, though. Substances that heat quickly also cool down again quickly.

During the day, the desert rock and sand absorb heat from the Sun. Their temperature rises and they reradiate their energy into the sky, but at the same time they continue to absorb solar radiation. The balance between the energy they absorb and the energy they radiate allows the surface temperature to rise to a peak in the early afternoon, after which it remains steady. Then, as the Sun sinks toward the horizon, the balance starts to shift. Radiation from the surface remains constant, but less solar energy is absorbed. The surface starts to cool, but slowly. Once the Sun sinks below the horizon and darkness falls, there is no more sunshine for the desert to absorb. The surface temperature then plummets. Desert nights are cold. Sometimes they are very cold indeed.

Movies and TV programs sometimes give the impression that in a desert the ground surface is everywhere the same. The Sahara, for example, is portrayed as an endless sea of sand dunes. True, a large area of certain deserts is like this, but most of the Sahara is not. The ground is stony and there is not much sand, because over hundreds of years it has been blown away by the wind and piled up in the dunes.

During the day, the Sun heats the ground and its temperature rises. It does not rise at the same rate everywhere, however, nor does it reach the same maximum temperature. There is another way the properties of surfaces differ. Some reflect more heat and light than others. The proportion of the radiation falling on it that a surface reflects is known as the *albedo* of that surface and it is reported as a percentage. Dry sand, for example, reflects 35–45 percent of the sunshine falling on it, so it has an albedo of 35–45 percent, which is usually written as 0.35–0.45. The average albedo of desert surfaces is 0.25–0.30. This means that sand is more reflective than solid rock.

In fact, sand has an albedo about 75 percent higher than that of rock. Because it reflects more of the heat falling on it, sand warms more slowly than rock. Sand in the central Sahara reaches a peak temperature of about 145°F (63°C) around noon. Sandstone and basalt rock both reach a peak temperature of about 175°F (79°C) a little later, at about 2 P.M. By that time the sand is starting to cool rapidly, but the rock does not start to cool until around 5 P.M. The surfaces all cool at different rates. By about 6 A.M., when the temperature is at its lowest, sand is at about 80°F (27°C), basalt at 100°F (38°C), and sandstone at 110°F (43°C). In California, granite rock surfaces can reach 125°F (52°C) at noon, but by 6 P.M. they have cooled to 72°F (22°C).

Above ground, the air is much cooler. Two feet (60 cm) above a desert surface that heats to a maximum of 135°F (57°C), the air temperature through the day ranges between about 65°F (18°C) and 85°F (29°C). Wind speed 2 feet (60 cm) above the ground also varies through the day, from about 2 MPH (3 km/h) in the early morning to 18 MPH (29 km/h) at noon.

# Whirlwinds rise when the air is calm

Deserts are usually windy places, but sometimes there is a calm day, and that is when whirlwinds may appear. Wind blowing across the surface mixes the air and cools the ground. Those are two things no whirlwind can endure.

As the Sun rises, the ground starts to heat and by early afternoon it has reached the highest temperature it will attain. Because the day is calm, with no wind to cool the ground, the surface is very hot, but it is markedly hotter in some places than in others. Patches of bare rock are about 30°F (17°C) hotter than nearby sand dunes.

Air in contact with the surface is warmed by it. The air expands and becomes less dense as it warms and so it rises through the cooler, denser air above it. Over the rock patches, however, air rises faster than it does over the sand, because it is hotter. The expansion of the air reduces the surface air pressure everywhere, but pressure falls faster and lower over the rock than over the sand.

Some of the air over the sand dunes then starts flowing toward the rock patches, where the atmospheric pressure is lower. The difference in pressure is very small indeed, but it is enough to set up a flow of air. When it comes close to a rock patch, the inflowing air is warmed by the rock and joins the rising air current.

Its own vorticity makes the moving air turn and, because it is converging toward a center of low pressure, it turns counterclockwise in the Northern Hemisphere. Air is now spiraling into the low-pressure region and then rising, still in a spiral. As it spirals inward, its speed increases to conserve its angular momentum (see "Vortices and angular momentum," on pages 77–83).

The ground is very dry, which means that individual sand and dust particles are not sticking to one another. Quite a light wind is sufficient to lift them. A wind of 12 MPH (14 km/h) will move medium-sized sand grains (about one-thousandth of an inch, 0.025 mm, in diameter) and dust particles, which are much smaller than this, are raised even more easily. The smallest particles are carried upward in the spiraling vortex, along with leaves and any other loose material light enough to be lifted. It is these particles that make the whirlwind visible.

Although dust devils occur most often in deserts, they can occasionally rise up in the most unlikely places. On farms they have been known to raise loose hay, forming "hay devils." They can lift volcanic ash, as "ash devils," and they sometimes put in an appearance during forest fires, as "fire devils."

# Why they rise without warning and die suddenly

The size of the whirlwind and the strength of the wind around its center depend on the difference in air pressure inside and outside its core. This depends, in its turn, on the difference in temperature between different surfaces. There are often many different types of surface within a fairly small area, so the temperature differences vary markedly from place to place.

Without warning, a whirlwind rises from a spot where the ground is especially hot. When conditions are right for one whirlwind to rise, they are usually right for a whole group of them, so a moment later another whirlwind appears not far away, over its own hot patch. Most reach a height of about 100 feet (30 m) and some rise to 300 feet (90 m). Really fierce ones, with winds powerful enough to do real damage, may be giants more than 6,000 feet (1,830 m) tall.

Whirlwinds share with tornadoes their formation by convection, but there is no condensation to sustain them by releasing latent heat, and there is no high-level wind shear to disperse the rising air and draw more air from below. The supercell that produces tornadoes has about 10,000 times more energy than a dust devil.

As it rises, the hot air carries heat away from the ground, cooling it. After a time, what had been a hot patch is at much the same temperature as its surroundings. Air pressure above it then rises, and air ceases to flow toward it. The whirlwind dies, vanishing as suddenly as it came.

How long this takes depends on the vigor of the original convection currents. Many dust devils last no more than seconds, but the strongest can survive for several hours.

# WATERSPOUTS AND WATER DEVILS

Almost everyone has heard of "Nessie," the Loch Ness monster. According to legend, the first person to have reported seeing it was St. Columba (c. 521–597), the Irish prince and monk who brought Christianity to Scotland. He is said to have encountered Nessie in the year 565 and he forbade it from harming a person swimming in the loch. Since then, thousands of people have described sightings of what they took to be Nessie. If there has only ever been one monster, it must be rather elderly by now, but it seems to be remarkably fit for its age. It continues to appear—many people claim to know someone who knows someone else whose close relative has definitely seen it—and the stories about it have attracted millions of visitors to the loch and given rise to a thriving souvenir industry. You can buy Nessie models, toys, buttons, neckties, and postcards in gift shops throughout Scotland. Nessie is a true patriot.

Loch Ness is about 23 miles (37 km) long, a little more than one mile (600 m) wide, and its waters, 750 feet (230 m) deep, are stained almost black by peat washed into the loch from the hills on either side. It is mysterious, often gloomy, and it provides an entirely suitable home for a mythical monster. The loch is not unique, however. Almost every large lake in the world is said to harbor a monster, and monsters are alleged to inhabit several other Scottish lochs, although none has been searched for so thoroughly as the one in Loch Ness. Despite the searches, some of which involved the use of submersibles and one that comprised a full sonar scan by a fleet of boats sailing in formation, no evidence has been found for the existence of any large, unidentified animal. Nor has any physical evidence ever been found of this or any of the other lake monsters. There have been no bones, no skin, not even any otherwise inexplicable tracks left in soft mud near the shore.

## Is Nessie a water devil?

Many possible explanations of the sightings have been offered. One of them is that Nessie is nothing more than an unusual movement of the water itself, produced entirely by a freak of the weather. If this is correct and the "monster" consists only of water, it would explain why, when it subsides, or "submerges," it leaves not the slightest trace. The suggestion is that at least some of the sightings may have been of *water devils*. These cannot account for all the sightings, however, and while it is extremely

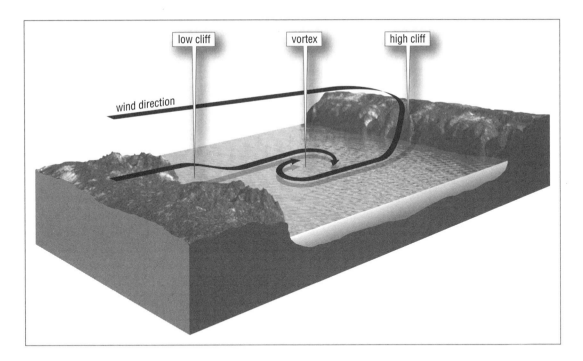

low cliff          vortex          high cliff

wind direction

unlikely that some unknown large animal lurks in the depths of this or any other freshwater lake, it is not altogether impossible.

*Eddy vortex due to wind deflection*

Water devils are the aquatic cousins of dust devils, but they are smaller and less violent. They may form by convection, but over certain lakes there is another mechanism that is capable of producing them—the wind.

In order for the wind to make a water devil appear, there must be steep, high cliffs bounding the lake on one side and low cliffs on another side. When a strong wind blows over the low cliffs, across the water surface, and into the high cliffs, air may be deflected along and down the face of the high cliffs and back over the lake, as a stream of air flowing in a different direction from the main wind. Somewhere over the lake the two streams may then meet and the resulting wind shear may start the deflected air rotating. A combination of vorticity and the conservation of its angular momentum (see "Vortices and angular momentum," on pages 77–83) may then be sufficient to produce a vortex. As the diagram suggests, the vortex is produced by eddying similar to that which occurs between buildings lining city streets, but on a larger scale.

The vortex is made visible by the water droplets it carries. Those near the base are whipped up from the surface into a small cloud. Droplets higher up are produced by condensation as moist air is drawn into the spiral, where the pressure is reduced. As the pressure falls, the air expands and cools adiabatically (see the sidebar "Adiabatic cooling and warming," on page 5) to below its dew point temperature, and water vapor condenses. In this case, the fall in pressure is due not to uneven heating of the surface and resulting convection, but entirely to the Bernoulli effect (see the sidebar "The Bernoulli effect," on page 170).

There are many lakes over which water devils may form. How often they occur depends on the frequency with which the wind blows from the right direction with sufficient force, but they are freak events and always unexpected. It is not hard to imagine that, seen from a distance, a water devil might be mistaken for the long neck of an unknown animal with a tiny head, the cloud of spray and foam at its base suggesting a bulky body just below the surface. If you think you see a lake monster, look at the base of its "neck." If the water is frothing and bubbling, probably it is a water devil and its "body" is composed of water whipped up by air flowing into the spiral.

Most water devils are small and not especially dangerous, but there are exceptions and even mild ones can be frightening. A party of anglers is said to have encountered one in February 1978 on Loch Dionard, set in the mountains many miles north of Loch Ness. A rising wind had made them decide to head for the shore when they heard a strange noise behind them and turned. What they saw was a swirling column of water, about 10 feet (3 m) high. It was already close and heading straight for them. As it passed over them, the spiraling air lifted their boat from the water, spun it around, and then dropped it. The water devil continued for some way across the loch, then died and disappeared. The anglers were badly shaken, but unharmed.

# Waterspouts

Water devils resemble waterspouts, but these are very much bigger and it is convection that causes them, not eddies in a horizontal wind flow. They can occur anywhere, but are most often seen over warm water. Sometimes one forms over a very large lake, but most form over the sea. They are fairly common in the Caribbean and off the Florida Keys. Professor Howard B. Bluestein, a leading authority on tornadoes, records that in 1975 he was almost late for his own presentation at a conference on tropical meteorology at Key Biscayne because he was gazing enraptured at a group of waterspouts dancing outside his hotel.

Some waterspouts are true tornadoes, hanging beneath a cumulonimbus cloud that contains a mesocyclone. If the cloud drifts out over the sea, the tornado will turn into a waterspout called a *tornadic waterspout*. The only difference between a tornadic waterspout and a tornado over land is that while it crosses water there is no dust and other solid material to be drawn into the vortex. Instead, water is swept up and forms a swirling cloud called a *spray ring* around the base and, no matter what its color may have been over land, when it becomes a waterspout it will turn white, because its funnel then consists only of water.

A waterspout that is a true tornado can be powerful, and if it moves back over land it can cause a great deal of damage. In 1935 a tornado at Norfolk, Virginia, moved over the sea, where it destroyed part of a pier and threw small boats onto the shore. Then it moved back and started wrecking the town, demolishing several buildings before it died.

# How waterspouts form

Waterspouts can form without the help of a mesocyclone. These nontornadic waterspouts are called *fair weather waterspouts*. They form over open water—never over land—and are generally weaker than tornadic waterspouts. Most are less than about 300 feet (90 m) in diameter at the base and generate winds of no more than 50 MPH (80 km/h). You are most likely to see a waterspout of this kind over shallow water on a hot day. In deep water, there is usually enough mixing between the surface layer that is warmed by the Sun and cooler water below to prevent the water reaching a sufficiently high temperature. Shallow water, which can be heated all the way to the sea or lake bed, grows warmer than deep water. This explains why waterspouts are often seen close to the shore, especially in sheltered bays. Fair weather waterspouts often form over the Great Lakes in late summer, when the water is at its warmest.

The high surface temperature warms the air in contact with it and causes strong convective upcurrents. These are very moist, because a large amount of water evaporates into the warm air. As the air rises it cools adiabatically, water vapor condenses, and cumulus clouds develop. If the air is sufficiently unstable, inflowing air may start to rotate, and it is this rotating air that grows into the mature waterspout.

The first indication that a waterspout is forming is a distinctive dark circle with a pale disk at the center that appears on the surface of the water. The pale disk consists of spray being whipped up by the developing vortex. Alternating light and dark bands then appear, spiraling outward from the dark circle. Soon after that, the spray ring rises from the surface as a circle surrounding the dark area. It heralds the emergence of the mature funnel.

Watch a waterspout, or examine a photograph of one, and you might well suppose that it sucks water from below and carries it into the cloud in its upcurrents, rather like a vacuum cleaner. This is what your common sense might tell you, but it would be wrong. Except for the water that is whipped up from the surface to form the spray ring at the base, the funnel consists entirely of droplets that have condensed due to the drop in pressure as air spirals inward. It is freshwater, even if the waterspout forms over the sea, although it might contain some salt, because some spray droplets at the base evaporate, leaving solid salt crystals that are swept upward and dissolve as water vapor condenses onto them.

# Nonsupercell tornadoes and gustnadoes

It is not only waterspouts, water devils, and dust devils that can form in the absence of a mesocyclone. Professor Bluestein has described how he was hunting tornadoes in Texas in 1981, when he saw a tornado behind the car in which he was a passenger. He reported it to colleagues at the National Severe Storms Laboratory, in Norman, Oklahoma. They examined it with their radar and found, to their surprise, that the tornado was beneath a fairly weak storm cloud that was still developing and contained no mesocyclone. It closely resembled a fair weather waterspout that had developed over land. Some scientists call tornadoes of this kind *nonsupercell tornadoes*. They are also known as *landspouts* or *land waterspouts*.

They are something of a mystery. Meteorologists can explain tornadoes that develop from mesocyclones in supercells, but the fact that a tornado can also occur without a mesocyclone to start it rotating suggests that the usual explanation is incomplete. Whatever their cause, landspouts are weaker than true tornadoes and only faintly visible. The pressure in the core may not even be low enough to cause condensation, so the funnel can be seen only because of the dust it carries.

Other small tornadoes sometimes form in the gust front where the downcurrents spill out beneath a supercell. These often rotate anticyclonically (clockwise in the Northern Hemisphere), because they spin in diverging air. They are called *gustnadoes* (see the sidebar "Gustnadoes," on page 52).

# RAINING FISH

When it rains very heavily, we often say it is raining "cats and dogs." Some people believe this expression is a corruption of *catedupe*, an old French word for "waterfall," and it seems reasonable that someone might talk about it raining "like a waterfall." All the same, cats have often been associated with rain, and at one time people in many different parts of the world used to believe they could influence the weather. In parts of Java, people used to bathe two cats, one male and one female, when they wanted rain. In Europe, witches were believed to take the form of a cat when they rode on storms, and in Scotland witches were believed to raise sea storms with the help of cats. Probably this belief arose from Norse mythology, in which the world serpent, lying at the bottom of the sea, sometimes takes the form of a cat. Dogs and wolves were associated with the wind and with the god Odin. Together, therefore, cats and dogs symbolize heavy rain and strong winds.

Whatever the origin of the phrase may be, no one supposes that cats and dogs can really fall from the sky. The very idea of such a thing is clearly absurd. On the other hand, in the early 20th century the Irish writer and historian Patrick Weston Joyce included a strange story in his book *The Wonders of Ireland*. Like much of his book, this tale was taken from an early work called *Chronica Scotorum*. The event it describes took place on the feast day of St. George (April 23) in 1055 at Rosdalla, near Kilbeggan, today a small town about 50 miles (80 km) west of Dublin.

As Joyce retells it, the people of Rosdalla saw "a great steeple of fire, in the exact shape of a circular belfry, or what we now call a round tower. For nine hours it remained there in sight of all: and during the whole time, flocks of large dark-colored birds without number kept flying in and out through the doors and windows. . . . Sometimes a number of them would swoop suddenly down, and snatch up in their talons dogs, cats, or any other small animal that happened to lie in their way; and when they had risen again to a great height they would drop them dead to the ground."

Unless the story is entirely invented, this was a tornado. Observers have often likened tornadoes to steeples or towers, and they can look as though they are made of fire if lightning or some other electrical phenomenon illuminates them from inside. Debris carried swirling aloft by a tornado can look like a flock of birds. This is not the only time such a comparison has been made, although nowadays people usually know what it is they are witnessing.

It was clearly a powerful tornado, for it lasted a remarkably long time. Did it snatch up dogs and cats "in its talons," raise them to a great height, then drop them dead? It may well have, and the event was already so extraordinary it is hard to see why anyone would want to embellish it. If we believe the main claim, that a tornado struck Rosdalla in 1055, which is certainly believable, there seems no good reason to doubt the rest of the story. It appears, therefore, that on at least one occasion it has "rained cats and dogs," even if there were not very many of them and they were dead when they landed.

It can hardly be called "rain," but on May 17, 1983, a few sheep may have traveled by air to a field at Baileyhaulwen, in Powys, Wales. They came from another field several hundred feet away and the farmer who found them said they could not possibly have reached his field on foot. To do so, he said, they would have had to cross a river and stone walls.

We can imagine some dreadful disaster that kills birds, causing large numbers of them to fall to the ground, but we do not expect other animals to drop from the sky. Other animals, after all, have no business being in the sky in the first place. Yet it happens.

# Fishes from on high

On Sunday August 7, 2000, it rained sprats (small relatives of herring) in Great Yarmouth, Norfolk, a seaside resort on the east coast of England. According to eyewitnesses, there was a clap of thunder, a rip of lightning, and then the fishes began to fall into a garden belonging to Fred Hodgkins, a retired ambulance driver, who thought at first they were hailstones. Mr. Hodgkins said the 2-inch (5-cm) fish were all dead.

In 1666, on the Wednesday before Easter, there was a fall near the town of Wrotham, in Kent, England, of small fishes about the length of a man's little finger. These were judged to be young whiting. More fish fell at Mountain Ash, Glamorgan, Wales, on February 9, 1859. On this occasion there were two showers of them, each lasting about two minutes and with 10 minutes between showers, and the fish, mainly minnows and sticklebacks, covered an area of 8,640 square feet (803 m²).

Fish have been falling from the sky for a long time. Flounder and Dover sole fell on East Ham, London, in May 1984, but the falls are not confined to Britain. On the morning of October 23, 1947, A. D. Bajkov, a biologist who worked for the U.S. Department of Wildlife and Fisheries, was eating breakfast with his wife in a restaurant in Marksville, Louisiana, when the waitress told them fish were falling from the sky into the trees. "We went immediately to collect some of the fish . . . They were freshwater fish native to local waters: large-mouthed black bass, goggle-eye, and hickory shad." He said the individual fishes were 2–9 inches (5–23 cm) long.

Sometimes the weather delivers shellfish. On May 28, 1881, periwinkles fell on Worcester, England. These are edible winkles, up to 1 inch (2.5 cm) long, that live among rocks and seaweed on rocky shores. Worcester, however, is more than 50 miles (80 km) from the nearest seashore. Thirsk, in Yorkshire, is only 25 miles (40 km) from the sea. It also received a fall of winkles, in June 1984, this time accompanied by a starfish (which is not edible). Pond mussels fell on Paderborn, Germany, in 1892, snails fell on Chester, Pennsylvania, in 1870 and on Algiers, Algeria, in 1973, jellyfish fell on Bath, England, in 1894, and in 1954 crayfish landed on parts of Florida.

# Flying frogs

Frogs drop from the sky more often than fish, however, sometimes in very large quantities. Two steamers, the *Success* and the *Elliot*, moored at the Mississippi River levee at Cairo, Illinois, as well as the trees, fences, and the ground beside the river, were covered in small green frogs that fell on August 3, 1883. Frogs fell on Kansas City, Missouri, in 1873.

On June 12, 1954, Sylvia Mowday was with her two young children in a park at Sutton Coldfield, on the northern side of Birmingham, England, when the sky clouded over and it started to rain heavily. They ran for shelter and watched what Mrs. Mowday thought was soft hail, until Timothy, her 11-year-old son, said "It isn't hail, Mum, they're frogs, baby frogs," and so they were. Mrs. Mowday said they were "coming down like snowflakes." Frogs have also fallen on Arkansas, on January 2, 1973, on Southgate, London, on August 17, 1977, on Greece in 1991, and on September 24, 1973, toads fell on Brignoles, France. In 1864, a farmer in Quebec found a frog inside a hailstone.

# Turtles, nuts, and cans

Nor are these the only remarkable things to fall to the ground. On July 4, 1995, it rained unopened soda cans north of Keokuk, Iowa. The cans were labeled, so it was easy to trace them to the Double Cola Bottling Plant in Moberly—150 miles (241 km) to the south.

In 1930, during a severe hailstorm at Borina, a small town not far from Vicksburg, Mississippi, a gopher turtle fell from the sky. The turtle was 6 by 8 inches (15 × 20 cm) in size and completely encased in ice.

Hazelnuts fell on Bristol, England, on March 13, 1977, and in 1979 plant seeds and beans fell in Southampton, England. In 1976 live maggots rained on several yachts.

There are far too many of these stories for them to be hoaxes. The most likely explanation is that tornadoes cause them. Consider the account given by Mrs. Mowday. She and her children ran for shelter because the sky clouded over and it started to rain heavily. Until then it had been a fine summer day, just the day on which the air might have been very unstable. If it was a towering cumulonimbus cloud that produced the rain, the cloud may well have contained a mesocyclone. There could have been a tornado nearby. Had the tornado crossed a pond, and there is a large lake in that park, perhaps it could have caught up young frogs, only recently grown from polliwogs and emerging onto a bank that the rain had made wet.

The funnel of a tornado or waterspout is visible because water vapor has condensed in it, not because of water raised from the surface, but powerful vortices can and do pick up all kinds of objects and sometimes water. The 1935 tornado at Norfolk, Virginia, crossed a creek, removing all the water and some mud from the bed. The water would have merged with the moisture in the cloud and fallen again as rain, mixed with the mud, and neither water nor mud would have been noticed when they fell. Had it picked up fish or frogs, on the other hand, their fall would certainly have been noticed.

When strange objects fall from the sky, the event is bound to be reported, especially if those objects are animals, and the fall must always seem mysterious. So far as the people who observe the falls are concerned, there is no obvious explanation. Tornadoes often occur in remote, rural areas and go unnoticed. In any case, they will usually have disappeared by the time their parent cloud crosses an inhabited area and its upcurrents are no longer powerful enough to keep aloft whatever items they have collected.

Some puzzles remain, however. If a tornado picks up fish or frogs, why does it pick up nothing else? Gravel never seems to fall from the sky, for example, yet it is plentiful on the banks and beds of rivers and ponds. When they are wet, do the individual stones stick to one another too tightly to be lifted? Pond plants never seem to be dropped, either. Some water plants are rooted securely, but others float clear of the bottom, so why do tornadoes leave them behind? It is also odd that fish and frogs seem to land all together in particular places. Most tornado debris ends up scattered over a wide area.

These are questions that so far have no answers. There can be no doubt that occasionally frogs, fish, and other items, even cans of soda, do fall from the sky. They have been doing so throughout history, the falls continue to this day, and too many people have seen them for the phenomenon to be dismissed. It does happen, and tornadoes are the most likely cause. That certain features of these events remain unexplained does not mean that something other than tornadoes and waterspouts causes them, but only that scientists still have a great deal to learn about what goes on inside mesocyclones and the vortices that descend from them.

# WHEN AND WHERE TORNADOES HAPPEN

Tornadoes occur far more frequently in the United States than in any other country (see "Tornado Alley," on pages 120–127), but tornadic storms are by no means confined to North America. Europe has experienced many (see "Tornadoes in Europe," on pages 128–134) and cyclones moving north from the Bay of Bengal often bring violent twisters to the eastern part of the Indian subcontinent. Bangladesh suffered three in 1991, for example, one in April and two a couple of days apart in May. In 1993 there was one tornado in Bangladesh on January 9 and another on May 14. Each of them caused approximately 50 deaths and left thousands of people homeless. There was also a tornado in April in West Bengal.

Few tornadoes are reported from Africa, but this may be the only continent to escape them and even its apparent freedom may be due to lack of reports, rather than lack of tornadoes. There is no obvious reason why tornadoes should not occur in those parts of Africa where the climate is not too dry for them.

Much of Australia is desert, but about 15 tornadoes are reported there each year and the true number may be considerably greater, because away from the cities the country is so sparsely populated. The town of Mandurah, Western Australia, has suffered nine tornadoes over a period of 33 years, and when the area up to 12 miles (20 km) to the north of the town is included, the number increases to 18 in 33 years. Seven of those tornadoes were rated F-2 or F-3 on the Fujita Tornado Intensity Scale (see page 144).

# Tropical cyclones and tornadoes

It may be no more than a coincidence, but Africa also escapes hurricanes. Most Atlantic hurricanes begin as tropical thunderstorms over Africa. The storms create an atmospheric disturbance that moves westward, over the ocean, and produces a "kink" in the prevailing airflow, called an *easterly wave* (because it begins in the east). Easterly waves can intensify to produce small areas of low atmospheric pressure, and if these grow and intensify further, they turn into tropical depressions. Tropical depressions often dissipate, but when they intensify they can grow into tropical storms and then, when their winds exceed 75 MPH (121 km/h), the qualifying minimum, they become hurricanes. Hurricanes move from east to west in the tropical Atlantic and through the Caribbean. The huge storm clouds that produce hurricanes also trigger tornadoes.

What are called "hurricanes" in the Atlantic and Caribbean are known as "cyclones" in the Bay of Bengal and "typhoons" in the Pacific. These are just different names for the same kind of storm, and several more names are used locally in various parts of the world. The technical name for them, the one that meteorologists use, is *tropical cyclones*. No matter what people call them, they are huge, fierce storms and tornadoes are often associated with them. Any region that experiences tropical cyclones can expect tornadoes. Tropical cyclones occur in Madagascar, but they are rare over the continent of Africa, although some are recorded. There was a hurricane in Algeria on January 15, 1922, for example. The absence of tropical cyclones brings no guarantee that tornadoes will not strike, however, only that the absence of one of their causes may make them rather less frequent.

# Tornadolike winds

Winds that are known locally as "tornadoes" are common in the countries of West Africa south of the Sahara. They occur most frequently at the beginning and end of the rainy season, from March to May and in October and November near the coast, and from May to September inland. In fact, they are line squalls (see "Squall lines," on pages 49–56) that travel from east to west, sometimes as far as 500 miles (800 km), at about 30 MPH (50 km/h). They bring violent thunderstorms, and at the gust front, where downcurrents spill outward from the storm cloud, winds can reach 80 MPH (129 km/h) inland, although they seldom exceed 40 MPH (64 km/h) near the coast. The winds raise large amounts of dust, and when the gust front passes there is often, but not always, torrential rain. The winds are strong, but they do not form vortices around a low-pressure core.

In drier regions, dust devils (whirlwinds) are common (see "Dust devils and whirlwinds," on pages 100–105). The biggest of these, called *haboobs* (from the Arabic word for "wind"), form along fronts, often about 15 miles (24 km) long and moving at about 35 MPH (56 km/h). Haboobs are whirlwinds, but their winds seldom exceed about 30 MPH (50 km/h), except in gusts. The dust they carry penetrates everything, making them a serious nuisance, but haboobs are much gentler than full-scale tornadoes.

Tropical cyclones occur exclusively in the Tropics, but they are only one cause of tornadoes. Countries outside the Tropics also experience twisters, and Africa should receive its share, even if we do not get to hear about them.

# Conditions for a tornado

Three conditions are necessary to trigger tornadoes. Moist air must be very unstable, towering cumulonimbus storm clouds must form in the unstable air, and the high-level wind must blow at a different direction from the wind at lower levels to provide the wind shear that removes rising air. All of these conditions are common and it is not unusual for all three to coincide. This does not mean there will be tornadoes, but it does mean they are possible.

Strong but uneven heating of moist ground will make the air unstable. Air is warmed by contact with the ground and water vapor evaporates into it. The warm, moist air expands, rises, and starts to cool adiabatically (see the sidebar "Adiabatic cooling and warming," on page 5). The fall in temperature makes some of the water vapor condense, releasing latent heat and sustaining the instability. This is the way that summer thunderstorms develop in temperate climates, and in the Tropics and subtropics, such storms are much commoner and usually bigger.

Because the instability that triggers them is caused by heating of the ground surface, storms of this kind are most likely to occur in the late afternoon and early evening, when the ground has been warming for several hours, but has not yet started to cool. In the United States, the number of tornadoes reaches a maximum between May and September. Two-thirds of all tornadoes occur between 2 P.M. and 8 P.M., and about one tornado in every four occurs between 4 P.M. and 6 P.M. Tornadoes are least likely to form around dawn, when the air is at its most stable. This suggests that many tornadoes are triggered by isolated thunderstorms.

In the world as a whole, there are about 2,000 thunderstorms happening at any one time and every day there are something like 45,000. Not all of these, however, are caused by uneven heating of the ground. Anything that forces moist air to rise will render it unstable if it is raised higher than its condensation level. This is the height at which its temperature falls low enough for water vapor to condense and, if the air is moist enough, to release significant amounts of latent heat. An air mass that has crossed the ocean will be moist when it reaches land, and if it is forced over a mountain range it may well become sufficiently unstable for cumulonimbus storm clouds to form in it. Storm clouds may also develop along a front where warm, moist air is undercut by advancing colder, denser air. Frontal storm clouds of this kind can merge into squall lines. The violent storms associated with squalls often trigger tornado outbreaks.

Air masses move throughout the year, but vigorous frontal systems form only where the differences in the characteristics of the two air masses are fairly extreme. Fronts are commonest where polar and arctic air meet tropical air. This happens in eastern North America, in winter as far south as the Gulf of Mexico, in northwestern Europe, and in eastern Asia. In winter it also happens along a belt between the eastern Mediterranean and Caspian Seas.

Thunderstorms may develop along fronts at any time of year and some of them may be powerful enough to trigger tornadoes. This means that while spring and summer are the most likely seasons for tornadoes, they can also occur in fall and winter. Just as no part of the world is immune, neither is any time of year.

Whether or not tornadoes will form depends on the third necessary factor. There must be wind shear aloft, to disperse the air that rises by convection in the upcurrents. Fronts can supply wind shear, but often it is the jet stream that does so (see "Jet streams," on pages 27–36). The jet stream moves with the seasons and its location at any particular time provides a clue to the places where tornadoes are most likely.

In summer, the Polar Jet Stream lies across North America in the latitude of the Great Lakes, passes over Europe just to the south of Britain, and continues across central Asia. In winter it is further south and blows much faster. It crosses North America along a line from approximately the southern tip of Baja California to Chesapeake Bay. On the other side of the Atlantic it lies across the Sahara, continuing over Asia just to the north of the Indian subcontinent. In spring and fall it is moving between its summer and winter positions. These are its average locations, however, and on a shorter timescale the jet stream is quite variable in its direction and force, from time to time briefly disappearing altogether.

Add these factors together and a pattern emerges. Strong convection in moist, unstable air, with wind shear aloft, can occur almost anywhere at almost any time, but it is a little more likely in some places and at some times than others.

# Why there are more tornadoes in summer

Isolated storms that are vigorous enough to send upcurrents all the way across the tropopause and into the lower stratosphere are more frequent in summer than in winter. This is because they require strong surface heating and an abundant supply of moisture to trigger them.

The season for tropical cyclones begins in late summer and continues into the fall. Tropical cyclones cannot develop unless the sea-surface temperature is above 80°F (27°C) over a large area. The sea warms through the late spring and summer, but it is not until late summer that its temperature is high enough for convective storms to grow into tropical cyclones. They also require high-level wind shear to remove rising air. Strong convection then produces towering cumulonimbus clouds in which supercells can develop. The resulting storms are associated with tornadoes. There are, therefore, two reasons why tornadoes are more frequent in summer than at other seasons.

Tropical cyclones form in the Tropics, but they often move into higher latitudes. Tornadoes are likely to be more frequent along the tracks tropical cyclones usually follow than they are elsewhere.

Tornadoes may also be expected below the jet stream. Its position varies, but on any particular day during summer its location indicates where tornadoes may occur. Fast-moving cold fronts may also generate tornadic storms along squall lines. The speed of the front provides the best clue to the likelihood of tornadoes, because the faster the cold air advances, the faster it lifts the warm air ahead of it, and the more rapidly warm air is made to rise, the more unstable it is likely to become.

These are no more than very general indications, however. Tornadoes can be expected whenever and wherever the conditions needed to trigger them are met, but it does not follow that they will occur. Nowadays they can often be predicted (see "Tracking and forecasting tornadoes," on pages 155–163), but only by the presence of their parent mesocyclones and, since these are short-lived, by the time a warning can be given the danger is already very close. Tornadoes appear and disappear abruptly and they break every rule that might allow scientists to build a complete explanation of their behavior.

# TORNADO ALLEY

The United States suffers far more tornadoes than any other country in the world. On average, there are 810 every year and they kill 89 people and injure 1,500. There are good years and bad ones. There were only 463 tornadoes in 1963, for example. That was a good year, but in 1992, which was a very bad one, there were 1,297. The worst year of all was 1998, when there were 1,424. In April, May, and June of most years, which are the peak months in all states, there are often several tornadoes a day. In May 1991, for example, there were 335 tornadoes—more than 10 a day—and there were 399—13 a day—in June 1992, although this was the highest monthly total on record. The graph illustrates the annual figures from 1950 through 2000.

As the table shows, the annual number of tornadoes in the United States seems to be increasing, although the increase may be more apparent than real. Tornadoes were seriously underreported before 1953, the year that a national system for collecting tornado data was inaugurated. The reporting of tornadoes has increased since then due to technological improvements in monitoring equipment and to an increase in the population density of rural areas. More people living in what was formerly a remote area makes it likelier that a short-lived tornado will be observed and reported. The technology continues to improve, and so the apparent number of tornadoes may well increase still further in the coming years—but without there necessarily having been any more tornadoes.

As the map shows, however, American tornadoes are not distributed at all evenly. States vary greatly in area, so the best way to count tornadoes is as the average number each year for every 10,000 square miles (25,900 km²) of territory. This way of counting makes it possible to compare the importance of tornadoes in geographically small states, such as Delaware and Connecticut, with that in large states, like Texas and California.

No tornado has ever been reported in Alaska. This is not surprising, because of the climate, but Alaska is the only state to escape tornadoes completely. There is an average of at least one each year in every other state, but they are much rarer in the western states than in the East and South. They are also uncommon in Hawaii, which averages one tornado a year—1.55 for every 10,000 square miles (0.6 per 10,000 km²) of territory.

To some extent, tornadoes may be underreported in the more sparsely populated western states, but the extent of underreporting is probably not very important. There may be dust devils, but true tornadoes cannot form in deserts or regions where the climate is dry, because there is insufficient surface moisture to sustain the violent convection currents that are needed for a mesocyclone to form. In any case, most of California is not sparsely populated, yet it experiences annually only 0.31 tornadoes for every 10,000 of its square miles (0.1 per 10,000 km²)—an average of five a year for the entire state.

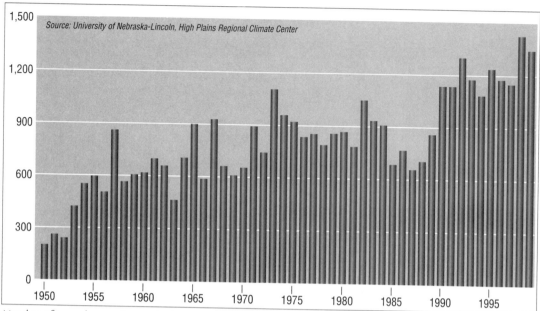

Number of tornadoes each year in the United States, 1950–2000.

## TOTAL NUMBER OF TORNADOES IN
## THE UNITED STATES, 1950–99

| Year | Tornadoes |
| --- | --- |
| 1950 | 201 |
| 1951 | 260 |
| 1952 | 240 |
| 1953 | 422 |
| 1954 | 550 |
| 1955 | 593 |
| 1956 | 504 |
| 1957 | 858 |
| 1958 | 564 |
| 1959 | 604 |
| 1960 | 616 |
| 1961 | 697 |
| 1962 | 657 |
| 1963 | 463 |
| 1964 | 704 |
| 1965 | 897 |

(continues)

## TOTAL NUMBER OF TORNADOES IN
## THE UNITED STATES, 1950–99 (continued)

| Year | Tornadoes |
|------|-----------|
| 1966 | 585 |
| 1967 | 926 |
| 1968 | 660 |
| 1969 | 608 |
| 1970 | 653 |
| 1971 | 889 |
| 1972 | 741 |
| 1973 | 1,102 |
| 1974 | 956 |
| 1975 | 919 |
| 1976 | 834 |
| 1977 | 852 |
| 1978 | 789 |
| 1979 | 855 |
| 1980 | 866 |
| 1981 | 782 |
| 1982 | 1,047 |
| 1983 | 931 |
| 1984 | 907 |
| 1985 | 684 |
| 1986 | 765 |
| 1987 | 656 |
| 1988 | 702 |
| 1989 | 856 |
| 1990 | 1,133 |
| 1991 | 1,132 |
| 1992 | 1,297 |
| 1993 | 1,173 |
| 1994 | 1,082 |
| 1995 | 1,234 |
| 1996 | 1,173 |
| 1997 | 1,148 |
| 1998 | 1,424 |
| 1999 | 1,342 |

Source: University of Nebraska—Lincoln, High Plains Regional Climate Center

# Where tornadoes are most frequent

Kansas, on the other hand, where the most famous of all fictional tornadoes carried away Dorothy and her dog, Toto, averages 5.71 tornadoes a year for every 10,000 square miles (2.2 per 10,000 km²). For the state as a whole, this works out at an average of 47 tornadoes a year. Despite its tornado-prone reputation, however, which was created by *The Wonderful Wizard of Oz*, Kansas is not quite the most sorely afflicted state. You are more likely to see a tornado to the south, in Oklahoma. That state suffers an average of 52 a year, or 7.44 for every 10,000 square miles (2.9 per 10,000 km²), and they are almost as frequent in Louisiana, Indiana, and Iowa. Florida is the most dangerous state of all. It has an average of 46 tornadoes a year, or 7.84 per 10,000 square miles (3.0 per 10,000 km²). Texas experiences more tornadoes than any other state—an average of 124 a year—but the size of the state means there are only 4.65 per 10,000 square miles (1.8 per 10,000 km²).

*Average number of tornadoes in the United States. 1961–1990.*

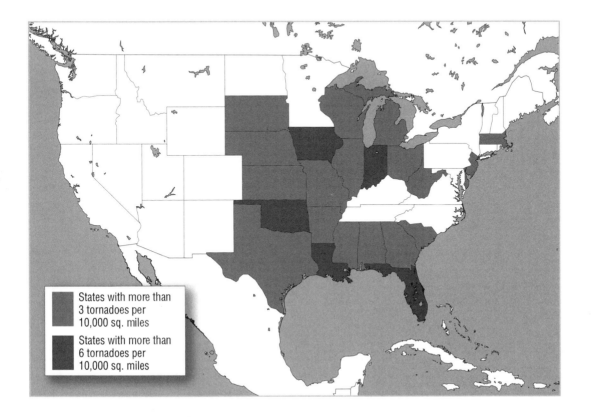

States with more than 3 tornadoes per 10,000 sq. miles

States with more than 6 tornadoes per 10,000 sq. miles

Tornadoes are rare to the west of the Rocky Mountains and north of latitude 45°, although Canada is no stranger to them, but there are 10 states in which they are fairly common: Alabama, Arkansas, Florida, Iowa, Kansas, Mississippi, Missouri, Nebraska, Oklahoma, and Texas. In the southern states, the monthly number of tornadoes peaks between March and May with a second peak in November. In the northern states most tornadoes are a little later, between April and June, and there is no second peak in the fall.

All of these ten states lie to the east of a line running from Nebraska to Texas. This line also marks the boundary of the Great Plains, with land to the west rising into the Rocky Mountains. The weather systems that generate tornadoes develop over the Great Plains and the area most severely affected by them is often known as "Tornado Alley."

# Tornado Alley

This is where the major tornado outbreaks occur. The 1925 outbreak, of possibly seven tornadoes, began in Missouri and crossed Illinois and Indiana. Of a total of 11 states affected by an outbreak in May 1973, Alabama and Arkansas were so ravaged by tornadoes that they were declared disaster areas. The Super Outbreak of 148 tornadoes in April of the following year struck all the states between Michigan and Alabama, and there was another outbreak in June 1974 in Oklahoma, Kansas, and Arkansas. A tornado destroyed a shopping mall in Mississippi on January 10, 1975, and in April 1977 there was a major outbreak in West Virginia, Virginia, Alabama, Mississippi, Georgia, Tennessee, and Kentucky. A single tornado, but one that killed 59 people in Wichita Falls, Texas, moved through the Red River Valley, on the border between Texas and Oklahoma, in April 1979. Year after year the story continues. In November 1992 an outbreak of up to 45 tornadoes struck 11 states from Texas to Ohio. In March 1994 there was an outbreak in Alabama, Georgia, the Carolinas, and Tennessee. On January 23, 1996, the Louisiana governor declared a state of emergency in Shreveport after a tornado had damaged about 200 buildings and injured 30 residents of a nursing home. One eyewitness reported that "the trees were bouncing around . . . trees a couple of hundred feet tall, they were absolutely tossing around like crazy." On February 14, 2000, a series of tornadoes killed 18 people and injured more than 100 in Georgia.

It is because of its geography that the United States suffers so badly from tornadoes. Compare North America with Russia and it becomes clear why this is so. Both are large continents in latitudes between the Arctic and about 25°N at the tip of Florida and about 35°N at the southern shore of the Caspian Sea. They are both about the same size—the United States and Canada together cover about 7.4 million square miles (19.2 million km²) and Russia covers about 6.6 million square miles (17.1 million km²). Both have a large plain, but in North America this occupies only the eastern half of the continent. To its west the land rises steadily towards the high peaks of the Rocky Mountains. Russia has no comparable north-to-south mountain range in the west to affect the inflow of maritime air, and its plain covers most of the country. North America is surrounded by sea, but Russia is bounded to the west by Europe and by the Asian landmass to the south.

In winter, the Russian landmass cools rapidly and a great mass of dense air subsides over it. This air mass is very stable and produces a region of high pressure (an anticyclone) covering most of the country. A pressure of 1,076 millibars once measured at Irkutsk is believed to be the highest atmospheric pressure ever recorded anywhere. Weather systems moving from west to east are pushed to the north, over Scandinavia, or south, over the Mediterranean, by air spilling outward from the anticyclone. In summer, the pattern reverses. The land warms rapidly and pressure falls until the winter anticyclone has been replaced by an equally large area of low pressure. This draws in air from surrounding regions. Atlantic air masses bring rain in summer and have some warming effect in winter over the western part of the country but, in general, pressure gradients are shallow and the climate is very stable.

Any large continental plain is likely to experience tornadoes and Russia is no exception. Tornadoes are well known there, especially in the south, where uneven heating of the ground generates strong convection leading to powerful thunderstorms. More than 400 people died from injuries caused by a tornado on June 9, 1984, and the damage was extensive. North America is different, however, because it is exposed to a much greater variety of air masses.

# Collision of air masses over the Great Plains

Maritime polar air masses (see the sidebar "Air masses and the weather they bring," on page 3) form over the North Pacific and move eastward. As it crosses the Rockies, the cool, moist air cools further and loses much of its moisture. Now fairly dry, the air sinks down the eastern slopes of the foothills, but the descent is gentle, because high ground extends a long way to the east of the mountains. The air warms adiabatically a little during its descent, but by the time it reaches the plains it is still relatively dense and it advances, fairly slowly, behind a weak cold front aligned approximately from southwest to northwest. The jet stream is similarly aligned directly above it.

Farther south, over Texas, New Mexico, and Mexico, continental tropical air masses form and move north. In spring and summer, as the land

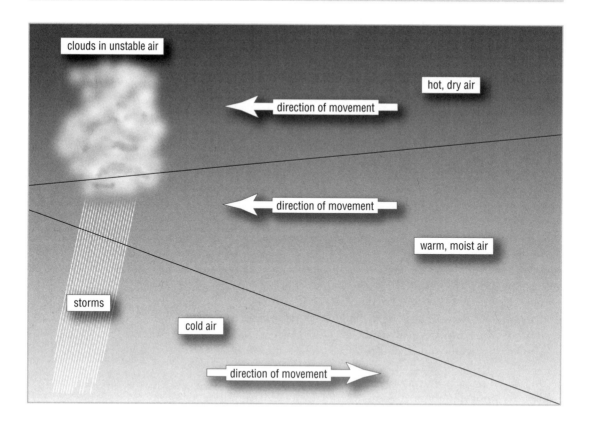

clouds in unstable air

hot, dry air

direction of movement

direction of movement

warm, moist air

storms

cold air

direction of movement

The Great Plains
"sandwich"

warms rapidly, these bring hot, dry air into the plains. At the same time, maritime tropical air masses are moving northwestward from the Gulf of Mexico. This air is warm and moist, but the continental tropical air is warmer, so when they meet over Mexico and the southern United States, the maritime air is held beneath the less dense continental air. The moist air warms further as it crosses the hot land surface. Ordinarily, this would trigger strong convection and much of its water vapor would condense to form clouds, but the overlying layer of even warmer air forms a temperature inversion that prevents this. Only small clouds can form, and they are confined to the lower part of the atmosphere.

When this air reaches the western side of the Great Plains, it meets the cold air moving down from the high ground. The cold air undercuts the warmer air. Now there is a "sandwich" made from air derived from three distinct air masses. The drawing shows how these are arranged. At the base is maritime polar air that has lost much of its moisture, at the top is very dry, hot, continental tropical air, and between them is very moist, warm, maritime tropical air from the Gulf.

As the warm, moist air is forced to rise up the advancing cold front, it expands and cools adiabatically. Its water vapor starts to condense, and the change of temperature with height decreases from the dry to the saturated adiabatic lapse rate (see the sidebar "Evaporation, condensation, and the formation of clouds," on page 38). The air is already unstable, but the front increases its instability by making it continue to rise. Now really big clouds form and the convection becomes so vigorous that upcurrents break through the overlying layer of continental tropical air and the cumulonimbus clouds tower all the way to the tropopause and sometimes across it.

These events produce the biggest, most violent thunderstorms in the world. Above them, aligned with the cold front, is the jet stream, which provides strong wind shear at high altitude. All the ingredients for creating mesocyclones are assembled, and the tornadoes follow inevitably.

The "sandwiching" of air masses begins along the western boundary of the Great Plains and continues, usually in a southeasterly direction, with the advance of the cold front. This is what turns the region into Tornado Alley and it makes the United States unique. No such collision of air happens routinely anywhere else in the world. Tornadoes can and do strike anywhere and at any time, but it is because of this particular collision that they are so frequent on the eastern side of the United States.

# TORNADOES IN EUROPE

Bognor Regis is a seaside resort on the south coast of England, approximately 50 miles (80 km) southwest of London. It is a quiet place, where visitors enjoy strolling gently beside the sea and relaxing in a tranquil environment. The tranquility was rudely shattered, however, a little after 5 P.M. one Saturday afternoon in October 2000. The weather was not good that afternoon. It was windy and it had been raining heavily for some time.

Then there was a loud bang. One eyewitness said it felt like "being inside a walnut that was being crushed." The lights went out, the windows shattered, and slivers of glass flew through the house. Another resident had just left home to visit friends. He returned 20 minutes later to find that the chimneys had been ripped from his house and his living room filled with rubble. Not far away, another man was working in his loft when the roof began shaking—"like it was a tent," he said, "and the timbers were being thrown around like matchsticks"—and he heard the tiles being torn away. A man and his wife were driving along the road when their car was struck by torrential rain and, no more than 30 feet (9 m) in front of them, there was a wall of flying debris. Small tree branches battered the car. Then the car left the ground. It took off, traveling sideways, then landed with a bump on the opposite side of the road.

Bognor had been struck by a tornado. It lasted for no more than five minutes, but during that short time it carved a swath of destruction about 1.5 miles (2.4 km) long. More than 100 homes were damaged, some so seriously that their owners could not return to them. Narrowly missing a supermarket, where shoppers were sheltering from the rain, the twister finally reached a trailer park. Before it died it managed to lift one mobile home into the air and drop it on top of another. Six people were in the mobile homes at the time. They were rescued once the wreckage had been stabilized. Fortunately they were only slightly hurt and the Bognor tornado killed no one.

It was not the first tornado to strike the area. There was another a few miles away in January 1988. Weather conditions that are capable of triggering tornadoes in the United Kingdom occur on an average of 15 days every year. Sometimes there are tornadoes on those days, sometimes not, and sometimes there is a tornado outbreak. On November 23, 1981, a vigorous cold front attached to a deep depression produced 105 tornadoes in England and Wales during the six hours it took to cross the country. The United Kingdom experienced 152 tornadoes in 1981. In 1989, on the other hand, only 11 were recorded.

About 20 miles (32 km) southwest of Bristol, England, is the village of Congresbury. There, at about breakfast time one January morning in 1991, people noticed a big, dark cloud approaching. Obviously, a storm was about to break out, but most people were busy getting ready for work or school and no one took much notice. Then suddenly, with no warning, tiles were ripped from roofs, debris flew everywhere, and a huge wind rushed through the houses. Moments later, when it had passed, power lines were down, trees were uprooted, and homes were demolished. A tornado had passed through the village.

# Tornadoes can happen anywhere

Europeans do not expect their weather to behave in this way. What they know of tornadoes they learn mainly from the American experience of them, and people tend to assume they are an exclusively American phenomenon. Indeed, many Europeans might dismiss stories of home-grown tornadoes as pure fantasy. Yet, while it is true that tornadoes are much less common in Europe than they are in America and those that do occur are mild by comparison with their cousins across the ocean, Europe does not escape. No one can be sure just how many there are, but estimates put the figure for Britain at between 30 and 60 in most years, with an average of 33. The map shows the approximate location of British towns that have experienced tornadoes in modern times. A study over a 25-year period found that there are an average of 10 tornadoes a year in Italy.

Weather systems usually reach western Europe from the Atlantic. They are associated with maritime air masses in which frontal systems and depressions develop (see the sidebar "Weather fronts," on page 6). These systems encounter continental air masses further east, and the continental air sometimes extends westward as an anticyclone or ridge of high pressure. Storms often develop in summer and fall, when anticyclones bring clear skies and light winds, allowing strong convection currents above moist ground to produce cumulonimbus clouds. Nowhere in Europe, however, does the geography of the continent cause the kind of collision of air masses that brings such violent squall-line storms to the Great Plains of the United States (see "Tornado Alley," on pages 120–127).

To the east, the European climate is continental, with hot summers and cold winters. In the west it is maritime, with rainfall distributed fairly evenly throughout the year, mild winters, and cool summers. This is not a type of climate that is capable of great violence, except on rare occasions. Nevertheless, vigorous cold fronts and uneven summer heating can affect it, and both of these can generate thunderstorms that are powerful enough to trigger tornadoes.

Tornadoes do occur, and in Europe they can strike at any time of year and there is no season in which the likelihood of them increases. Some of the most severe, including those that may have caused a major disaster in Scotland in 1879 (see "Tornadoes of the past," on pages 135–140), have happened in winter, but there is no pattern to their occurrence. Most of them pass unremarked, because they affect remote, rural areas and are gone before anyone sees them.

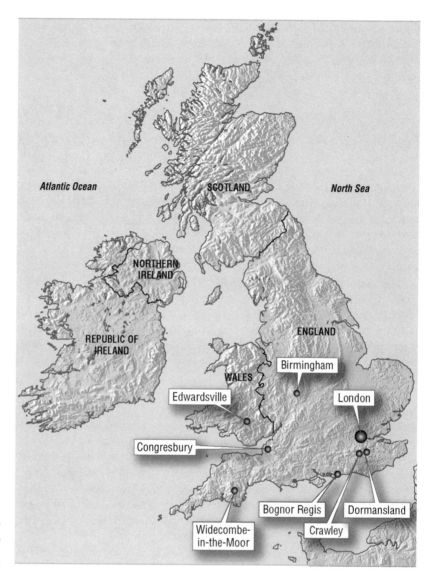

*Places in Britain that have experienced tornadoes*

People who do witness tornadoes are often reluctant to talk about them for fear of ridicule. A farmer who watched a small tornado scatter his hay and lift one of his cows into the air found no one believed him when he tried to tell them what he had seen. He was relieved when, years later, he listened to a talk about extreme weather given by someone who could reassure him that he had not imagined the whole thing. It is possible that tornadoes in rural areas are sometimes observed but not reported for this reason.

Occasionally, though, people are forced to take notice when tornadoes strike an important center of population. This happened in Russia on June 9 and 10, 1984, when an outbreak of tornadoes struck Ivanovo, Gorky, Kalinin, Kostroma, and Yaroslavl, five important towns. Hundreds of people were killed, trees were uprooted, and brick houses and factories were demolished.

On December 8, 1954, a Londoner described seeing a car fly past his shop window, 15 feet (4.5 m) above the ground, and land upright without so much as bursting a tire. Its flight was caused by one of those tornadoes that could not be ignored. The twister struck west London during the afternoon rush hour and left a nine-mile (14.5-km) track of devastation varying between 300 and 1,200 feet (90–370 m) in width through Chiswick, Gunnersbury, Acton, Golders Green, and Southgate. The roof was torn from Gunnersbury train station and a factory in Acton was demolished. Remarkably, given that so many people were present, there were few injuries and no deaths.

Doors and windows were blown out when a small tornado crossed the southern suburbs of Birmingham, England, in June 1937 and, earlier still, an outbreak of tornadoes accompanied a cold front that crossed south Wales in October 1913. The 1913 outbreak included the worst British tornado of the 20th century. It struck Edwardsville, Wales, on October 27, killing six people. What were probably small tornadoes have been recorded as extremely violent but very local weather disturbances in many parts of England, especially in central and eastern regions, where the land is generally flat.

# Widecombe-in-the-Moor and its encounter with a fireball

One of the most curious accounts of a tornadic storm concerns the church of St. Pancras, in the village of Widecombe-in-the-Moor, in Devon. The "moor" of the name is Dartmoor and Widecombe lies on its eastern side, about 20 miles (32 km) northeast of Plymouth.

During the morning service on Sunday, October 21, 1638, with the church packed with worshipers, an event took place that was far beyond anything the villagers had ever experienced. Richard Hill, the village schoolmaster, recorded it in *A true Relation of most strange and lamentable accidents happening in the Parish Church of Wydecombe in Devonshire, on Sunday, the 21st of October 1638*. Hardly surprisingly, it was said to have left the church smelling of fire and brimstone. One of the pinnacles on the church tower was destroyed (it was replaced later) and the roof collapsed.

The damage was caused by what is now thought to have been a tornado, but the twister did not arrive alone and it was its companion that savaged and terrified the congregation. The interior of the church was set ablaze in a way that, according to the schoolmaster's account, "so affrighted the whole Congregation that the most part of them fell downe into their seates, and some upon their knees, some on their faces, and some on one another, with a great cry of burning and scalding they all giving themselves up for dead." Mr. Ditford, the parson, escaped injury but, said Mr. Hill, "the lightning seized upon his poor wife, fired her ruff, and linnen next to her body, and her clothes, to the burning of many parts of her body in a very pitiful manner." A parishioner, "adventuring to run out of the church, had her clothes set on fire, and was not only strangely burnt and scorched, but had her flesh torn about her back, almost to the very bones." Some of the coins melted in one man's purse. In all, 62 people were injured and, according to different reports of the event, somewhere between five and 50 were killed. One of those was said to have died when his head was "rent into three pieces."

Tornadoes accompany severe thunderstorms, and the companion to the 1638 tornado seems likely to have been an even rarer electrical phenomenon associated with such storms—a *fireball*. Little is known about fireballs, except that they really happen and they can be dangerous. There are descriptions of them from all over the world and they seem invariably to set fire to the first flammable material they touch, which would explain how clothes burst into flames at Widecombe. In the modern world they also burn out electrical wiring, causing any appliance connected to a power supply to explode.

# What are fireballs?

In 1984 a fireball fell to the ground in Leeds, Yorkshire, penetrated to below the surface, and set fire to a gas pipe, which exploded and burst a water main. At least two fireballs caused damage when violent and probably tornadic thunderstorms crossed southern England on July 20, 1992. A house in Crawley, Sussex, burst into flames, and in Dormansland, Surrey, a fireball was seen to descend and strike a house. Observers said it was like a large, red ball that fell from the sky. It made a hole 6 feet (1.8 m) wide in the roof and started a fire in the loft and a bedroom. The storm was very fierce that night and there may well have been a tornado, although it caused no evident damage.

Whatever they are, fireballs are not ordinary lightning. Nor are they ball lightning, the glowing spheres that float horizontally, passing through walls and windows, and usually disappear suddenly with a loud "pop."

In 1999 two New Zealand researchers, John Abrahamson and Peter Coleman, made a tornado fireball deliberately. They constructed a circular chamber, about 3.3 feet (1 m) wide, with openings near the base that allowed air to enter at different angles. An extraction fan mounted above the chamber drew air upward, creating a vortex 4 inches (10 cm) across. The experimenters injected liquefied petroleum gas into the bottom of the vortex, where the air was moving relatively slowly, and ignited it with a spark. Provided that air entered the vortex at an angle of 66°, they found that the burning fuel was drawn into the air eddying at the base of the vortex. It formed a sphere and remained there as a stable fireball.

Their experiment suggests a way a fireball might occur. If the tornado draws some combustible material into the base of the vortex and then lightning or sparks from a falling power line ignite it, the burning fuel might form a stable sphere. The fireball would be hot enough to burn anything it encountered, its precise temperature depending on the nature of the fuel, and it would survive until it had exhausted its fuel supply.

# Suction vortices and crop circles

Tornadoes and waterspouts move erratically across the surface and suction vortices that form around the center of a tornado sometimes leave behind them a spiraling trail of flattened crops. When suction vortices form at all, usually there are several, but not always. There can be just one that forms and then dissipates almost at once. During the few seconds that it lasts, the vortex may not have time to wander. Instead of a spiraling trail, it leaves behind an isolated swirl of leveled plants.

During the 1980s Dr. Terence Meaden of the Tornado Research Organization proposed that brief, stationary vortices might be the cause of "crop circles." These had been delighting journalists for some years, as well as attracting believers in flying saucers and giving rise to extraordinary stories of strange lights in the sky and weird noises. At first, the circles themselves were circular areas of flattened crops inside fields growing cereals, with no track or footprints linking them to the edges of the fields. They have been seen in Japan and other countries, but it was in southern England that they were most abundant. At their peak, several new ones were appearing every night during late summer, when the cereal crops were almost ripe enough for harvesting and the circles were clearly visible.

As the enthusiasm of the ufologists grew wilder, the circles started to become more elaborate. Circles had smaller circles around their edges, circles were linked by straight lines, and eventually crops were being laid flat in patterns resembling scientific formulae. The craze came to an end in September 1991, when two middle-aged men explained how they had been making the circles and other patterns, equipped with string, stepladders, and boards. Making the circles was very simple, called for very little equipment, and it was quick. Their confession did not deter the UFO hunters, however. They continued to believe in alien visitations, even while the hoaxers were making patterns in full view of them.

These men did it for fun, but there were far too many for the two of them to have been responsible for all the circles. There must have been many other hoaxers and, besides the hoaxes, a few circles that were not hoaxes at all.

Some witnesses said they had watched as short-lived, stationary vortices flattened circles of vegetation. These were far short of full-scale tornadoes, but at least some may have formed as eddies, much like those that generate water devils on some lakes (see "Waterspouts and water devils," on pages 106–110). Eddy vortices are especially common on the lee side of high ground, and once air starts spiraling, the conservation of its angular momentum (see "Vortices and angular momentum," on pages 77–83) tends to accelerate it toward the center. This mechanism might well flatten a circular area inside a field of wheat or barley.

# TORNADOES OF THE PAST

Look at the map showing part of eastern Scotland, and you will see that just north of Edinburgh there is a wide estuary (or firth). This is the Firth of Forth and to its north lies the county of Fife. Fife is bounded to the north by the Firth of Tay, with the city of Dundee on its northern shore. Roads and railroads linking Dundee and Edinburgh must either cross the two firths or make a long detour inland to cross the rivers Forth and Tay farther upstream, where they are narrower. In the last century, railroads were expanding rapidly to link every part of Britain, and a bridge was built across the Forth. Then, on June 20, 1877, the north coast of Fife was linked to Dundee by another bridge, across the Tay.

In those days, engineers knew less than they do now about the effects of wind on bridges, and the Tay Bridge was not stressed in the way all bridges have been since. Nevertheless, it was proudly boasted that the new bridge, a little over 1 mile (1.6 km) long, was strong enough to withstand the worst weather imaginable.

On the evening of Sunday, December 28, 1879, the mail train departed on time from Edinburgh, carrying passengers bound for the north. By the time it reached the Tay Bridge, there were between 75 and 90 people on board. The weather was stormy, with gale force winds and heavy rain. When the train was about halfway across, 13 spans of the bridge collapsed. The train fell into the River Tay, far below. There were no survivors. This was the Tay Bridge Disaster.

Despite the strong wind, the bridge should have stood, although some engineers now think there was a flaw in the design. Others believe that some other factor must have caused the tragedy. These scientists believe that the bridge was struck simultaneously by two tornadoes. The design may have been faulty, and the bridge had already been weakened by severe gales, but it was the tornadoes that destroyed it. Two waterspouts were seen in the vicinity at around the time of the accident.

## European tornadoes

The first tornado to be recorded in Britain—and one of the most severe—struck Bow, London, on October 23, 1091. It demolished several houses and churches. In June 1233, two waterspouts appeared off the coast of southern England. These were the first waterspouts recorded anywhere in Europe.

The Grand Harbor at Valetta, Malta, was severely damaged in September 1556 when a waterspout first destroyed a fleet of warships preparing to go into battle and then crossed over land. At least 600 people died in that storm.

Any tornado that crosses a populated area will cause severe damage and injury, but as the years turn into centuries, the details of such events are often lost. We know no more about the tornado that struck Welles-bourne, Warwickshire, England, in 1140 than that it caused extensive damage. A little more is known about the one that struck Nottingham, England, on July 7, 1558. It destroyed every house and church within a mile (1.6 km) of the city and trees were thrown more than 200 feet (61 m). One child was lifted to a height of 100 feet (30 m), then dropped.

One night in September 1669 a tornado formed at La Rochelle, on the Atlantic coast of France, and traveled all the way to Paris, a distance of 248.5 miles (400 km). This may be the longest tornado track ever known in Europe. Indeed, if the tornado began as a waterspout over the sea, the track may be even longer. On the other hand, what is recorded as a single track may in fact have been made by two or more tornadoes that occurred on the same night.

Tornadoes are usually narrow, but there are exceptions. On the after-noon of June 3, 1902, a tornado formed in western France that was almost 2 miles (3 km) across.

European tornadoes are mild compared with American ones. Five or six people were killed by the 1558 Nottingham tornado, but in June 1865 the tornado that moved through Viroqua, Wisconsin, claimed more than 20 lives.

Tornadoes struck Britain again in August 1979, in the form of tornadic waterspouts, when a tornado outbreak originating in the U.S. midwestern and New England states crossed the Atlantic. The storms reached the Irish Sea during the Fastnet Race, in which yachts sail from the Isle of Wight, off the south coast of England, to the Fastnet Rock, off southwestern Ireland, pass around the rock, and sail back to Plymouth. In that year, of the 306 vessels that entered the race, only 85 completed it. The storms whipped up by the tornadoes were so severe that 23 yachts sank or had to be abandoned and 18 sailors died.

# Outbreaks

Tornado outbreaks have afflicted Tornado Alley (see "Tornado Alley," on pages 120–127) many times. In the 1925 outbreak, about seven tornadoes killed a total of 689 people in Missouri, Illinois, and Indiana. There was another major outbreak, affecting 11 states, in May 1973, and, of course, the Super Outbreak of April 1974, which was followed by a second outbreak on the night of June 8.

There was another outbreak on April 4, 1977, affecting West Virginia, Virginia, Alabama, Mississippi, Georgia, Tennessee, and Kentucky. That outbreak caused 40 deaths and damage costing an estimated $275 million. At least 65 people were hurt and five died in a smaller outbreak that passed through Kalamazoo, Michigan, on May 13, 1980. On April 2 and 3, 1982, an outbreak affected Ohio, Texas, Arkansas, Mississippi, and Missouri, and on May 11 and 12 another outbreak struck Kansas, Oklahoma, and Texas, causing damage estimated to cost $200 million. On March 28, 1984, more than 70 people died in an outbreak in the Carolinas, and from May 6 to 9 storms in Kentucky, Louisiana, Tennessee, Ohio, Maryland, and West Virginia cost at least 14 lives and left 6,000 people homeless when floods added to the tornado damage.

Severe outbreaks continue. Most years see one or two. One of the most serious of recent years occurred from May 18 to 20, 1983, when at least 59 tornadoes moved through Texas, Tennessee, Missouri, Georgia, Louisiana, Mississippi, and Kentucky. In Houston, Texas, 350 homes were destroyed and more than 20 people died. Another outbreak, in the Great Plains and midwestern states on June 8, 1984, generated 49 tornadoes. Barneveld, Wisconsin, was totally demolished. A Kansas outbreak, on April 26, 1991, produced more than 70 tornadoes. Up to 45 tornadoes affected 11 states, from Texas to Ohio, in an outbreak from November 21 to 23, 1992.

An outbreak crossed Pennsylvania, Ohio, and New York on May 31, 1985, then crossed into Ontario, Canada. Several Pennsylvania towns were almost totally destroyed and at least 88 people died. Texas, the Carolinas,

Virginia, Louisiana, and Oklahoma were affected by an outbreak on May 6, 1989, that also caused severe flooding. There was an outbreak in Indiana, Illinois, and Wisconsin on June 2 and 3, 1990, and Alabama, Georgia, the Carolinas, and Tennessee were struck on March 27, 1994, by tornadoes that killed 42 people.

The 1985 tornadoes were not the only ones to affect Canada. On July 31, 1987, five of them struck a trailer park and nearby industrial center at Edmonton, Alberta. The tornadoes were relatively mild, with winds of only 60 MPH (96 km/h), but their target was vulnerable—trailers are fragile—and more than 25 people died.

Tornadoes can form in winter as well as summer, provided the storms that trigger them are violent enough. From December 12 to 16, 1987, storms that generated blizzards in Arkansas also produced tornadoes.

# Most tornadoes are short-lived

Outbreaks last for hours or days, but individual tornadoes seldom last for longer than seconds or minutes. That they can wreak such appalling havoc in so short a time is a measure of their ferocity.

In 1973, for example, a fairly weak tornado, with winds of only 100 MPH (160 km/h), struck San Justo, Argentina. It lasted for only three minutes, but in that time it killed 60 people and injured more than 300.

At Maravilha, Brazil, about 10 people died in a tornado on October 9, 1984. The tornado that destroyed a Mississippi shopping mall on Friday, January 10, 1975, was also brief, but it had time to kill 12 people and injure a further 200. A tornado killed at least 10 people in Marion, Illinois, on May 29, 1982, during the few minutes before it died.

Several tornadoes struck Water Valley, Mississippi, on April 21, 1984, killing 15 people, and five days later more than half the buildings in Morris, Oklahoma, were demolished by a tornado that killed a total of 14 people in and near the town. Saragosa, Texas, suffered a tornado on May 22, 1987, that killed 29 people, and 119 homes were destroyed and 18 people were killed by one in Hunstville, Alabama, on November 15, 1989. Plainfield, Illinois, was struck on August 28, 1990, by a tornado that killed 29 people and injured 300.

Major tropical cyclones are often accompanied by tornadoes. Hurricane Gilbert, which crossed the Caribbean and Gulf of Mexico from September 12 to 17, 1988, generated nearly 40 tornadoes in Texas alone. In 1989 Hurricane Hugo, which crossed the Caribbean islands and the eastern United States from September 17 to 21, also triggered tornadoes at Awendaw, South Carolina.

Tornadoes are uncommon in Africa, but on May 20, 1977, Moundou, Chad, was struck by one. Again it was soon over, but not before 13 people had died and 100 had been injured.

# Bangladesh and India

Away from the cyclones moving north from the Bay of Bengal, tornadoes are not common in India, either, but the subcontinent is not altogether immune. It took no more than two minutes for 32 people to die and 700 to be injured when a tornado struck northern Delhi on March 17, 1978.

During the spring and fall cyclone season, however, Bangladesh and the Indian states of West Bengal and Orissa, bordering the Bay of Bengal, are regions almost as dangerous as Tornado Alley. A tornado 500 feet (153 m) wide struck the western edge of Dhaka, Bangladesh (then part of India), on April 7, 1888. That storm killed 188 people and injured approximately 1,200. Up to 500 people died on April 11, 1964, when a tornado demolished several villages. Another tornado injured more than 200 people and killed 19 when it struck at least 12 villages in Bangladesh on April 10, 1976, and on April 1 of the following year an even more destructive one killed more than 600 people and injured about 1,500 in Madaripur and Kishorganj. About 70 people were killed, 1,500 injured, and 15,000 homes destroyed at Noakhali, on April 12, 1981, and 12 died and 200 were hurt at Khulna on April 26, 1983. A tornado at Sripur, on April 10, 1991, destroyed a textile mill, and the country suffered two tornadoes the following month, on May 7 at Tungi and on May 9 at Sirajganj. A tornado in the Sylhet and Sunamganj districts on January 8, 1993, lasted only five minutes, but in that time it killed 32 people and injured more than 1,000.

The worst tornado to strike Bangladesh in recent times struck more than 20 villages on April 26, 1989. It left about 1,300 people dead, 12,000 injured, and nearly 30,000 homeless. A series of violent thunderstorms struck western Bangladesh on the afternoon of Monday, May 13, 1996. The winds demolished more than 80 villages. By the time the storms abated, between 500 and 1,000 people had lost their lives, more than 30,000 had been injured, and about 100,000 were homeless. At least some of those storms are believed to have been tornadic.

In April 1978 Orissa State, India, was struck by a tornado that killed nearly 500 people and wounded more than 1,000. Later the same month, about 100 people died in a tornado in West Bengal. Orissa was struck again on April 12, 1981, when a tornado devastated four villages, killing more than 120 people, injuring hundreds, and destroying 2,000 homes. On April 9, 1993, 100 people died when a tornado destroyed five villages in West Bengal.

# Tornadoes in China

Most typhoons originating in the South China Sea form in summer and fall. They sometimes bring tornadoes to eastern China but like tornadoes everywhere, those in eastern Asia observe no rules. They should not happen as early as April or May, but on April 11, 1983, a tornado killed 54 people in Fujian Province, China, just across the strait from Taiwan, and in May of that year, several tornadoes in central Vietnam killed nearly 80 people.

Farther north, off the East China Sea, 14 towns were seriously damaged and at least 16 people were killed and more than 400 injured when a tornado struck Heilongjiang Province, China, on July 31, 1987.

Throughout the world and throughout history, tornadoes have appeared with little or no warning and have wreaked havoc in communities they have crossed. There are more in some years than in others, but there is no evident pattern to their changing frequency. It is possible, however, that tornadoes may become more frequent in the future. Many scientists believe that, by releasing into the atmosphere carbon dioxide and a range of other gases that absorb heat, we may cause an enhanced "greenhouse effect." This would make climates generally grow warmer and might lead to more large-scale thunderstorms, some of which would be tornadic.

# MEASURING THE SEVERITY OF TORNADOES

Any tornado that crosses a populated area will cause damage, but not every tornado causes the same amount of damage. Tornadoes vary quite widely in strength. Some generate winds of only 60 MPH (96 km/h) or even less, others, admittedly extremely rare ones, of 300 MPH (483 km/h) or more, and in the great majority of cases the wind speed lies somewhere between these extremes.

Obviously it would be very useful if scientists could arrange tornadoes in categories according to their force. This would allow them to see whether, on average, tornadoes are stronger in certain regions than they are in others. The resulting information would provide guidance for builders and emergency services, by telling them the worst conditions that structures and communities are likely to encounter. This information could be provided to prospective buyers of property, accompanied by a warranty that the property was built to the requisite standard. When a tornado warning is issued, it might also make it possible to include a forecast of the wind force people should expect. Not least, a comprehensive categorization of tornadoes as they occur would provide meteorologists with valuable data to help in their studies of tornadic storms.

Unfortunately, the scientific study of tornadoes is extremely difficult (see "Tracking and forecasting tornadoes," on pages 155–163). The vortices appear very briefly and without warning, so there is a large element of luck in whether a team of tornado-hunters just happens to be present when one occurs, even if they have accurate weather forecasts to guide them to likely locations.

Even if scientists are in the right place at the right time, by no means are their problems solved. They must then find some way to measure conditions at the center of the tornado vortex and in the funnel immediately around it. The conventional instrument for measuring wind speed is called an *anemometer*. There are several designs, but the commonest, shown in the illustration, consists of small cups mounted at the end of horizontal arms attached so they can turn freely about a vertical axis. When the wind blows, the arms spin and their rate of spin is converted into wind speed. Alternatively, the anemometer may measure the pressure exerted by the wind, with a vane to keep the instrument facing into the wind. Anemometers work well with most of the winds we experience, but the winds inside a tornado would demolish them instantly and scatter their remains over a vast area.

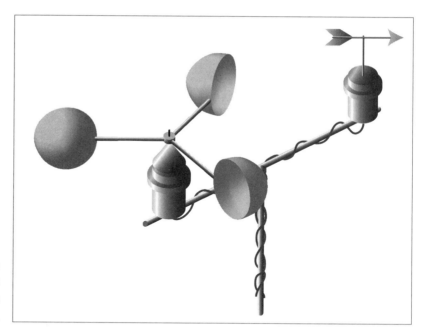

*Anemometer. The rotating cups design is one of several anemometers in common use.*

# Calculating wind speed from the pressure gradient

There is another way to approach the problem. It still requires direct measurement, but at least the instruments can be made more robust.

Wind is the movement of air from a region of relatively high atmospheric pressure to one where the pressure is lower. The wind does not flow in a straight line, directly from high to low, but spirals inward (see the sidebar "Christoph Buys Ballot and his law," on page 14) near the surface and at higher levels flows around the center of low pressure. The speed of the wind is determined by the *pressure gradient*, which is the difference in atmospheric pressure between the high- and low-pressure centers. The greater the pressure gradient, the stronger the wind will be, and the relationship between the two is determined by well-known physical laws. If you know one value, the other can be calculated. To calculate the wind speed inside a tornado, therefore, all you need to do is measure the atmospheric pressure some distance away from the tornado and the pressure at its center. It is still necessary to place a barometer inside the tornado, but at least barometers have no moving parts that must be exposed to the wind.

This method would work in principle, but the original difficulties are not really resolved. Scientists still have to find the tornadoes they wish to examine and then install their instruments directly in the path of the approaching storm without being killed, and the instruments themselves must survive to be recovered later. A barometer can be made much stronger than an anemometer, but it is doubtful whether any instrument could withstand a wind of more than 200 MPH (322 km/h).

Nevertheless, it has been attempted. TOTO, developed by Alfred J. Bedard and Carl Ramzy at the National Oceanic and Atmospheric Administration (NOAA) Environmental Technology Laboratory in Boulder, Colorado, represents one attempt. TOTO is a robust cylinder in a casing of half-inch (25-mm) aluminum set in a frame of angle iron, with arms holding instruments to measure wind speed, pressure, temperature, and electrical discharges. It carries its own batteries and it records the data it obtains. The initials of its name stand for Totable Tornado Observatory. (They also spell the name of Dorothy's dog in *The Wonderful Wizard of Oz.*) TOTO weighs 400 pounds (182 kg) and has made many measurements of mesocyclones, but it is designed only for winds up to 200 MPH (322 km/h). Winds stronger than this would probably topple it.

# Inferring wind speed from its effects

Suppose, though, that scientists were able to infer the conditions inside a tornado from the effects it caused. The force needed to uproot a mature tree, for example, or to demolish a building can be calculated accurately, so it might be possible to work out the force of a tornado by the damage it caused. This was the approach adopted by T. Theodore Fujita (1920–98). As professor of meteorology at the University of Chicago, he spent half a century studying tornadoes.

Fujita began by making detailed examinations of the trails left by some 250 tornadoes and tornado outbreaks. With his colleague Allen Pearson, formerly the chief tornado forecaster for the National Weather Service, in 1971 he devised what is now known as the Fujita Tornado Intensity Scale, shown in the table below. It is a six-point scale that relates wind speed to the extent of the damage the wind is likely to cause and it is often used to describe tornadoes.

In the United States, 69 percent of all tornadoes are weak, 29 percent are strong, and only 2 percent are violent. An F-0 tornado causes very little damage. Branches may be broken from trees and loose tiles ripped from roofs. At F-1, windows may be broken and some trees blown down. F-2 indicates a much more serious event. Mature trees may be uprooted and flimsy structures, such as mobile homes, are likely to be demolished. With winds approaching 200 MPH (322 km/h), an F-3 tornado will overturn cars, demolish walls, and flatten trees. Beyond these categories, tornadoes are described as violent. An F-4 tornado can demolish a house, leaving it as a pile of rubble, and one rated F-5 has the power to demolish houses and scatter the debris over a wide area. Even steel-framed buildings will be severely

| FUJITA TORNADO INTENSITY SCALE | | | |
|---|---|---|---|
| Rating | Wind speed (mph) | (km/h) | Damage expected |
| Weak | | | |
| F-0 | 40–72 | 64–116 | Light damage |
| F-1 | 73–112 | 117–180 | Moderate damage |
| Strong | | | |
| F-2 | 113–157 | 182–253 | Considerable damage |
| F-3 | 158–206 | 254–331 | Severe damage |
| Violent | | | |
| F-4 | 207–260 | 333–341 | Devastating damage |
| F-5 | 261–318 | 420–512 | Incredible damage |

damaged and cars may be picked up and carried several hundred feet. Some scientists have proposed additional ratings of F-6 to F-12, that would describe tornadoes with wind speeds of 319–700 MPH (513–1,126 km/h). Speeds of F-6 might occasionally be attained in suction vortices, but it is doubtful that they could be encountered in a tornado itself.

# Doppler radar

The Fujita scale is based not on measurements of wind speed but on assessments of the effects of tornadoes and calculations of the force that is needed to produce those effects. Nowadays, however, meteorologists often observe tornadoes with Doppler radar, which allows direct measurement of wind speed from a distance.

Radar exploits the fact that all forms of electromagnetic radiation travel at the speed of light and that at certain wavelengths (the distance between one wave crest and the next) radiation is reflected by objects it strikes. Water droplets strongly reflect radiation with a wavelength of about 10 cm, so this is the wavelength used for weather radar. It can reveal the structure of clouds by showing where their water is concentrated and the level at which rising water freezes and falling ice melts. By measuring the time that elapses between a radiation pulse leaving the transmitter and the receipt of its reflection, it is possible to calculate the distance between the radar transmitter and the reflective water droplets.

Doppler radar is based on the fact that the wavelength of radiation emitted by a source will decrease if the source is moving toward an observer and increase if the source is moving away. Discovered in 1842 by the Austrian physicist Christian Doppler (see the box), this is called the *Doppler effect*. It applies to radiation of any kind (Doppler proposed it for the case of light, but tested it only with sound) and to reflected radiation as well as radiation from a primary source.

# Discovery of the Doppler effect

Christian Johann Doppler (1803–53) was an Austrian physicist who spent many years as professor of mathematics at the University of Prague. He became intrigued by the way the pitch of a sound changes when the source of the sound is moving with respect to the observer. Like many people in the days when railroads were expanding all over Europe and America, Doppler had noticed that the sound of a train whistle rises in pitch when the train is approaching and falls in pitch as the train recedes.

In 1842 Doppler suggested why this happens and worked out a set of mathematical equations describing the phenomenon. Sound travels as waves that propagate through the air. He proposed that the movement of a vehicle must affect sounds that emanate from it while it is moving. As the source of the sound approaches an observer the sound waves have a progressively shorter distance to travel. This, Doppler believed, would "compress" the waves, shortening their wavelength—the distance between one wave crest and the next. Without altering the speed of the sound, shortening the wavelength increases the number of wave crests passing a fixed point each second. In other words, it raises the frequency of the sound. We hear an increase in the frequency of a sound as a rise in pitch. When the source recedes, the opposite happens. Sound waves now have progressively further to travel. This "stretches" them, increasing their wavelength and reducing the frequency. We hear a reduction in frequency as a lowering of pitch.

Christoph Buys Ballot tested the idea in 1845, with an unusual experiment he conducted at Utrecht, in the Netherlands. Buys Ballot hired a locomotive and a flatcar and employed a group of trumpeters, and also a group of musicians who were picked because of their sense of perfect pitch. He placed the trumpeters on the flatcar and had the other musicians stand close to the track. For two days the train moved back and forth at different speeds. As it moved, the trumpeters played sustained notes—a different note each time. The musicians beside the track wrote down the note they heard and the way that it changed as the train approached, passed, and receded. When he studied the results, Doppler found that his equations were correct.

He believed that the effect he had observed with sound waves should also be true of light. In this case, however, some details of his explanation were not quite correct, although his basic idea was. The Doppler effect on light—and all electromagnetic radiation, including radar—was explained correctly in 1849 by the French physicist Armand-Hippolyte-Louis Fizeau (1819–96). Fizeau said that the effect should be visible as a change in the spectrum of light from the moving source. If the source is receding, the wavelength of light should increase, shifting the spectrum in the direction of red light. If the source is approaching, the wavelength should be reduced and the spectrum should be shifted in the direction of blue.

This was confirmed by observation in 1868 by the English astronomer Sir William Huggins (1824–1910). The chemical elements in the outer layers of a star absorb radiation, each at a particular wavelength. This absorption appears as black lines in the spectrum of light from the star. Huggins detected a small red shift in one of the lines corresponding to hydrogen in the spectrum of the star Sirius, and calculated from this the rate at which Sirius and Earth are moving apart.

If you transmit a pulse of radiation at a wavelength that is known very precisely, measure equally precisely the wavelength of its reflection, and compare the two, you will find whether the source of the reflection is moving toward or away from the observer and at what speed. The diagram illustrates the principle. If the object reflecting the pulse is approaching, the wavelength received will be shorter than the wavelength transmitted. It is said to be *blue-shifted*, because when this happens to visible light, the change is toward the shorter-wave, blue end of the light spectrum. If the object is receding, the wavelength received will be longer than that transmitted, or *red-shifted*, toward the long-wave, red end of the spectrum. The amount by which the radiation has been blue- or red-shifted indicates the speed with which the object is approaching or receding. In the case of rapidly rotating raindrops, obviously the water does not change color; the terms *blue-shifted* and *red-shifted* are used by convention.

If an object is scanned in this way, and if the Doppler radar indicates that one side of the object is approaching and the other side retreating, clearly the object must be rotating, and the amount of wavelength shift reveals its speed of rotation. That is how Doppler radar is used to tell whether there is a rotational motion of water droplets inside a cloud. If there is, and the rotation is big and fast enough, the cloud contains a mesocyclone.

Doppler radar is now used to study weather systems from a distance of 100 miles (160 km) or more, but there are a few disadvantages. Not every cloud with rotating currents develops into a mesocyclone and generates tornadoes, for example, so the instrument readings need careful interpretation. Also, the curvature of the Earth limits the range of any radar. Distant objects close to the ground are below the transmitter's horizon and therefore hidden from radiation that travels in a straight line. Radar instruments may also have difficulty with line-squall storms moving across the field of view, from left to right or right to left. This is because the Doppler effect refers only to objects that are moving toward or away from the observer. This problem is resolved by using two

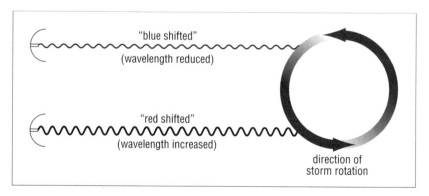

*Doppler effect. The reflection from the side of the storm approaching the instrument is "blue-shifted"; the reflection from the receding side is "red-shifted."*

Doppler radars, observing from different positions to give a more three-dimensional view.

As technology continues to improve, meteorologists will have an increasing number of tools at their disposal. In years to come these will allow them to make much more detailed observations of the conditions inside tornadic storms and to measure the severity of tornadoes much more precisely.

# STUDYING TORNADOES

Tornado hunters have a hard time. Working on the ground, they must drive to likely areas and then cruise along remote country roads, constantly searching the sky for storm clouds that look promising. It is a somewhat hit-or-miss operation, and if they are lucky enough to spot a tornado they have only a few minutes in which to unload the instruments from their van, install them in the path of the approaching storm, and get out of the way before it arrives.

They have clues, of course. Before setting out they will have analyzed information from the National Weather Service. What interests them is not so much the ordinary weather forecast, but the data returned from meteorological balloons, called *radiosondes* or, if they are used primarily to study high-altitude winds, *rawinsondes* (see the box). Meteorologists first began using radiosondes in 1927 and nowadays they are routinely released from weather stations all over the world. In order to ensure that the data they provide can be built into a comprehensive picture of the weather at a particular time, every participating weather station, no matter where it is in the world, releases two radiosondes each day, one at midnight and one at noon Universal Time (UT). Universal Time is the time at Greenwich, England, counting the hours from midnight. The name was adopted officially in 1928 to replace Greenwich Mean Time.

The tornado hunters based at the National Severe Weather Laboratory in Norman, Oklahoma, tune into the early-morning broadcast of radiosonde data. These start arriving at the National Meteorological Center, in Washington, D.C., soon after 7 P.M., which is midnight UT. The hunters look for places where the air temperature drops very sharply with increasing height and the wind increases in speed and changes direction rapidly. A steep environmental lapse rate—the rate at which temperature decreases with height—suggests that the air is very unstable (see the sidebar "Lapse rates and stability," on page 71). If the wind speed and direction in the upper troposphere differ from those in the air below, rising air will be carried away, drawing more air behind it to feed the upcurrents.

Supported by data about the movement of weather systems, this profile of the atmosphere indicates a collision between three air masses, where potentially unstable air is held trapped beneath a stable layer, and with strong wind shear aloft. These are ideal conditions for the formation of severe thunderstorms that may link into squall lines (see "Squall lines," on pages 49–56). Some of the storms may become tornadic.

As they drive, the team of hunters keeps in contact with the changing meteorological situation by radio, cellular telephones, and a miniature TV. The information they received before setting out guides them to the general area in which tornadic storms may be expected. Constant updates include the results of Doppler radar scans of cloud patterns (see "Measur-

# Radiosondes and rawinsondes

Weather stations throughout the world use balloons to study atmospheric conditions above ground level and to a height of about 80,000 feet (24.4 km), in the middle of the stratosphere. Balloons were first used for this purpose in 1927. Modern versions are called *radiosondes*, because they take soundings (measurements, originally of the depth of water beneath a ship, for which the French word is *sondes*) and transmit them to receiving stations by radio. To make sure that measurements from around the world can be combined to produce a comprehensive picture of atmospheric conditions at a particular time, every weather station, no matter where it is, releases one radiosonde every day at midnight and a second at noon Universal Time. The U.S. National Meteorological Center, in Washington, D.C., receives about 2,500 sets of radiosonde data every day.

The balloon itself is spherical, about 5 feet (1.5 m) in diameter, and filled with hydrogen. Beneath it there is a cable nearly 100 feet (30 m) long with a package of instruments attached to its lower end. The cable must be this long to make sure that air movements around the balloon do not interfere with instrument readings. The standard instrument package comprises a very sensitive thermometer, a hygrometer to measure humidity, and a barometer to measure air pressure. There are also timers, switches to turn the instruments on and off at predetermined times, a radio transmitter, batteries to supply power, and a parachute to return the instruments safely to the ground.

After it is released, the radiosonde climbs steadily, at about 15 feet (4.58 m) per second. As it rises, its hydrogen expands, and when it reaches a height of about 80,000 feet (24.4 km) the balloon bursts and its instruments parachute to the ground, from where they are recovered and returned to the weather station that launched them. During its flight, the radiosonde broadcasts its measurements to the ground station.

In addition to its instruments, the radiosonde carries a radar reflector immediately below the balloon. This strongly reflects radar pulses and allows the movement of the radiosonde to be tracked from the ground. Before radar was invented, balloons were tracked visually, but, of course, they disappeared from view as soon as they entered cloud.

As it ascends, the radiosonde moves horizontally with the wind, which usually changes direction and speed in different layers of air. Tracking the radiosonde provides accurate information on the wind speed and direction in each atmospheric level through which the device passes. Balloons that are tracked to study winds at very great heights are sometimes called *rawinsondes* (for radar wind sounding). In years to come, these will probably broadcast their precise locations using the Global Positioning System.

ing the severity of tornadoes," on pages 141–147). These will identify cumulonimbus clouds and the location of thunderstorms that have developed mesocyclones and supercells.

# Preparing to record a tornado

Even at this stage, finding a tornado is a matter of chance, and when one is found it may start to chase the hunters, forcing them to flee before they have time to set up their instruments. Even with the help of radiosonde data and constantly updated weather reports, most hunters can expect to see no more than one or two tornadoes a year and none at all in some years. Capturing pictures and data from those few twisters involves driving long distances—sometimes thousands of miles. If you live in Tornado Alley (see "Tornado Alley," on pages 120–127) you have probably seen tornadoes and know firsthand what they can do. If you live in any other part of the country, you may never see a tornado in your entire life unless you go looking for one.

You should hope never to see a tornado and on no account must you ever go out in pursuit of them. Professional tornado hunters are highly trained. They can judge the way a tornado is moving and they know when and how to keep out of its way. Lacking their experience, you might be caught, and even the mildest tornadoes are extremely dangerous.

While they search, the scientists record a running commentary, describing their location and the weather conditions they can see. Once they locate a tornado, they prepare to make their observations and measurements. The team carries a video camera to provide a visual record and for some years they used the TOTO (Totable Tornado Observatory) to measure temperature, wind speed, and pressure inside the vortex (see "Measuring the severity of tornadoes," on pages 141–147). Today there is an improved version of TOTO called "Turtle" or "TOTO II." The Turtle was designed by Fred Brock, a meteorologist at the University of Oklahoma, who also built the first ones. Turtles earned their name because of their shape. They are smaller, lighter, and more robust than TOTO, with their instruments housed inside a dome-shaped metal shell that stands about ankle-high when it is placed on the ground. TOTO recorded its data on charts. Turtles record them digitally. This makes Turtles more reliable and, because of their small size, easier to transport and set up than TOTO.

Portable Doppler radar is also available to the tornado hunters. At one time, some scientists believed winds inside the most powerful tornadoes might blow faster than the speed of sound (in air at 68°F, 20°C, this is about 770 MPH, 1,239 km/h). Portable Doppler radar instruments have measured wind speeds close to 300 MPH (483 km/h) and scientists now believe this is about as fast as they ever blow.

# Resolution

A radar signal travels like a beam of light and it has the same limitation as a flashlight beam. A flashlight is very good at illuminating nearby objects, but objects farther away are not nearly so well lit. This is because the beam diverges. As the illustration shows, the farther the beam travels the wider it becomes, so its light is spread over an area that increases with distance.

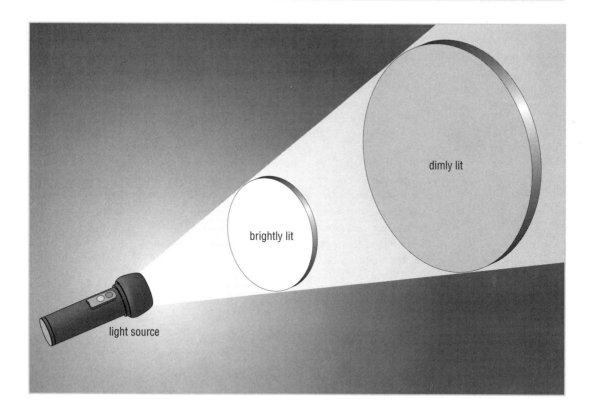

The amount of light does not change, so as the area covered increases, the amount of light received at each small part of it must decrease. The size of objects it will reveal clearly is called the *resolution* or *resolving power* of the flashlight or radar.

Resolution is especially important for Doppler radar, because the technique relies critically on highly accurate measurements of the wavelength of signals reflected from different parts of the object being examined. In the early years of their use, portable Doppler radars were unable to resolve details as small as an average tornado from a distance of a few miles, which is often as close as tornado hunters can get. Increasing the size of the transmitting and receiving antennas would improve resolution, but it would also make the apparatus much more cumbersome and prone to damage in the strong winds along the gust front of a squall line. Instead, a group of engineers at the University of Massachusetts at Amherst made a set of radar equipment that works at a much shorter wavelength. The short wavelength allows the radar to transmit a much narrower beam, with less divergence. The narrow beam provides the needed improvement in resolution without increasing the size of the antennas, but at a price. The equipment costs more and uses more power, and under certain weather conditions the reflections it receives can be difficult to interpret.

*Image resolution. An object close to the source of light is illuminated more intensely than one farther away, because the beam of light diverges. Consequently, the resolution of the image decreases with distance from the light source.*

# Studying tornadoes from the air

No pilot would willingly fly through a tornado, but tornadic storms are studied from the air using specially equipped and strengthened airplanes. Planes fly over, around, and through cumulonimbus clouds along carefully planned routes, recording vertical air currents, winds, temperatures, pressures, electrical activity, and a range of other characteristics. The information they gather helps scientists to understand how thunderstorms develop and to discover what goes on inside huge storm clouds.

Rawinsondes are also used. These balloons can be launched directly into storms and their movements tracked. In 1986 this technique, in those days using radiosondes and tracking them visually, resulted in the first direct measurements obtained from inside a tornadic storm. These showed that the upcurrents were rising at more than 100 MPH (160 km/h).

# Computer models

Nowadays scientists have an entirely different approach to studying the way in which events occur naturally. They can use computers to construct models that simulate the phenomenon. The first computer models were made in the 1960s, but it was not until the 1980s, with the invention of supercomputers, that scientists had access to sufficient computing power and speed to begin modeling weather systems.

Computer models are entirely mathematical. Models of weather phenomena begin with the equations that describe the known physical behavior of air under specified conditions of temperature, pressure, density, and humidity. Once the initial data describing the state of the atmosphere have been fed into it, the model is set to run. It then depicts the way the weather system will evolve over time. A model can show, for example, what happens when air is warmed from below and how it cools as it rises and expands. It can modify this by adding the effects of its water vapor condensing or evaporating. It can indicate how air masses at different temperatures and densities may react when they meet, and how pressure gradients, vorticity, and the Coriolis effect influence wind speed and direction.

For modeling purposes, the atmosphere is divided into "blocks" by means of a three-dimensional grid of vertical and horizontal lines, all of which meet at right angles. All the equations are used to make calculations at every point where grid lines intersect. The finer the grid, the more accurate the model will be, but the finer the grid, the more intersections it will have and, therefore, the more calculations that must be made. Computer modelers strive constantly to improve their accuracy by working with ever-finer grids.

Once the basic equations have been programmed and the grid constructed, data must be fed into the computer so that numbers can be substituted for the symbols in the equations. The numbers must be genuine, obtained by making measurements of the actual conditions at a particular place and time. This is how the measurements made by tornado hunters are used. The data they collect are passed on to the modelers and fed into computers.

When this task is completed, the model can be set running. At each grid intersection, the condition of the air will be calculated and the results passed to neighboring intersections as data that alter the conditions there. Alterations mean that the relevant values must be recalculated, producing changed conditions that pass as input data to more intersections. Step by step, the entire system changes its characteristics as the computer calculates and recalculates the changes taking place at every grid intersection. Millions of calculations are needed to show changes that would take only a few minutes in a real weather system, so if the model is to produce useful results in a reasonable time, it must work very fast indeed. That is why such models can be made only with the fastest, most powerful supercomputers in the world.

When the computer run ends, the result will be a system that is in a different condition from the one in which it commenced. In a sense, the model will have predicted that if the weather, or developing storm, starts in the way the input data described, after so many minutes or hours this is what will have happened to it. Perhaps it will have dissipated, leaving a clear sky. Or maybe it will have grown into a huge and violent storm. Or, if conditions are right, perhaps it will have formed a supercell and caused one or more tornadoes.

# The need for "ground truth"

This is all very well, but before scientists can trust the results from all these millions of calculations, they must check to see what happened out in the real world. This is what scientists call *ground truth*—information they obtain by observing what really happens outside, "on the ground." This is another job for the tornado hunters, although in their case it is a job they have already done. As well as recording conditions in and around a tornadic storm, they will also have monitored its progress. They will know what really happened to it, and this can be compared with what the computer predicted should have happened. If the two agree, and if they continue to agree after many tests of this kind, the model will be accepted as reliable.

Then the model can be used to simulate the real world by performing experiments. Scientists can ask it direct questions. Is this what starts an upcurrent rotating? How fast must that rotation become before it extends downward in a tornado funnel? What happens as the upcurrents and downcurrents separate and the storm becomes a supercell?

Supercells can now be accurately modeled in this way. As finer and finer grids are used, the models reveal increasing amounts of detail. Very lifelike tornado vortices have been produced inside computers. Because the modelers had to feed in the data to produce those "virtual" vortices, they are very close to understanding the way they occur. A scientific picture of the birth, life, and death of a tornadic storm is being painted, detail by ever-finer detail.

It does not mean tornado hunters can pack up their vans and go home. Ground truth will always be needed, partly to keep a check on the models as they continue to develop. Left to themselves, the models could easily diverge from reality until they came to generate simulations that were very convincing, but quite wrong—and therefore harmful, because they would seriously mislead forecasters. Observers will also be needed to supply more and more data. Tornadoes are not bound by rules, and a complete understanding of one "average" tornado does not necessarily mean the mechanisms of all tornadoes have been mastered.

In the coming years, modelers and tornado hunters will continue to collaborate. The practical result of their efforts will be improved tornado forecasts.

# TRACKING AND FORECASTING TORNADOES

Tornadoes are unpredictable, almost by definition. Despite this, once they have appeared their progress can be tracked and people can be warned whenever there is a likelihood that one will come close to them. Not so many years ago, and well within the memory of people who are still alive, the first sign of an approaching tornado was often the distinctive roar it made or its actual appearance. Everyone able to do so would run for shelter and hope they reached it in time. There was no time to do much that might have made their homes more secure.

Tornadoes are still far from being tamed, or even fully understood, but meteorology has advanced greatly in modern times. Today there is usually, although not always, time to prepare for the onslaught. At present, the National Weather Service can provide about six minutes warning between the time a tornado funnel touches the ground and its arrival in a populated area. It sounds little enough, but it comes after an earlier warning that tornadoes are likely, and in six minutes lives can be saved. This safety margin is likely to improve considerably in the next few years.

## Mapping weather systems

Weather systems move and each one affects an area of hundreds of square miles. There is no possibility of plotting its movement or forecasting how it will behave unless the system can be seen as a whole, with all of it displayed at once on a map. Regardless of how many people record measurements of temperature, wind, pressure, and rainfall in different places, no overall picture can emerge until their observations have been collected and plotted on a map.

Scientists realized as long as two centuries ago that there was a need to collect information from scattered locations at a central point, but in those days the fastest travel was by galloping horse, so the task was impossible. They did what they could, even so, collecting measurements all made at about the same time and compiling them to produce *synoptic charts*, much like the weather maps you see today in newspapers and on TV. A synoptic chart is one recording the situation at a particular time (the word is from the Greek *sunoptikos*, meaning "seen all together"). Charts of this kind were being compiled in France by the late 18th century, but by the time they could be drawn, the situation they recorded was 10 years old. Scientific weather forecasting was out of the question.

What the meteorologists needed was some means of communicating the results of measurements as fast as they were obtained. The breakthrough for which they had been waiting so long came in 1844. That was the year when the first telegraph line in the world was constructed. It ran only between Baltimore, Maryland, and Washington, D.C., but it was so successful that similar lines were soon linking towns in many countries, and once they were installed, meteorologists began to use them to compile weather reports and forecasts.

Samuel Morse, who claimed to have invented the telegraph, also devised the code used to transmit messages along it. The code, bearing his name, is little used today, but it was simple, easy to learn, and transmitting it required very little electrical power. It was based on combinations of only two signals, one short (called a "dot" and conventionally written as .), the other long (called a "dash" and conventionally written as _). A dash was a signal sustained three times longer than a dot, and a rather longer interval served to separate letters. In Morse code, for example, the word "tornado" is:

$$\_ \ \_\_\_ \ \cdot\_\cdot \ \_\cdot \ \cdot\_ \ \_\cdot\cdot \ \_\_\_$$
$$t \quad o \quad r \quad n \quad a \quad d \quad o$$

It looks cumbersome, but a skilled operator could transmit and read Morse code very fast. Because it uses only two signals, it is known as a *binary* code and it demonstrated the versatility of binary codes generally. In modern times this versatility has led to the use of another binary code, written using 0 and 1 to symbolize the "on" and "off" positions of a switch, as the basis for all digital computer programming.

Meteorologists could now communicate and weather stations were established all over America and Europe. Eventually these formed a network covering the whole world, although still rather unevenly. There are now about 2,500 surface weather stations throughout the world, and in addition some 1,500 ships also report meteorological observations. To ensure that the observations can be combined to produce a description of the weather at the same time everywhere, stations try to report readings taken at midnight, 0600, noon, and 1800 hours Universal Time (Z) every day. The data they obtain are coordinated and analyzed by a system called World Weather Watch (WWW), organized by the World Meteorological Organization (WMO), which is a United Nations agency.

# Observations of the upper atmosphere

For a long time observations were made only from the ground. Then, when lightweight but robust instruments became available in the 1920s, balloons came into use for measuring conditions above the surface, and eventually in the upper atmosphere (see the sidebar "Radiosondes and rawinsondes," on page 149). Today there are about 500 weather stations reporting upper-air measurements. Between their two ascents at noon and midnight to collect full data, at 0600 and 1800 Z wind balloons carrying only radar reflectors are launched and tracked simply to monitor wind direction and strength.

Aircraft are also used. Some civil airliners carry instruments to monitor atmospheric conditions. Such aircraft reports are irregular, however, because their timing and location are controlled by flight schedules and routes, and this reduces their scientific value. Airplanes are much more useful for direct observation than for routine monitoring. By the late 1940s there were planes strong enough to fly into thunderstorms, and today there are specially strengthened aircraft, equipped with sensitive instruments, that fly regularly through cumulonimbus clouds and around the central cores of storms. Different types of plane work at each altitude up to 30,000 feet (9 km) and beyond.

Even then, an overall picture had to be compiled from many local observations. Each weather station, balloon, ship, or aircraft can report only the conditions at a particular place. It was impossible to see and measure a weather system the size of a continent or ocean all at once, but the next major step brought that wide view much closer.

# Orbiting satellites

On April 1, 1960, the first *Television and Infrared Observation Satellite (TIROS-1)* was launched into Earth orbit. It circled the Earth, transmitting to ground stations television pictures of the narrow strips of land and sea over which it was passing. *TIROS-1* observed only part of the Earth, missing the polar regions, and its pictures were somewhat fuzzy, but it revealed new possibilities. In particular, it provided much more detail than had been obtainable earlier. Surface weather stations are many miles apart and upper-air observation stations are even more widely dispersed, so scientists had to guess what was happening between them, in the gaps where no observations could be made. Satellite pictures resolve details only a mile or two (1.5–3 km) across, and there are no gaps. They show patterns of cloud, great swirls of cloud around depressions, individual cumulus causing showers, and entire frontal systems. There are now many weather satellites orbiting the Earth and delivering large amounts of detailed, very accurate data (see the box).

Weather satellites are placed in either a *polar orbit*, which may be *sun-synchronous*, or in a *geostationary*, or *geosynchronous*, or *Clarke*, orbit (after the author Sir Arthur C. Clarke, who first thought of it). A polar orbit, shown in the diagram, is at a height equal to one-seventh the radius of the

# Weather satellites

Orbiting satellites are widely used to augment the information collected by surface weather stations. Satellites transmit instrument measurements to ground stations, as well as photographs taken in one or more visible light wavelengths or in the infrared. The *Television and Infrared Observation Satellite* (*TIROS-1*) was the first to be launched, on April 1, 1960, by the United States.

TIROS-1 was also the first weather satellite to enter polar orbit. A total of 10 *TIROS* satellites completed the series, and in 1966 the first of nine Environmental Science Services Administration (ESSA) satellites was launched, using a *TIROS* operating system. The United States also operated the *Nimbus* satellites, launched between 1964 and 1978. Currently the United States uses the *Advanced TIROS-N* and *National Polar-Orbiting Environmental Satellite System* (*NPOESS*) series of satellites operated by the National Oceanic and Atmospheric Administration (NOAA). Russian polar-orbiting weather satellites all belong to the *Meteor* series, the first of which was launched successfully (one earlier launch failed) in 1969. There are also three Chinese *Feng Yun* (FY) satellites.

Many weather satellites are in geostationary orbit. The *Applications Technology Satellite-1* (*ATS-1*), owned by the United States, was the first of these to be launched, in December 1966. The *ATS* series was replaced in 1974 by the first in the *Synchronous Meteorological Satellite* (*SMS*) series, and the first *Geostationary Operational Environmental Satellite* (*GOES-1*) was launched on October 16, 1975.

A total of 12 *GOES* satellites have been launched (although one launch failed). Two are operational at any time. One, orbiting at 75°W, observes eastern North America, the western Atlantic Ocean, and western South America. The other, at 135°W, observes western North America, the eastern North Pacific Ocean as far as Hawaii, and the eastern South Pacific. Both satellites transmit data at half-hour intervals.

The European Space Agency is responsible for the *Meteosat* and *Meteosat Second Generation* satellites. The Japanese operate a series of five *Geostationary Meteorological Satellites* (*GMS*) and two *Multi-functional Transport Satellites* (*MTSat*). The Indian government operates the series of 11 *Indian National Satellites* (*INSat*). Russia operates the *Geostationary Operational Meteorological Satellite* (*GOMS*) series, which has been renamed *Elektro*. China has two *Feng Yun* (*FY*) satellites.

Satellite images show the distribution of clouds, but they reveal little about what is happening below the cloud tops. This should change as a result of CloudSat, a project forming part of the NASA Earth System Pathfinder Mission. The *CloudSat* spacecraft is due to be launched in 2004 on a *Delta* rocket from Vandenberg Air Force Base, in California, and it will spend two years measuring the height and thickness of clouds, as well as the amount of water and ice they contain and the way they develop. The spacecraft, carrying very advanced equipment, including radar especially designed to study clouds, will fly as part of a formation of other satellites. These will include the *Aqua* and *Aura* satellites operated by NASA, the French Space Agency's *PARASOL* satellite, and the *CALIPSO* satellite, operated jointly by NASA and the French Space Agency.

Earth—about 534 miles (860 km)—and is at a slight angle to the lines of longitude. The satellite takes 102 minutes to circle the Earth, passing close to both poles (but not exactly over them). As the satellite orbits, the Earth is turning beneath it, so each swath it covers, 1,700 miles (2,735 km) wide, lies beside the one over which it passed in its previous orbit. In the course of 12 hours, the satellite passes over every point on the Earth's surface. A polar orbit may also be sun-synchronous. In that case the satellite remains permanently in the same position in relation to the Sun and passes over every point on the surface at the same time every day. Surface stations can tune into transmissions from the satellite as it passes overhead to obtain current information about conditions in their area.

A geostationary orbit, shown in the diagram, is at a height equal to 5.6 times the radius of the Earth, about 22,370 miles (36,000 km), above the equator. The satellite moves in the same direction as the Earth rotates and at the same speed (at that height, 6,850 MPH, or 11,022 km/h), so it remains permanently above the same point on the surface. It has a view of almost an entire hemisphere, although its resolution at the edges is poorer than that closer to the center of its field of view and the North and South Poles are below the horizon for a satellite over the equator. World Weather Watch maintains five satellites in geostationary orbit, spaced

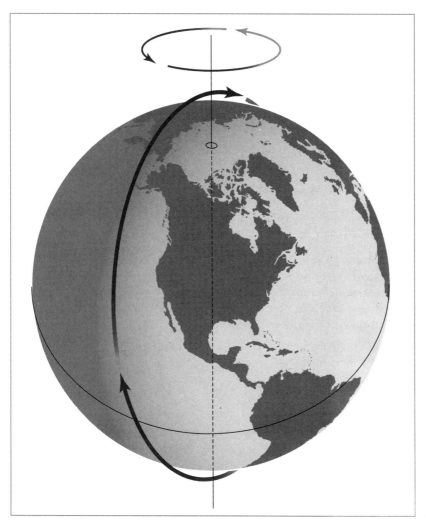

*Polar orbit*

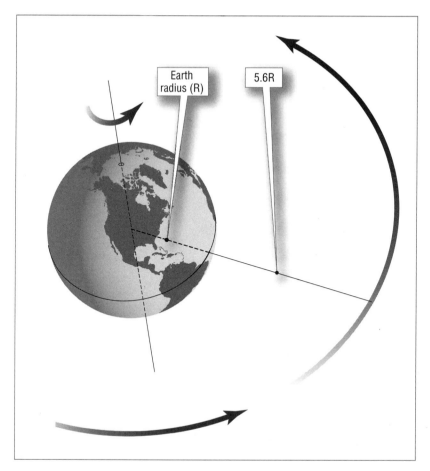

Earth radius (R)

5.6R

*Geostationary orbit*

evenly around the equator to provide a good view of the entire world. Instruments on a satellite in geostationary orbit scan its field of view slowly, taking 20 minutes to complete a scan. The resolution is almost as good as that from satellites in much lower polar orbits, and pictures can be taken at night using infrared cameras.

# Doppler radar

The latest recruit to the observational network over the United States is a nationwide Doppler radar cover called NEXRAD (Next Generation Weather Radar). The first installations came into operation in the early 1990s, and by 1996 the completed system comprised 175 of them, located at weather stations, airports, and military bases. Each one looks like a large golf ball mounted on top of a tall tower made from scaffolding, and it can provide three-dimensional images with clear resolution of weather up to 125 miles (200 km) away and rather poorer resolution of weather at distances up to 200 miles (322 km). These installations are fixed, of course, and much more powerful than the portable Doppler radars used by tornado hunters (see "Measuring the severity of tornadoes," on pages 141–147).

Already Doppler radar has improved the reliability of tornado prediction. Previously, radar was used to study storm clouds. The radar reflection indicated the location of raindrops and, because the more raindrops there are, the stronger the reflection will be, it also showed their concentration. Sometimes a characteristic hook shape can be seen in the rain pattern, to one side of the cloud. In the 1950s meteorologists came to recognize this as a sign of a mesocyclone, possibly heralding tornadoes. Today they rely on Doppler radar. This measures directly the speed at which air is rotating inside a cloud and is a much more reliable indicator of mesocyclones.

# Assembling and interpreting the data

All of the information from surface stations, upper-air soundings, ships, aircraft, satellites, and the NEXRAD network is processed in order to produce the forecasts issued by the National Weather Service. It is a formidable task and one that must be performed quickly if the forecast is to be of any use. In 1980 the Forecast Systems Laboratory at the NOAA Environmental Research Laboratories in Boulder, Colorado, launched PROFS— the Program for Regional Observing and Forecasting Systems (later changed to Services). Its aim is to find increasingly efficient ways of assimilating incoming information and displaying the result at interactive workstations, then to transfer the technologies to wherever forecasters need them. This is especially important for improving the quality of forecasts issued for the weather up to two hours ahead, called *nowcasting*. These are the forecasts that can give warning of approaching tornadoes.

Meteorologists are constantly watching the skies by studying pictures transmitted from orbiting satellites. These pictures show where large thunderstorms are developing. Wind measurements at various heights in the area around the thunderstorm will reveal the presence of high-level wind shear, and surface reports of changing temperature and pressure will allow the scientists to locate air masses and the fronts where different air masses meet. The situation changes as air masses move, vertically as well as horizontally, and their development is reported to the forecasting centers more or less as it occurs, in real time. Large, isolated thunderstorms and squall lines are also watched carefully.

The meteorologists of the National Weather Service are quick to recognize vigorous squall lines and large, isolated cumulonimbus clouds. Incoming reports tell them if these are producing severe weather conditions. If they think it necessary, the forecasters will issue a warning to communities in the path of the advancing storms. These may take the form of a *severe thunderstorm watch*, if thunderstorms are approaching you, followed some time later by a *severe thunderstorm warning*, when they have reached your area.

Really big thunderstorms can be dangerous in their own right. Lightning kills an average of 93 people a year in the United States and injures 300—and it is not true that it never strikes twice in the same place. Scientists at the University of Arizona made video recordings of 386 cloud-to-ground lightning flashes during the summer of 1997. They found that about one-third of all flashes hit the ground in two or more places, confirming research findings from France and other parts of the world. This means that certain places are struck more than once and that the chance of being struck by lightning is markedly higher than many people suppose. The National Severe Storms Laboratory now recommends that 6–8 miles (10–13 km) is a safe distance to be from a previous lightning strike. Previously, 2–3 miles (3–5 km) was considered safe.

Hail does not always fall as pellets not much bigger than rice grains. Hailstones can reach the size of softballs and fall with enough force to do serious damage. Wind gusts ahead of an advancing storm may not twist like the wind in a tornado, but they can briefly reach hurricane force. Storm winds of 140 MPH (225 km/h) have been measured. That is strong enough to strip away a roof or demolish a mobile home. Finally, storms bring torrential rain that can lead to flash floods, which kill more people than any other weather phenomenon.

# Warnings

Most national weather services issue warnings of severe weather, but it is only in the United States that meteorologists are especially alert to the risk of tornadoes. They pore over satellite photographs looking for the telltale "hook" in the cloud formation that indicates the presence of a mesocyclone and analyze Doppler radar images that tell them if the interior of a cloud is spinning, and how fast.

The first warning they broadcast is a *tornado watch*. It means that tornadoes have not yet been observed, but the conditions are right for them and they may develop in the next few hours.

You should always take this warning seriously. When you hear the message the sky may be blue, the Sun shining, and the air calm. Remember, though, that the forecasters are tracking a storm or squall line that is still a long way from you, but that may be moving fast in your direction.

Do not be deceived by the fine weather. If you hear on the radio or TV that storms are coming, believe what you hear. Even if the forecasters are wrong, which is unlikely, it is much better to be safe than sorry.

The second warning is a *tornado warning*. It means that a tornado has been reported in your area. If you hear this, you must find shelter immediately. You could be lucky, of course, and the tornado might never reach you, but it is foolish to take risks, and even if no tornado arrives, the rain, hail, and lightning almost certainly will.

# DAMAGE FROM TORNADOES

Forecasters can warn of an approaching tornado, but they can only guess at its severity. The Fujita Tornado Scale (see "Measuring the severity of tornadoes," on pages 141–147) ranks tornadoes by their wind speed and the damage they cause, but they are ranked only after the event. Scientists assess the damage the tornado caused and use this to work out its force. Obviously, they can do this only after the tornado has disappeared. Until it arrives, therefore, no one can tell whether it will merely break a few branches from trees and damage some chimneys or flatten well-built houses and throw cars around like toys.

A strong (F-2 and F-3) or violent (F-4 and F-5) tornado is likely to produce freak effects. A house was once transported 2 miles (3.2 km), and another was lifted, turned through 90 degrees, and gently set down again on the same spot. A car that traveled along a London street 15 feet (4.5 m) above the ground was set down gently, without being damaged. A car carrying two persons in Bognor Regis, England, was lifted into the air, moved sideways, and set down again on the opposite side of the road. Chickens have been stripped of all their feathers. A roof was once blown 12 miles (19 km). A woman living at El Dorado, Texas, is said to have survived being blown through a window of her house and carried 60 feet (18 m) by a tornado on June 10, 1958.

# Property damage

More commonly, though, tornadoes simply destroy property, and although improved forecasting and advice about how to survive have reduced the number of fatalities, the number of injuries and amount of property damage remain high. In the United States, property damage has tended to increase over the years. Damage is measured as monetary cost, so the increase is due partly to the rise in property values. Figures quoted for the cost of damage are based on estimates of insurance claims, so the rise in the total cost of damage to property also reflects the fact that more property is insured than was the case formerly. Increased property damage is also due to the growth in popularity of vacation homes, built to lower standards than would be demanded in cities, and of mobile homes. Outside the United States, in countries where warning systems are less advanced and large numbers of people live in poorly constructed housing in sprawling urban areas, the risk of death and injury is much higher.

Flying debris causes as much property damage as direct exposure to the wind and is probably responsible for most tornado injuries. The funnel itself is narrow, but winds around the core demolish anything in their path. This produces solid fragments of all sizes. At first these whirl around the vortex in upcurrents that are strong enough to keep them airborne. The fragments move in a circular path because the centripetal force, drawing them toward the center of the vortex, balances the momentum directing them in a straight line (see the sidebar). That balance is unstable, and after a few moments the momentum of the fragments exceeds the centripetal force. When that happens, fragments spray out from the funnel, each item flying in a straight line at a tangent to the vortex, as indicated in the diagram. As it advances, the tornado hurls debris outward in all directions, like a spinning gun—but a gun that possesses the capacity to reload itself constantly as it gathers fresh debris to spin and throw.

A moving object possesses energy due to its motion. This is called *kinetic energy*. If it collides with another object, the moving object loses part or all of its kinetic energy. This energy does not simply vanish, however. It

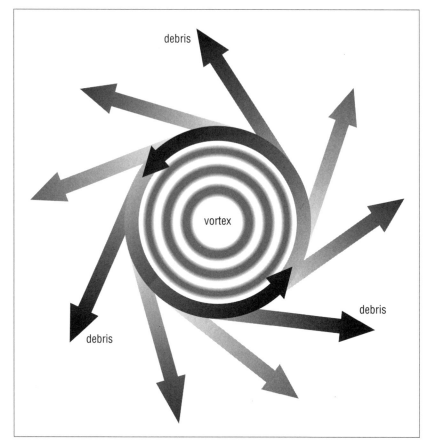

*How debris sprays out*
*from a tornado*

# Centripetal force

When an object moves along a curved path, there is a force that tries to propel it along a straight path at a tangent to the curve. This is sometimes incorrectly called "centrifugal force." Its correct name is *momentum*.

Newton's first law of motion states: Unless it is acted upon by external forces, a body at rest will remain at rest and a moving body will continue moving in a straight line. This tendency to remain at rest or in a state of uniform motion is called *inertia*. Momentum is the force propelling the body in a straight line. It is equal to the mass of the body multiplied by its velocity.

If the body continues in its curved path, a countervailing force must act against its momentum. In the case of an orbiting satellite, the gravitational attraction between the satellite and the Earth provides the force preventing the satellite from departing at a tangent to its orbital path. In the case of an object being swung in a circle at the end of a rope, tension in the rope itself supplies that force. A passenger in a car that corners at high speed is pushed outward against the side of the car. The pushing force is momentum and the side of the car, pushing in the opposite direction and holding the passenger in, supplies the countervailing force.

The force that holds a moving body in a circular path is called *centripetal force*. It acts between the body and the center of the circle its motion describes, in the direction of the center of the circle. The diagram shows how the two forces act.

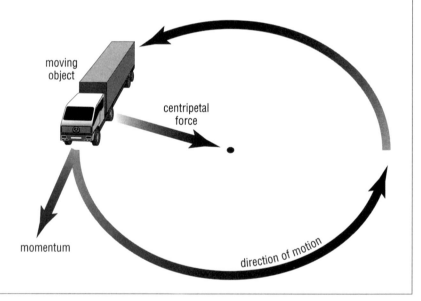

moving
object

centripetal
force

momentum

direction of motion

*Centripetal force*

may be transferred to the other object, setting it in motion. This is what happens on a pool table when one ball strikes another and makes it roll. Eventually, all the kinetic energy dissipates, converted into heat, but it is the transfer of kinetic energy that causes damage.

How much damage depends on the amount of kinetic energy the moving object possessed. This is proportional to the mass of the object and the square of its velocity (see the sidebar), which means that speed is much more important than mass. If, for example, a mass of 1 pound (0.5 kg) moves at 45 feet per second (13.7 m s⁻¹), its kinetic energy will be about 32 pounds (47J). Double the mass, to 2 pounds (1 kg), and the kinetic energy is 63 pounds (94J). Keep the mass at 1 pound (0.5 kg) and double the velocity, to 90 feet per second (27.4 m s⁻¹), and the kinetic energy is 126 pounds (188J).

It requires less energy to accelerate a small mass to high speed than it does to accelerate a large mass, so the speed of the fragments ejected from a tornado funnel depends on their size (strictly, their mass, but for most ordinary materials it amounts to roughly the same thing). Obviously, if you are struck by an object the size and weight of a car you will be injured, even if it is traveling quite slowly, but even the fiercest tornadoes throw out few cars. Contrary to what common sense might suggest, the small items, traveling very fast, are much more dangerous than the large ones. They are also much harder to see.

# Force of the wind

Walking on a windy day can be difficult. You can feel the wind pushing you this way and that. Air is a physical substance. It has weight (or mass). One cubic foot of air weighs about 0.08 pound (1.28 kg m⁻³). When air moves it also possesses kinetic energy, and the amount of kinetic energy is calculated in just the same way as for any other substance. The faster air moves, the more kinetic energy it has, and so the harder it pushes you. In a 30-MPH (48-km/h) wind, which is strong enough to push you around when you are out walking, the kinetic energy of the moving air is about 2 pounds per cubic foot (114J). If you are, say, 5.5 feet (1.7 m) tall

## Kinetic energy

Kinetic energy (KE), which is the energy of motion, is equal to half the mass ($m$) of a moving body multiplied by the square of its velocity (its speed and direction, $v$). Expressed algebraically:

$$KE = 1/2\ mv^2$$

This formula gives a result in joules if $m$ is in kilograms and $v$ is in meters per second. If you need to calculate the force in pounds that is exerted by a mass measured in pounds moving in miles per hour, the formula must be modified slightly to:

$$KE = mv^2 \div 2g$$

where $v$ is converted to feet per second (feet per second = MPH × 5280 ÷ 3600) and $g$ is 32 (the acceleration due to gravity in feet per second).

and 1 foot (0.3 m) wide (width, not waist measurement!) a 30-MPH (48-km/h) headwind will push against you with a force of about 12 pounds (5.5 kg). At the wind speeds common around the core of a tornado, the force can be huge. Near the core of a severe tornado (F-3) the wind may be 200 MPH (322 km/h), with a kinetic energy of about 94 pounds per cubic foot (5.120J). Try walking in that, and the wind will press against you with a force of nearly 520 pounds (236 kg), which is probably about four times the weight of your body. Obviously, you will not be able to remain on your feet, because the force pushing against you is much greater than your own weight.

When a 200-MPH (322-km/h) wind slams into the side of a trailer, it hits it with a force of approximately 10 tons (9 tonnes). That first blow smashes the side, opening up gaps for the wind to widen further, but the trailer is not hit from just one direction. Tornadic winds spiral, so the wind constantly changes direction as the tornado moves. Not surprisingly, the trailer disintegrates almost instantly—it simply flies apart.

# Pressure in the vortex

Air pressure at the center of a tornado vortex is very low. It used to be believed that if a tornado passed directly over a building, the sudden difference between the pressure inside and the pressure outside could make the building explode. People were advised that the way to prevent this was to open the windows before the tornado arrived, in order to allow excess air to flow out of the building and thereby equalize the pressure. Indeed, buildings do sometimes appear to explode, but it is the wind and flying debris that cause most of the damage. Once the structure has been breached and seriously weakened, wind blowing through it can make parts of it collapse outward. By that time, of course, the interior and exterior air pressures have equalized. Opening the windows actually increases the likelihood of severe damage, because it provides immediate access to the wind. In any case, there is no way even the fiercest tornado could make a building explode. The drop is pressure at the core of a tornado, compared with average sea-level pressure of 1,013 millibars (14.7 pounds per square inch), is unlikely ever to exceed about 100 millibars (1.45 pounds per square inch) and usually it is much smaller. This is nowhere near strong enough to make a house, or even a mobile home, explode.

Roofs are especially prone to damage in any strong wind. There are several reasons for their vulnerability.

Many homes have roofs covered with slates, tiles, or shingles. These are laid in an overlapping pattern and fastened at their upper edges. They cannot be fastened very tightly, because if one breaks it must be possible to remove and replace it without disturbing those around it. Wind can penetrate along the lower edge, exerting an upward force that may be strong enough to dislodge any loose tiles, and once a few have been removed the wind can quickly strip away more.

Some roofs are covered by single sheets of material, but often these are not fixed very securely to the frame of the building. Nails driven at right angles through the skin and into the roof timbers will hold under most conditions, but if a wind of tornadic force finds a gap under the eaves and pushes upward, they are not too difficult to withdraw.

Most roofs, especially on private homes, slope up to a central ridge. This shape is excellent for allowing rain to flow away quickly and for preventing snow accumulating in a layer thick and heavy enough to damage the structure. In really strong winds, however, ridged roofs do experience a force due to pressure differences above and below. The reason for the reduced pressure above the roof is the same as that which produces the very low air pressure at the center of a tornado vortex.

It is called the Bernoulli effect and it was discovered in 1738 by a Swiss mathematician called Daniel Bernoulli (see the sidebar). If you picture the wind as a mass of air flowing through an imaginary tube, a ridged roof constricts the tube. Air must flow up the roof, over the ridge, and down the other side. This accelerates the wind, because air crossing the roof must travel farther than air higher above the roof, but it must do so in the same length of time. In cross section, the roof forms a triangle and the air has to travel along two of its sides instead of straight across the base. Bernoulli found that when this happens, the pressure in the flowing air decreases as it accelerates past the constriction. This drop in pressure results in an upward force acting on the roof, because the pressure above the roof is markedly lower than the pressure beneath. Combine this force with the upward force from wind that has penetrated the building from below, and those nails will not hold for long. Once they give and the entire sheet starts to lift, it acts like a sail until it is completely free, then twists and turns chaotically until it falls to the ground.

# Winds ahead of and behind the tornado

Tornadoes are most likely to occur along the leading side of an advancing supercell storm (see "Supercells," on pages 69–76). When you see the huge black or slightly green cloud, with a mass of cloud rotating below part of it, expect a tornado.

As the storm comes closer, the straight-line wind will increase, often to a force that causes some damage to property. Then the tornado itself arrives, reducing buildings to rubble and hurling debris outward with great force. Within seconds, or at most minutes, the tornado has passed or dissipated, but the rest of the storm is still to come.

# The Bernoulli effect

In 1738 the Swiss mathematician Daniel Bernoulli (1700–82) published a book called *Hydrodynamica*, in which he showed that when the speed at which a fluid (liquid or gas) flows increases, the pressure within the flow decreases. He reached this conclusion while studying water flowing through a pipe from a tank where the water level was high to another where it was lower. In the end, of course, the water level is the same in both tanks, but while the water is flowing Bernoulli found that the pressure within the flowing stream is related to the speed with which it flows. This is summarized as:

$$p + 1/2rV^2 = \text{a constant}$$

where $p$ is the pressure, $r$ the density of the fluid, and $V$ its velocity (speed). Because the expression $p + 1/2rV^2$ is a constant, if one of the terms in the expression changes, one or more of the other terms must also change to compensate. The density ($r$) of a moving fluid is unlikely to change, so $p$ is directly related to $V$. If the pressure increases, then the velocity must decrease, and vice versa.

If, for example, the fluid flows through a tube with a constriction in it, assuming the fluid is not compressed (which would increase its density), the rate of flow must increase at the constriction, because the same volume of fluid must pass there in a given time as passes every other point in the tube. It follows from Bernoulli's equation that the pressure must decrease at the constriction.

The Bernoulli effect explains how an aerofoil, such as the wing of an aircraft, generates lift and how it is possible for a strong wind to lift the roof from a building. As the diagram shows, the movement of air across the curved upper surface of the aerofoil or ridged roof generates a region of reduced pressure above the surface. The higher pressure below the surface then exerts an upward force—in the case of an aircraft, called "lift."

The wind no longer twists, but behind the tornado lies the *gust front*, where winds reach gale force. Behind them there is the hailstorm, followed by the heaviest of the rain—and all of these accompanied by lightning. Finally, at the rear of the storm, downcurrents carrying air away from the cloud at ground level produce winds that can reach hurricane speeds. Buildings are exposed to a sequence comprising huge wind gusts, the tornado, severe hail, torrential rain, and winds perhaps of hurricane force, and they may also be struck by lightning.

After a storm generating an F-2 tornado, trailer homes will have been shattered and most buildings will have lost their roofs. An F-3 tornado will also demolish some walls, even of well-built houses. A violent tornado, F-4 or F-5, will leave very few buildings standing and the debris will be so thoroughly mixed there is no way to tell which rubble belonged to which house. Some houses will have been lifted bodily from their foundations and carried away, only to crash again. They will not even leave a pile of ruins as a memorial, because their bricks, mortar, timber, and plaster—not to mention their contents—are likely to have

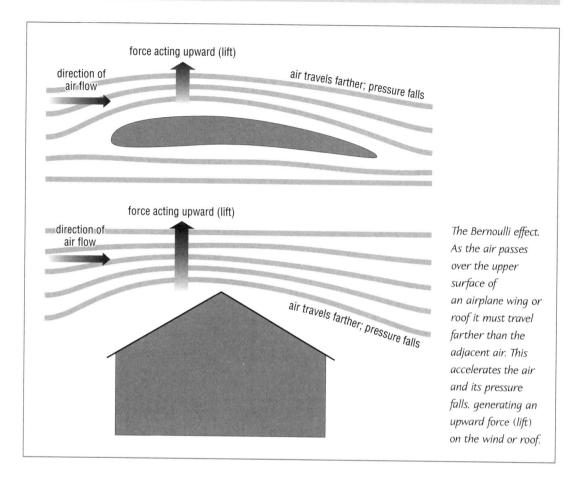

force acting upward (lift)

direction of air flow

air travels farther; pressure falls

force acting upward (lift)

direction of air flow

air travels farther; pressure falls

*The Bernoulli effect. As the air passes over the upper surface of an airplane wing or roof it must travel farther than the adjacent air. This accelerates the air and its pressure falls. generating an upward force (lift) on the wind or roof.*

been carried aloft into the funnel and scattered over a vast area. Some trees will have been stripped of their bark before being torn from the ground. Trains will be overturned, cars thrown hundreds of feet, and, battered by wind and debris, whole areas will have been pounded almost to dust, then drenched by the rain.

# WILL CLIMATE CHANGE BRING MORE TORNADOES?

Climates are constantly changing. Obviously, during a full-blown ice age North America and Europe look very different from the way they look today. During the coldest part of the most recent ice age, Canada and the northern half of the United States, as well as northern Europe, had a climate very like that of present-day Greenland. Regions beyond the edges of the ice sheets supported tundra, like that of northern Canada today. Prior to the commencement of that ice age, however, about 100,000 years ago, elephants, rhinoceroses, and hippopotamuses roamed and wallowed over what is now the center of London.

All of this was a very long time ago, of course. The most recent ice age ended about 10,000 years ago. Temperatures then rose, and it is tempting to assume that they have remained fairly constant ever since. It is tempting, but quite wrong. Around 10,800 years ago, for example, the average temperature in England was rather higher than it is today, although a small ice sheet still covered part of Scotland. Then, probably in the space of about 50 years, the temperature in England fell by 7–9°F (4–5°C) and conditions remained cold for the next 600 years. Glaciers appeared in some parts of the country.

During the Middle Ages the English climate was approximately 1.3°–1.8°F (0.7°–1.0°C) warmer than it is today, and the climate was 1.8°–2.5°F (1.0°–1.4°C) warmer in central Europe. The medieval warm period was followed by the Little Ice Age, lasting from the 16th to the early 20th centuries. Temperatures fluctuated during the Little Ice Age, but in 1687 the average temperature in Switzerland was 7°–9°F (4°–5°C) cooler than it is now.

## Identifying the changes

The idea that climates are unchanging is quite recent. Scientists were unable to forecast the weather until there were telegraph networks to transmit measurements and observations from a wide area to a central point (see "Tracking and forecasting tornadoes," on pages 155–163). They were collecting and collating meteorological information much earlier, however, and examining it intensively. Scientists had been doing this since about 1775. They obtained their data from nationwide observational networks established for the purpose, and their reason for all this effort was a widespread suspicion that the climate was changing. There were sudden variations in the behavior of the seasons, and these departures seemed to be increasing. If this were so, those variations might have serious consequences for public health and agricultural output.

The fears being expressed in the early part of the 19th century were identical to those being expressed today. Warmer weather might bring more disease. Cooler weather might cause deaths from hypothermia and an increase in demand for fuel—in those days principally coal, burned on open hearths (by those who could afford it) and producing copious amounts of smoke that would exacerbate respiratory illnesses. A sudden increase in yields, due to favorable weather, meant bumper harvests and a fall in food prices, but price fluctuations might destabilize the markets. Harvest failures were much worse. In the 18th and 19th centuries they often meant famine.

By the end of the 19th century, scientists had access to weather records going back about 100 years. These had been obtained using standard instruments and they had been made in many of the major cities of the world. The records were reliable. Unfortunately, their interpretation was not.

Scientists compared the records for recent years with those relating to a century earlier. What they found was that there had been very little change. The climate of the late 19th century was little different from that of the late 18th century. Naturally enough, they concluded from this that despite all the fears about the changing seasons, climates are essentially constant. They do not change very much at all.

What the scientists failed to notice was that there had been a number of very cold episodes during the 19th century, some of them lasting several decades. Alpine glaciers advanced markedly between about 1820 and 1850, for example. But then temperatures recovered and the glaciers began retreating. The retreat that began then is still continuing—and causing alarm about climate change. Temperatures rose and fell through the 19th century, but by the end of the century they chanced to have returned to the values of a century earlier. They were back where they began and no one noticed they had been on several excursions in between.

It was convenient to believe that climate is constant—and it is still convenient. All planning depends on the predictability of conditions. Builders need to know the range of temperatures and precipitation their houses should experience. Houses built for the Vermont climate would not be suitable in Mexico. Some communities are wise to buy snowplows even though these machines are very costly, but other communities would be foolish to do so. We rely on averages, usually calculated over about 30 years, and prefer to ignore the extent to which climates change on a rather longer scale.

# Present climate change

At present the global climate is growing warmer. The warming is not distributed evenly. Some places, such as India, southern China, and parts of the United States, are experiencing no change or are actually becoming colder. The Antarctic Peninsula is growing warmer, but much of the interior of Antarctica is growing colder. Much the same is happening in the Northern Hemisphere. The southern coastal region of Greenland and the adjacent sea have cooled by 2.32°F (1.29°C) since 1959, although they have become warmer since about 1993. The warming is a global average, and temperatures are increasing by about 0.027°F (0.015°C) a year, or 2.7°F (1.5°C) a century. Associated with this, total precipitation is increasing in the Northern Hemisphere outside the Tropics.

Several factors are contributing to this change. Part of it may be a general warming as the world emerges from the Little Ice Age. This idea is supported by evidence linking the Little Ice Age with variability in the intensity of solar radiation and the fact that the Sun has been especially active in recent years. The present phase of warming, which began in the late 1970s, also appears to be linked to the emergence of a large pool of warm water in the Pacific Ocean.

Most climatologists believe that some of the warming, and possibly most of it, is due to the increasing atmospheric concentration of carbon dioxide and certain other gases. The Sun radiates energy across a wide spectrum of wavelengths (see the sidebar), but predominantly at short wavelengths. This is the energy that warms the Earth's surface. When the surface warms, it radiates the heat away, but at long wavelengths, because the wavelength is inversely proportional to the temperature—the hotter the radiating body, the shorter are the wavelengths of its radiation.

These gases absorb part of the long-wave radiation emitted by the Earth's surface, thereby warming the air. This warming comprises the *greenhouse effect*, and the gases are known as *greenhouse gases*. The Intergovernmental Panel on Climate Change (IPCC), which is the body advising governments, estimates that if the atmospheric concentration of greenhouse gases increases until it is double the concentration of preindustrial times, the consequent warming will be 2.5°–10.4°F (1.4°–5.8°C). The IPCC thinks that this point may be reached by about 2100. Many scientists believe the actual warming is much more likely to be close to the lower figure and that the upper figure is much too high.

# Is warmer weather also stormier?

Tornadoes are triggered by extremely severe storms. Such storms represent a vast release of energy. A warming climate suggests that the atmosphere

# The solar spectrum

Light, radiant heat, gamma rays, X rays, and radio waves are all forms of electromagnetic radiation. This radiation travels at the speed of light as waves. The various forms differ in their wavelengths, which is the distance between one wave crest and the next. The shorter the wavelength, the more energy the radiation has. A range of wavelengths is called a *spectrum*. The Sun emits electromagnetic radiation at all wavelengths, so its spectrum is wide.

Gamma rays are the most energetic form of radiation, with wavelengths of. $10^{-10}$–$10^{-14}$ $\mu$m (a micron, $\mu$m, is one-millionth of a meter, or about 0.00004 inch; $10^{-10}$ is 0.00000000001). Next come X rays, with wavelengths of $10^{-5}$–$10^{-3}$ $\mu$m. The Sun emits gamma and X radiation, but all of it is absorbed high in the Earth's atmosphere and none reaches the surface. *Ultraviolet* (UV) radiation is at wavelengths of 0.004–4 $\mu$m; the shorter wavelengths, below 0.2 $\mu$m, are absorbed in the atmosphere but longer wavelengths reach the surface.

Visible light has wavelengths of 0.4–0.7 $\mu$m, *infrared* radiation 0.8 $\mu$m–1 mm, and *microwaves* 1 mm–30 cm. Then come *radio waves*, with wavelengths up to 100 km (62.5 miles).

will possess more energy—higher temperatures mean more heat—and so severe storms might become more frequent.

This sounds reasonable, but it is too simple. Tornadic storms require a strong wind shear in the upper atmosphere. This is most often supplied by the jet stream. Consequently, a strong jet stream tends to be associated with more tornadoes. The jet stream is produced by the strong difference in temperature between polar and tropical air on either side of the polar front (see the sidebar).

Global warming is predicted to be most pronounced in high latitudes. Tropical and equatorial temperatures are not expected to rise by the same amount. This suggests that the difference in temperature between tropical and polar air will decrease, as polar air becomes warmer but tropical air remains much closer to its present temperature. If that happens, the jet stream—generated by that temperature difference—is likely to become weaker and less regular. This might have several consequences, one of which would be a marked decrease in midlatitude storms.

On the other hand, higher temperatures would increase the rate of evaporation. This would supply more moisture, and it is the condensation of water vapor in air that is rising strongly by convection that supplies the energy that drives supercell storms. So moister air might make severe storms more frequent, and with more frequent storms there would be more tornadoes.

Supporting the idea of a link between warming and severe storms, during the 1990s two research teams found a relationship between thunderstorms and average minimum temperatures and wet-bulb temperatures. The *wet-bulb temperature* is measured by a thermometer that has its bulb wrapped in wet muslin, so the thermometer reading is affected by the loss of latent heat as water evaporates from around the bulb. Subtracting the wet-bulb temperature from the *dry-bulb temperature* shown by an ordinary thermometer gives the *wet-bulb depression*, from which the relative humidity and dew point temperature can be calculated. The researchers discovered that a 1.8°F (1°C) worldwide increase in the wet-bulb temperature would produce a 40 percent increase in lightning over the world as a whole, and a 56 percent increase over land areas in the Northern Hemisphere. The studies used data from only three years, however, and there have been few studies of trends over longer periods.

# Jet stream

During World War II, when high-altitude flying was new, aircrews sometimes found their journey times radically different from those they had calculated prior to takeoff. The effect was not reliable enough to predict, but when flying from west to east they could find their speed over the ground increased dramatically and when flying in the opposite direction they were just as dramatically slowed. They had discovered a narrow, wavy ribbon of wind blowing at speeds comparable to those of their aircraft. They called it the *jet stream*.

If they approached the jet stream from above or below, pilots found the wind speed increased by about 3.4–6.8 MPH for every 1,000 feet of altitude (18–36 km/h per 1,000 m). If they approached from the side, it increased by the same amount for every 60 miles (100 km) of distance from the core of the jet stream. At the center of the stream, the wind speed averages about 65 MPH (105 km/h) but it sometimes reaches 310 MPH (500 km/h).

There are several jet streams. The polar front jet stream is located between about 30°N and 40°N in winter and about 40°N and 50°N in summer. There is an equivalent jet stream in the Southern Hemisphere. The subtropical jet stream is located at about 30° throughout the year in both hemispheres. These jet streams blow from west to east in both hemispheres. In summer there is also an easterly jet at about 20°N extending across Asia, southern Arabia, and into northeastern Africa. This jet stream blows from east to west.

The jet streams are *thermal winds*. That is to say, they are generated by the sharp difference in temperature across the front separating two air masses. This difference is greatest close to the tropopause, which is why the jet streams occur at high altitude—the polar front jet stream at about 30,000 feet (9 km) and the subtropical jet stream at about 40,000 feet (12 km). The polar front jet stream is associated with the polar front, separating polar air and tropical air. The temperature difference responsible for the subtropical jet stream occurs only in the upper troposphere, on the high-latitude side of the Hadley cells.

The polar jet stream is quite variable and often it is not present at all. The subtropical jet stream is more constant. Consequently, the term *jet stream* often refers simply to the subtropical jet stream, and this is the one that is usually shown on maps.

# Are tornadoes becoming more frequent?

Given the uncertainty, climate scientists seek clues in the recent record. The number of tornadoes reported in the United States has increased greatly since the 1920s, but this does not mean there have been more tornadoes. The observational network, improved technology, increasing population in formerly remote areas, and a higher level of public education and interest in weather phenomena have combined to increase the number of reported sightings. So the number of reported tornadoes tells us very little.

There is a way around the problem. Most of the tornadoes that went unreported in the past were probably weak ones—F-0 to F-2 on the Fujita scale. If so, those are the tornadoes that are now being noticed. Strong and violent tornadoes, F-3 to F-5, on the other hand, are difficult to ignore. Even in remote areas they cause damage that is clearly visible. So most of those probably were reported, and removing the F-0 to F-2 tornadoes from the recent reports should produce figures that are more directly comparable with those from earlier years. When the search is restricted to the strong and violent tornadoes, there is no trend over the years. Some years saw an unusually large number—1974 was especially bad—but if anything, the number of strong and violent tornadoes is decreasing very slightly.

Another way of checking for change is by studying the record of *tornado days*. These are days on which at least one tornado was reported somewhere in the United States. This record shows that the annual number of tornado days increased from the early 1920s to the 1960s, but since then the number has been decreasing.

Tornadic storms are also associated with heavy falls of hail. Hailstorms damage crops and farmers claim on the insurance, so there are records of severe hailstorms. These can be added to the records from weather stations. The records show that over the 20th century, hailstorms became less frequent over most of the United States, but increased over the High Plains. The scientists of the IPCC conclude that "despite an increase in minimum temperature of more than 1°C since 1900 and an increase in tropospheric water vapor over the United States since 1973 (when records are deemed reliable), no systematic increase in hail or thunder days was found." (*Climate Change 2001: The Scientific Basis*, p. 162.)

The answer seems to be, therefore, that if global warming continues there is no reason to fear that tornadoes will become more frequent. It is more likely that their frequency will decrease.

# SAFETY DURING A TORNADO

In any kind of emergency, ignorance can lead to panic, panic to inappropriate action, and inappropriate action can result in injury or even death. Your chance of emerging unscathed increases dramatically if you know what to do and calmly carry out a well-rehearsed plan.

Obviously, we cannot anticipate everything that could happen, but it is only common sense to prepare in advance for those life-threatening events that may occur. At one time or another, tornadoes have occurred in 49 of the 50 states (Alaska remains tornado-free), but the risk is not the same everywhere. Oklahoma City, for example, seems to average around three tornadoes a year.

The first step, therefore, is to find out how great the risk is where you live. How often have tornadoes occurred in your area in the past? If there have been several, then tornadoes could strike again, so be ready for them. If you are new to the neighborhood, check with the nearest office of the National Weather Service or emergency service. If you learn that tornadoes are recognized as a local hazard, find out what plans your community has made. How will people be warned? Where are the safe places to shelter? How would an evacuation be organized? How would everyone be notified?

## Make sure family members keep in touch and know what to do

Your family may not be at home when a tornado strikes. Some members might be at school, others at work or driving. Agree on a place to meet if you are dispersed and cannot return home. Ask a friend who lives a long way away to act as a communication link. If the family is separated, members can telephone the friend to report their position and the friend can pass on the information to the next person who calls. Make sure the friend's number is taped to every telephone in your home and that all members of the household carry it with them. Naturally, your family can perform the same service for the friend.

Make sure everyone, including young children, knows how to call the emergency services. Make sure all adults and older children know how to turn off the electricity, gas, and water supply.

Know your surrounding area. If there is a "tornado watch" warning, use an up-to-date highway map to plot the location and movement of storms and to plan an escape route if you have to evacuate.

# Laying in supplies

You may be trapped in a shelter for some time, so you will need supplies and should keep them ready. Prepare emergency stores and keep them in or close to where you will shelter. This will be the basement if your home has one; if not, it should be a small room on the lowest floor, such as a bathroom or closet, or a hallway.

Your emergency store should contain supplies for three days. For each person you will need a blanket or sleeping bag, a change of clothing, three gallons (11 liters) of water in airtight containers, and dry or canned food. In addition, your store should have a first aid kit, battery-powered radio and flashlight with spare batteries for both, spare car keys, and a few basic tools such as a hammer, screwdrivers, wire cutters, and pliers. If anyone takes prescription medicines, remember to include a supply, and also include any special items needed for infants or elderly or disabled people.

The store should be kept in containers that you are able to carry easily in case of evacuation. Use holdalls, backpacks, or duffel bags. Check the contents from time to time and change the water and food every six months.

Keep important family documents in a waterproof wallet somewhere safe but easily accessible. If you have to seek shelter, take them with you. Also take cash or credit cards and personal identification. If you have to leave your home, the authorities may not allow you to return unless you can identify yourself.

# When you hear a tornado watch

If there is a "tornado watch" alert, keep the radio or TV on and tuned to a local station for weather updates. Ideally, you should have an NOAA weather radio with a warning alarm. Be ready to switch to battery-powered radio if necessary.

Outside, the weather may look fine and everything may be peaceful. The "watch" alert usually covers an area of about 140 miles by 200 miles (225 × 322 km) and you may be perfectly safe, but if the weather looks stormy, start taking precautions. If you are at home, make sure you know where in the house all other members of the family are. Shut all windows and exterior doors.

Take warnings of severe thunderstorms seriously. These are issued as a preliminary "watch" followed by a "warning," like those for tornadoes. It is possible for a severe thunderstorm suddenly to develop a mesocyclone and trigger a tornado.

# When you hear a tornado warning

"Tornado warnings" are issued for much smaller areas than "watches." If you hear a warning it means tornadoes have been seen quite close to you.

Watch the sky from indoors. Expect a tornado if the sky becomes very dark and the cloud seems slightly green, or if you see a wall cloud rotating beneath the main cloud. You may hear a loud roar of an approaching tornado. Not all tornadoes are predicted, and it is possible that you may see these weather signs without having heard a broadcast warning. Believe what you see. If you delay it may be too late.

Act immediately. If you are at home, gather everyone who is also at home with you and go to the safest place. Keep as far as you can from windows. If possible, shelter beneath a heavy table, workbench, or mattress.

If you hear a tornado approaching, have everyone who is not sheltering in this way adopt the safest position. Kneel, then squat on your heels, bend fully forward, and place your hands over the back of your head. If your home is damaged, turn off the electricity, gas, and water supplies as soon as it is safe to do so.

# Mobile homes, trailers, cars, and public spaces

No matter how strongly built you may think it is, or how firmly it is secured to the ground, no mobile home or trailer is safe. If you are in one when you hear a warning or if the sky looks threatening, leave at once. If you are in a trailer park, the owners should have a storm shelter and there should be a warden to pass on warnings and make sure everyone is safe. If there is no designated shelter, seek safety in the open. Go to the lowest ground and if a tornado is coming towards you, lie flat, face down, and cover your head with your hands.

Tornadoes have been known to travel at 70 MPH (113 km/h), and they can wreck cars. If you are driving, do not try to outrun one. Stop the car, get out, look for the nearest low ground and lie face down. If there is a ditch or dry gully or riverbed, lie on the bottom of it and cover your head with your hands.

Workplaces, schools, public buildings, and shopping malls should have designated safe areas and staff members to see that everyone moves to them. Follow the instructions you are given calmly, but at once and precisely.

The basement is the safest part of any building. If there is no basement, the refuge will be on the lowest floor, in one or more small rooms or hallways with no external walls. Everyone should be moved away from large, open rooms, such as assembly halls, cafeterias, and gymnasiums. These often have single-span roofs covered with large sheets of exterior skin and they afford very little protection against a tornado. It may be that engineers have judged the entire building to be unsafe in a tornado. In that case, the safest place will be outdoors on the lowest ground, and staff members should be available to direct everyone to it.

Do not try to get home if you are at work or in a public building when you hear the warning and, above all, on no account return to your car. Parking lots are especially dangerous places. Schools should keep students on the premises until the danger has passed and they should not be sent home early in an attempt to "beat the storm" if there has been a tornado watch alert. They are far safer in school than they would be on the streets or in a school bus.

# Avoid complacency

Planning what you would do in an emergency makes obvious sense. Emergencies are rare, however, and even in the areas that are most prone to them, tornadoes do not happen often. It is easy to grow complacent, neglecting to check your emergency store, for example, or the batteries in your smoke alarms.

Worst of all, perhaps, in the rush of ordinary, everyday life it is easy to forget that not everyone may be familiar with the procedures. From time to time, schools and workplaces hold drills to make sure everyone knows where they should go and that the premises can be evacuated quickly. When you travel by air, your attention will be drawn to the safety instructions, and flight attendants may demonstrate the use of life jackets and oxygen masks. This routine is followed every time a civil airliner sets out on a journey. Ships carrying passengers display safety instructions prominently in every part of the vessel, and before the ship sails a loudspeaker announcement is made, drawing passengers' attention to the notices. These include clearly marked assembly areas. Accidents with ships and civil aircraft are also rare events, but this emphasis on safety is a requirement of international maritime and aviation law, and it is a sensible one. This is what the professionals do, and you should be guided by their example.

Check your stores regularly. Make sure that the contact number remains displayed close to every telephone. Every so often, make sure every member of your family is familiar with the emergency arrangements. Ask each one directly. Hold drills.

So much attention to things that may never happen may seem excessive. You may find it embarrassing to keep reminding people. Remember, though, that airline cabin staff do not find this repetition embarrassing—and on short-haul routes they have to repeat it several times a day. They are concerned about saving lives, including their own.

That should be your aim, too, and experience shows that it works. You can survive a tornado if you have prepared a plan of action, rehearsed it, and then follow it.

# SI UNITS AND CONVERSIONS

| Unit | Quantity | Symbol | Conversion |
|------|----------|--------|------------|
| Base units | | | |
| meter | length | m | 1 m = 39.37 inches |
| kilogram | mass | kg | 1 kg = 2.205 pounds |
| second | time | s | |
| ampere | electric current | A | |
| kelvin | thermodynamic temperature | K | 1 K = 1°C = 1.8°F |
| candela | luminous intensity | cd | |
| mole | amount of substance | mol | |
| | | | |
| *Supplementary units* | | | |
| radian | plane angle | rad | $\pi/2$ rad = 90° |
| steradian | solid angle | sr | |
| | | | |
| *Derived units* | | | |
| coulomb | quantity of electricity | C | |
| cubic meter | volume | $m^3$ | 1 $m^3$ = 1.308 $yards^3$ |
| farad | capacitance | F | |
| henry | inductance | H | |
| hertz | frequency | $H_z$ | |
| joule | energy | J | 1 J = 0.2389 calories |
| kilogram per cubic meter | density | $kg\ m^{-3}$ | 1 $kg\ m^{-3}$ = 0.0624 lb. $ft.^{-3}$ |
| lumen | luminous flux | lm | |
| lux | illuminance | lx | |
| meter per second | speed | $m\ s^{-1}$ | 1 $m\ s^{-1}$ = 3.281 ft. $s^{-1}$ |
| meter per second squared | acceleration | $m\ s^{-2}$ | |
| mole per cubic meter | concentration | $mol\ m^{-3}$ | |
| newton | force | N | 1 N = 0.225 lb. force |
| ohm | electric resistance | $\Omega$ | |

*(continues)*

## SI UNITS AND CONVERSIONS (continued)

| Unit | Quantity | Symbol | Conversion |
|---|---|---|---|
| Derived units | | | |
| pascal | pressure | Pa | 1 Pa = 0.145 lb. in.$^{-2}$ |
| radian per second | angular velocity | rad s$^{-1}$ | |
| radian per second squared | angular acceleration | rad s$^{-2}$ | |
| square meter | area | m$^2$ | 1 m$^2$ = 1.196 yards$^2$ |
| tesla | magnetic flux density | T | |
| volt | electromotive force | V | |
| watt | power | W | 1 W = 3.412 Btu h$^{-1}$ |
| weber | magnetic flux | Wb | |

## PREFIXES USED WITH SI UNITS

Prefixes attached to SI units alter their value.

| Prefix | Symbol | Value |
|---|---|---|
| atto | a | $\times 10^{-18}$ |
| femto | f | $\times 10^{-15}$ |
| pico | p | $\times 10^{-12}$ |
| nano | n | $\times 10^{-9}$ |
| micro | μ | $\times 10^{-6}$ |
| milli | m | $\times 10^{-3}$ |
| centi | c | $\times 10^{-2}$ |
| deci | d | $\times 10^{-1}$ |
| deca | da | $\times 10$ |
| hecto | h | $\times 10^{2}$ |
| kilo | k | $\times 10^{3}$ |
| mega | M | $\times 10^{6}$ |
| giga | G | $\times 10^{9}$ |
| tera | T | $\times 10^{12}$ |

# Bibliography and further reading

Allaby, Michael. *A Chronology of Weather, Revised Edition*. New York: Facts On File, 2003.

———. *Encyclopedia of Weather and Climate*. 2 vols. New York: Facts On File, 2001.

———. *Hurricanes, Revised Edition*. New York: Facts on File, 2003.

Anderson, Mason. "Tornado Season Ends with Low Activity, Fewer Deaths." Disaster Relief. Available on-line. URL: www.disasterrelief.org/Disasters/020730tornadoseason. Posted July 31, 2002.

"April 3, 1974." Available on-line. URL: www.april31974.com. Accessed November 26, 2002.

Barry, Roger G., and Richard J. Chorley. *Atmosphere, Weather & Climate*. 7th ed. New York: Routledge, 1998.

BBC World Service. "Giant Hailstones Lash Australia." Available on-line. URL: news.bbc.co.uk/1/hi/world/asia-pacific/1123857.stm. January 18, 2001.

Bell, Ian, and Martin Visbeck. "North Atlantic Oscillation." Columbia University. Available on-line. URL: www.ldeo.columbia.edu/NAO/main.html. Accessed November 27, 2002.

Bluestein, Howard B. *Tornado Alley: Monster Storms of the Great Plains*. New York: Oxford University Press, 1999.

Bolton, Nigel, Derek M. Elsom, and G. Terence Meaden. "Forecasting Tornadoes in the United Kingdom." Tornado and Storm Research Organisation (TORRO). Available on-line. URL: www.chmi.cz/ECSS2002/abstracts/78.html. Accessed February 28, 2003.

Burroughs, William James. *Climate Change: A Multidisciplinary Approach*. Cambridge, U.K.: Cambridge University Press, 2001.

Coastal Observation Lab. "Mesocyclone Strikes New Jersey." Rutgers University, Institute of Marine and Coastal Sciences. Available on-line. URL: marine.rutgers.edu/mrs/news/020513_cyclone.htm. Accessed December 6, 2002.

Cohen, Philip. "Ball Lightning Experiments Produce UFOs." Available on-line. URL: home.dmv.com/~tbastian/balite.htm. May 26, 1999.

Cooksley, Peter G. *Wellington: Mainstay of Bomber Command*. Yeovil, U.K.: Patrick Stephens, 1987.

Elsom, Derek M. "British and European Tornado Extremes." Tornado and Storm Research Organisation. Oxford, U.K.: Oxford Brookes University. Available on-line. URL: www.torro.org.uk/whirlextreme.htm. Last modified January 22, 2003.

———. "Severe Storm Definitions and Whirlwind Classification." Tornado and Storm Research Organisation. Oxford, U.K.: Oxford Brookes University. Available on-line. URL: www.torro.org.uk/stormclassification.htm. Last modified December 2, 2002.

Fehlberg, Ira. "Recent Tornadoes in Western Australia." Inflow Images. Available on-line. URL: www.inflowimages.com/TornadoesInWa/TornadosInWa.htm. Accessed February 27, 2003.

Fenn, Beverley Billings. "It's Raining Frogs and Toads!" Available on-line. URL: www.conservation.state.mo.us/conmag/1996/decoi/3.html. Last revised December 17, 1996.

Fraser, David. "The Life Cycle of a Waterspout." Available on-line. URL: www.met.fsu.edu/Classes/Met4301/reports/fraser.htm. December 8, 1998.

Goodman, Jason. "Statistics of North Atlantic Oscillation Decadal Variability." Massachusetts Institute of Technology. Available on-line. URL: www.mit.edu/people/goodmanj/NAOI/NAOI.html. February 23, 1998.

Goodwin, Brian. "Kugelblitz!—The Fire in the Sky." Available on-line. URL: free-space.virgin.net/brian.goodwin/Kugelblitz!.htm. Accessed February 28, 2003.

Houghton, J. T., Y. Ding, D. J. Griggs, M. Noguer, P. J. van der Linden, X. Dai, K. Maskell, and C. A. Johnson. *Climate Change 2001: The Scientific Basis.* Cambridge, U.K.: Cambridge University Press, 2001.

"Inside Tornadoes." The Weather Channel Interactive, Inc. Available on-line. URL: www.weather.com/newscenter/specialreports/tornado/inside/about.html. Accessed February 25, 2003.

Lamb, H. H. *Climate, History and the Modern World.* 2d ed. New York: Routledge, 1995.

Lash, Gary. "Thunderstorms and Tornadoes." Fredonia State University. Available on-line. URL: www.geocities.com/CapeCanaveral/Hall.6104/tstorms.html. Accessed November 29, 2002.

Lutgens, Frederick K., and Edward J. Tarbuck. *The Atmosphere.* 7th ed. Upper Saddle River, N.J.: Prentice Hall, 1998.

Mandics, P. A. "Advanced System for the Interactive Analysis and Presentation of Geophysical Data." Program for Regional Observing and Forecasting Services, Environmental Research Laboratories, National Oceanic and Atmospheric Administration, July 1998. Available on-line. URL: www-fd.fsl.noaa.gov/papers/GeoData/pm7-98g.html. Accessed February 4, 2003.

Mantua, Nathan. "The Pacific Decadal Oscillation and Climate Forecasting for North America." Joint Institute for the Study of the Atmosphere and Oceans, University of Washington, Seattle. Available on-line. URL: www.astmos.washington.edu/~mantua/REPORTS/PDO/PDO_cs.htm. August 1, 2000.

———. "The Pacific Decadal Oscillation (PDO)." NOAA Climate Prediction Center. Available on-line. URL: tao.atmos.washington.edu/pdo. January 2000.

"May 3rd Remembered." The Weather Channel Interactive, Inc. Available on-line. URL: www.weather.com/newscenter/specialreports/tornado/may3rd/may3_1999.html. Accessed February 25, 2003.

McIlveen, Robin. *Fundamentals of Weather and Climate.* London: Chapman & Hall, 1992.

Murray, Lucas. "Mesocyclone." Available on-line. URL: www.geo.arizona.edu/~/lmurray/g256/vocab/mesocyclone.html. Updated December 3, 2001.

NOAA. "Giant Hailstones." Available on-line. URL: www.spc.noaa.gov/faq/tornado/hailjim.htm. Accessed November 29, 2002.

———. "Hurricane Andrew." Available on-line. URL: www.noaa.gov/hurricane-andrew.html. Updated August 22, 2002.

———. "Hurricane Beulah, September 1967." Available on-line. URL: www.srh.noaa.gov/crp/docs/research/hurrhistory/beulah/beulah.html. Accessed December 5, 2002.

———. "Tornado Outbreaks of 1999." USA Today. Available on-line. URL: www.usatoday.com/weather/news/1999/w99tor.htm. January 4, 2000.

———. "Tornado Outbreaks 1999." National Weather Service. Available on-line. URL: www.srh.noaa.gov/ftproot/lzk.html/outbreaks99.htm. Accessed December 3, 2002.

————. "Weather Service Commemorates Nation's Worst Tornado Outbreak." Available on-line. URL: www.publicaffairs.noaa.gov/storms/release.html. March 31, 1999.

OK-First. "Weather Fronts." Oklahoma Climatological Survey. Available on-line. URL: okfirst.ocs.ou.edu/train/meteorology/Fronts.html. Accessed November 26, 2002.

Oliver, John E., and John J. Hidore. *Climatology, an Atmospheric Science.* 2d ed. Upper Saddle River, N.J.: Prentice-Hall, 2002.

Palmer, Chad. "How the Jet Stream Influences the Weather." USA Today. Available on-line. URL: www.usatoday.com/weather/wjet.htm. August 11, 1997.

Ramby, Homer G. "Xenia, Ohio—Tornado—April 3, 1974." Available on-line. URL: www.interaxs.net/pub/hgr/tornado.htm. Accessed November 26, 2002.

Schneider, Stephen H., ed. in chief. *Encyclopedia of Climate and Weather.* 2 vols. New York: Oxford University Press, 1996.

Science and Technology. "Structure and Dynamics of Supercell Thunderstorms." National Weather Service. Available on-line. URL: www.crh.noaa.gov/lmk/soo/docu/supercell.htm. Accessed December 9, 2002.

————. "Structure and Evolution of Squall Line and Bow Echo Convective Systems." National Weather Service. Available on-line. URL: www.crh.noaa.gov/link/soo/docu/bowecho.htm. Accessed December 3, 2002.

Smith, Bruce B. "Waterspouts." Available on-line. URL: www.crh.noaa.gov/apx/science/spouts/waterspouts.htm. Accessed February 26, 2003.

Srinivasan, Margaret, and Kristy Kawasaki. "Science—El Niño/La Niña & PDO." Jet Propulsion Laboratory, NASA. Available on-line. URL: topex-www.jpl.nasa.gov/science/pdo.html. Updated May 14, 2002.

Teague, Dan G. "The Easter Sunday Tornado Outbreak." National Weather Service. Available on-line. URL: www.srh.noaa.gov/shv/Easter2000.htm. Accessed December 5, 2002.

"Tornadoes." Available on-line. URL: www.icomm.ca/hazards/meteorological/tornado.html. Accessed February 27, 2003.

"Tracking Tornadoes." The Weather Channel Interactive, Inc. Available on-line. URL: www.weather.com/newscenter/specialreports/tornado/tracking/toto.html. Accessed February 25, 2003.

Turnage, T. J., Robert R. Lee, and E. Dewayne Mitchell. "WSR-88D Mesocyclone characteristics of selected thunderstorms during the southwest Georgia tornado outbreak on 13–14 February 2000." NOAA. Available on-line. URL: www.srh.noaa.gov/tlh/tlh/mm5/SLS/turnage_sls.html. Accessed December 6, 2002.

Valine, William C., and E. Philip Krider. "Lightning Really Strikes More than Twice in the Same Place." University of Arizona, January 16, 2003. Available on-line. URL: www.newswise.com/articles/2003/1/LIGHTNG.UAZ.html.

Warren, J. "Giant Hailstones Kill 15 in Central China." WeatherMatrix. Available on-line. URL: www.cybervox.org/archive/stormreports/200206-200207/0095.html. July 20, 2002.

Williams, Jack. "VBX Jet Stream Information." *The USA Today Weather Book.* USA Today. Available on-line. URL: www.junction.net/norac/vbx/jet.htm. Accessed November 29, 2002.

Willis, Bill. "Weather Fronts." Available on-line. URL: www.wcscience.com/weather/fronts.html. Accessed November 26, 2002.

# Index

Page numbers in *italic* refer to illustrations.